2023

中国残疾人事业统计年鉴

China Statistical Yearbook on the Work for Persons with Disabilities

2023

（总第22期 No.22）

中国残疾人联合会 编

Compiled By China Disabled Persons' Federation

中国统计出版社
China Statistics Press

图书在版编目（CIP）数据

中国残疾人事业统计年鉴. 2023：汉英对照 / 中国残疾人联合会编. -- 北京 ：中国统计出版社, 2023.11
ISBN 978-7-5230-0337-4

Ⅰ. ①中… Ⅱ. ①中… Ⅲ. ①残疾人－社会福利事业－统计资料－中国－2023－年鉴－汉、英 Ⅳ. ①D669.69-66

中国国家版本馆 CIP 数据核字(2023)第 219033 号

中国残疾人事业统计年鉴 2023
China Statistical Yearbook on the Work for Persons with Disabilities 2023

作　　者/中国残疾人联合会
责任编辑/冯燕玲
封面设计/张　然
出版发行/中国统计出版社有限公司
通信地址/北京市丰台区西三环南路甲 6 号　邮政编码/100073
发行电话/邮购（010）63376909　书店（010）68783171
网　　址/http://www.zgtjcbs.com
印　　刷/河北鑫兆源印刷有限公司
经　　销/新华书店
开　　本/880×1230mm　1/16
印　　张/13.75　彩页 0.5
字　　数/464 千字
版　　别/2023 年 11 月第 1 版
版　　次/2023 年 11 月第 1 次印刷
定　　价/180.00 元

《中国残疾人事业统计年鉴 2023》编委会和编辑工作人员

编者说明

《中国残疾人事业统计年鉴2023》系统收录了全国和各省、自治区、直辖市2022年残疾人工作各方面的统计数据，是一部全面反映中国残疾人事业发展的资料性年鉴。

本年鉴内容由六部分组成：第一部分为主要指标数据图；第二部分为2022年中国残疾人事业发展统计公报；第三部分为综合统计资料，是历年统计情况的综合反映；第四部分为2022年度分省统计资料，记录2022年各省（自治区、直辖市）任务指标执行情况和全国汇总情况；第五部分为分省统计报告，包括全国31个省（自治区、直辖市）和新疆生产建设兵团的残疾人事业统计公报；第六部分为附录，介绍中国残疾人事业统计有关的政策法规文件。

本年鉴涉及的全国性统计数据均不包括香港、澳门特别行政区和台湾省数据。

本年鉴是根据各地残联报送的统计年报和部分专项业务项目统计结果编制而成。表格中"空格"表示该项统计指标数据不足本表最小单位数、数据不详或无该项数据。

2023年10月

目　录

Contents

第一部分　主要数据图

Part Ⅰ　Charts

图-1　2022 年各类残疾人接受基本康复服务情况……3

Chart1　Rehabilitation Services Received by Persons with Disabilities in 2022

图-2　2018-2022 年残疾人康复机构建设情况……3

Chart 2　Development of Rehabilitation Facilities for Persons with Disabilities during 2018– 2022

图-3　2022 年持证残疾人就业形式……4

Chart 3　Employment of Registered Persons with Disabilities in Urban and Rural Areas in 2022

图-4　2018-2022 年农村残疾人扶持情况……4

Chart 4　Poverty Alleviation for Persons with Disabilities in Rural Areas during 2018-2022

图-5　2018-2022 年残疾人接受托养服务情况……5

Chart 5　Persons with Disabilities Receiving Fostering Service during 2018-2022

图-6　2018-2022 年省、地级电视手语栏目播出情况……5

Chart 6　Sign Language Displayed In Provincial and Municipal TV Programs during 2018- 2022

图-7　2018-2022 年残疾人群众体育健身活动情况……6

Chart 7　Fitness Sports Activities for Persons with Disabilities during 2018-2022

图-8　2018-2022 年省级残疾人体育比赛情况……6

Chart 8　Sports Events for Persons with Disabilities at Provincial Level during 2018-2022

图-9　2018-2022 年残疾人专职委员选聘情况……7

Chart 9　Appointment of Commissioners for Disability Issuses at Grass-roots during 2018-2022

图-10　2022 年残疾人服务设施建设情况……7

Chart 10　Development of Service Facilities for Persons with Disabilities in 2022

第二部分　统计公报

Part Ⅱ　Statistical Communique

2022 年残疾人事业发展统计公报……11

Statistical Communiqué on the Undertaking for Persons with Disabilities in 2022……14

第三部分　综合统计资料

Part Ⅲ　Overall Statistics

3-1　中国残疾人事业主要业务进展情况(2018－2022)……20

Summary on the Development of the Work for Persons with Disabilities (2018－2022)

3-2 全国残疾人人口基础库主要数据 …… 28
Statistics of the National Basic Information Database of Persons with Disabilities

第四部分 分省统计资料
Part Ⅳ Provincial Statistics

一、康复
Rehabilitation

4-1-1 社区康复 …… 35
Community-Based Rehabilitation(CBR)
4-1-2 残疾人接受基本康复服务总体情况 …… 36
Basic Rehabilitation Services Received by Persons with Disabilities
4-1-3 辅助器具适配服务 …… 38
Provision of Assistive Devices
4-1-4 康复机构 …… 41
Rehabilitation Institutions
4-1-5 康复人才 …… 43
Rehabilitation Professionals

二、教育
Education

4-2-1 高中教育阶段 …… 51
Senior High Education
4-2-2 高等教育 …… 58
Higher Education

三、就业
Employment

4-3-1 残疾人就业状况 …… 65
Employment of Persons with Disabilities
4-3-2 农村困难残疾人实用技术培训及就业帮扶基地建设 …… 67
Training on Practical Skills and Technologies for PWDs in Rual Areas

四、社会保障
Social Security

4-4-1 残疾人参加社会保险情况 …… 68
Social Insurance Coverage of Persons with Disabilities
4-4-2 托养服务 …… 70
Institutional Care Services

五、专门协会
Specialized Associations

4-5-1 省(自治区、直辖市)专门协会建立情况 …… 73
Establishment of Special Associations at Provincial Level

4-5-2 市(地、州、盟)专门协会建立情况 …… 74
Establishment of Specialized Associations at Municipal Level
4-5-3 县(县级市、市辖区)专门协会建立情况 …… 75
Establishment of Specialized Associations at County/District Level

六、盲人按摩
Massage by the Blind
4-6-1 盲人按摩 …… 76
Massage by the Blind

七、宣传文化
Publicity and Cultural Activities
4-7-1 宣传文化 …… 78
Publicity and Cultural Activities

八、体育
Sports
4-8-1 体　育 …… 84
Sports

九、维权
Rights Protection
4-9-1 法规体系 …… 86
Legal System
4-9-2 执法检查 …… 87
Law Enforcement Inspection
4-9-3 法治宣传 …… 89
Publicity on Laws
4-9-4 法律救助 …… 90
Legal Aid
4-9-5 参政议政 …… 92
Participation of Persons with Disabilities in Administration and Discussion of State Affairs
4-9-6 无障碍环境建设与残疾人机动轮椅车燃油补贴 …… 94
Promotion of Accessible Environments and Gas Subsidy for Motorized Wheelchairs
4-9-7 残疾人信访 …… 95
Petitions from Persons with Disabilities

十、组织建设
Disabled Persons' Organizations
4-10-1 省(自治区、直辖市)级残联 …… 99
Disabled Persons' Federations at Provincial Level
4-10-2 地级残联 …… 101
Disabled Persons'Federations at Municipal Level

4-10-3 县(县级市、市辖区)级残联……103
Disabled Persons' Federations at County/District Level
4-10-4 乡(镇、街道)残联……105
Disabled Persons'Federations at Township Level
4-10-5 村(社区)残疾人组织……107
Disabled Persons' Federations at Village /Community Level

十一、残疾人服务设施建设
Service Facilities for Persons with Disabilities
4-11-1 残疾人综合服务设施……109
Comprehensive Service Facilities for Persons with Disabilities
4-11-2 残疾人康复设施……113
Rehabilitation Service Facilities for Persons with Disabilities
4-11-3 残疾人托养设施……117
Institutional Care Service Facilities for Persons with Disabilities

十二、信息化建设
Application of IT
4-12-1 残疾人事业信息化建设……121
Application of IT in the Work for Persons with Disabilities

第五部分 分省统计报告
Part Ⅴ Provincial Statistical Reports

北京市……125
Beijing
天津市……128
Tianjin
河北省……130
Hebei Province
山西省……133
Shanxi Province
内蒙古自治区……135
Inner Mongolia Autonomous Region
辽宁省……137
Liaoning Province
吉林省……139
Jilin Province
黑龙江省……141
Heilongjiang Province
上海市……143
Shanghai
江苏省……145
Jiangsu Province

浙江省 ······ 148
Zhejiang Province
安徽省 ······ 150
Anhui Province
福建省 ······ 152
Fujian Province
江西省 ······ 154
Jiangxi Province
山东省 ······ 156
Shandong Province
河南省 ······ 158
Henan Province
湖北省 ······ 160
Hubei Province
湖南省 ······ 162
Hunan Province
广东省 ······ 166
Guangdong Province
广西壮族自治区 ······ 168
Guangxi Zhuang Autonomous Region
海南省 ······ 170
Hainan Province
重庆市 ······ 172
Chongqing
四川省 ······ 174
Sichuan Province
贵州省 ······ 176
Guizhou Province
云南省 ······ 178
Yunnan Province
西藏自治区 ······ 181
Tibet Autonomous Region
陕西省 ······ 183
Shaanxi Province
甘肃省 ······ 186
Gansu Province
青海省 ······ 188
Qinghai Province
宁夏回族自治区 ······ 190
Ningxia Hui Autonomous Region
新疆维吾尔自治区 ······ 192
Xinjiang Uygur Autonomous Region
新疆生产建设兵团 ······ 194
Xinjiang Production and Construction Corps

第六部分　附　　录
Part Ⅵ　Appendix

关于使用 2010 年末全国残疾人总数及各类、不同残疾等级人数的通知……199
Notice on Quoting Statistical Numbers of Persons with Disabilities by the End of 2010
中国残联统计调查项目目录……200
Catalogue of Statistics and Survey Projects by China Disabled Persons' Federation
全国残联系统统计工作管理办法……202
Management of Statistical Work by China Disabled Persons' Federation
中华人民共和国统计法……205
The Statistics Law of the People's Republic of China
部门统计调查项目管理办法……210
Provisional Regulations on Management of Statistics and Survey Projects

主要数据图

Charts

图-1 2022年各类残疾人接受基本康复服务情况

Chart1 Rehabilitation Services Received by Persons with Disabilities in 2022

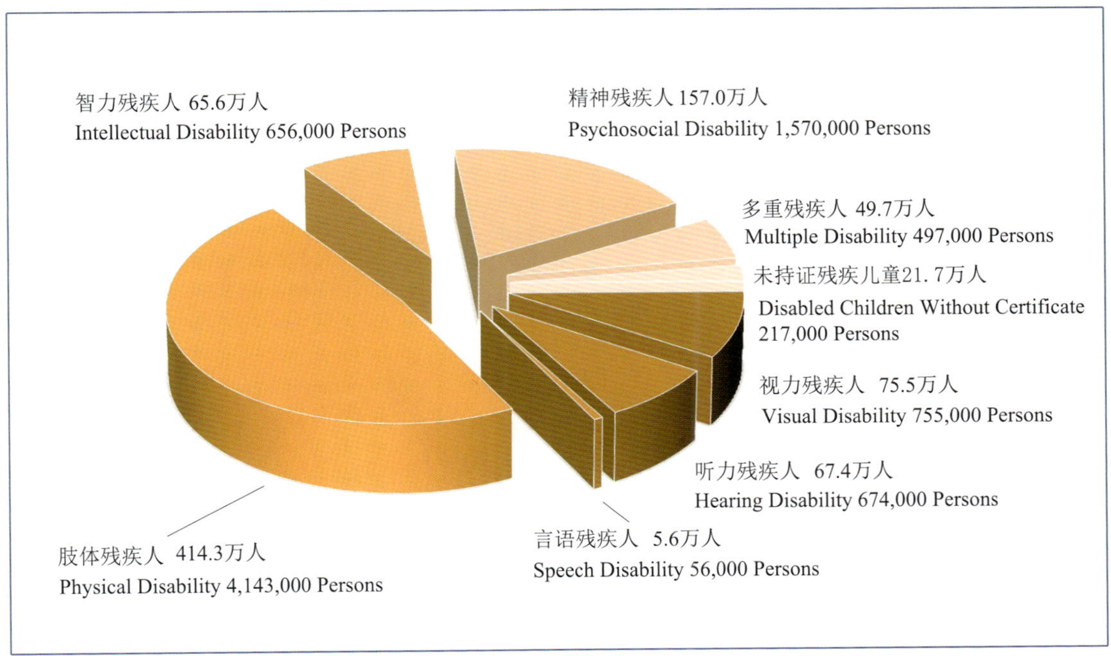

图-2 2018-2022年残疾人康复机构建设情况

Chart 2 Development of Rehabilitation Facilities for Persons with Disabilities during 2018 - 2022

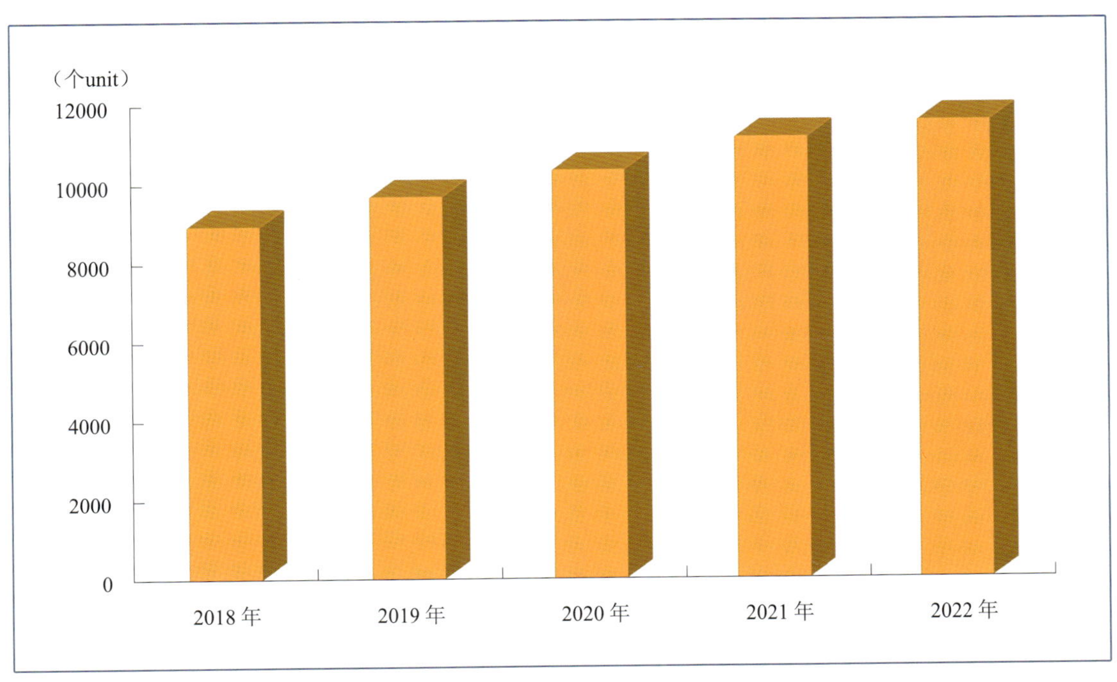

图-3 2022年持证残疾人就业形式

Chart 3 Employment of Registered Persons with Disabilities in Urban and Rural Areas in 2022

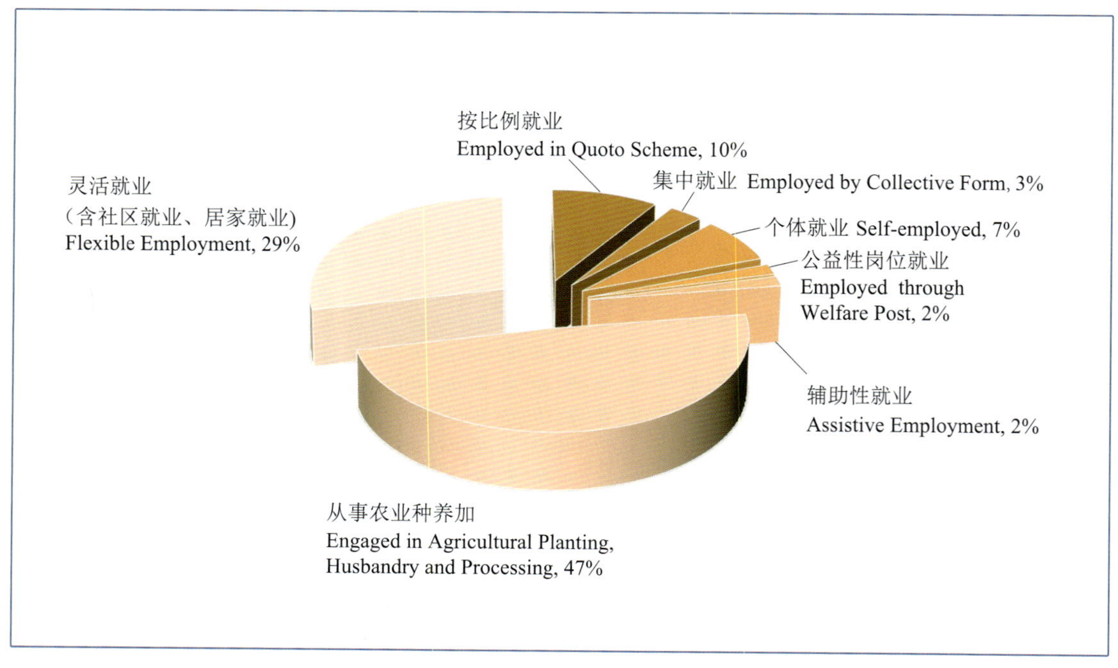

图-4 2018-2022年农村残疾人扶持情况

Chart 4 Poverty Alleviation for Persons with Disabilities in Rural Areas during 2018-2022

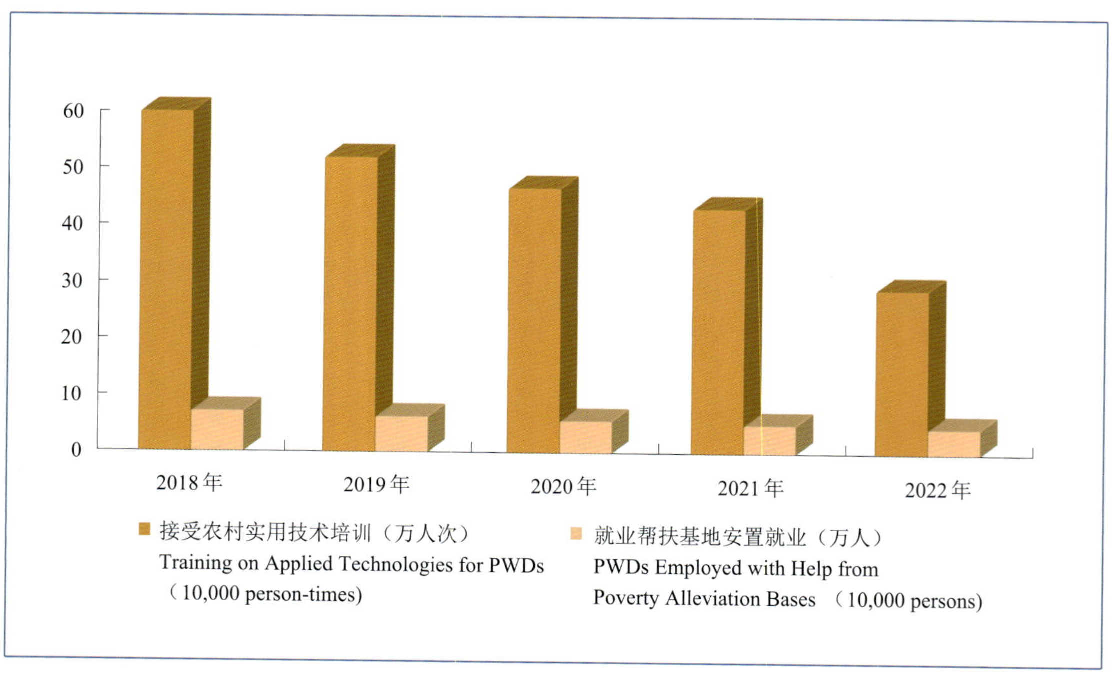

图-5 2018-2022年残疾人接受托养服务情况

Chart 5 Persons with Disabilities Receiving Fostering Service during 2018-2022

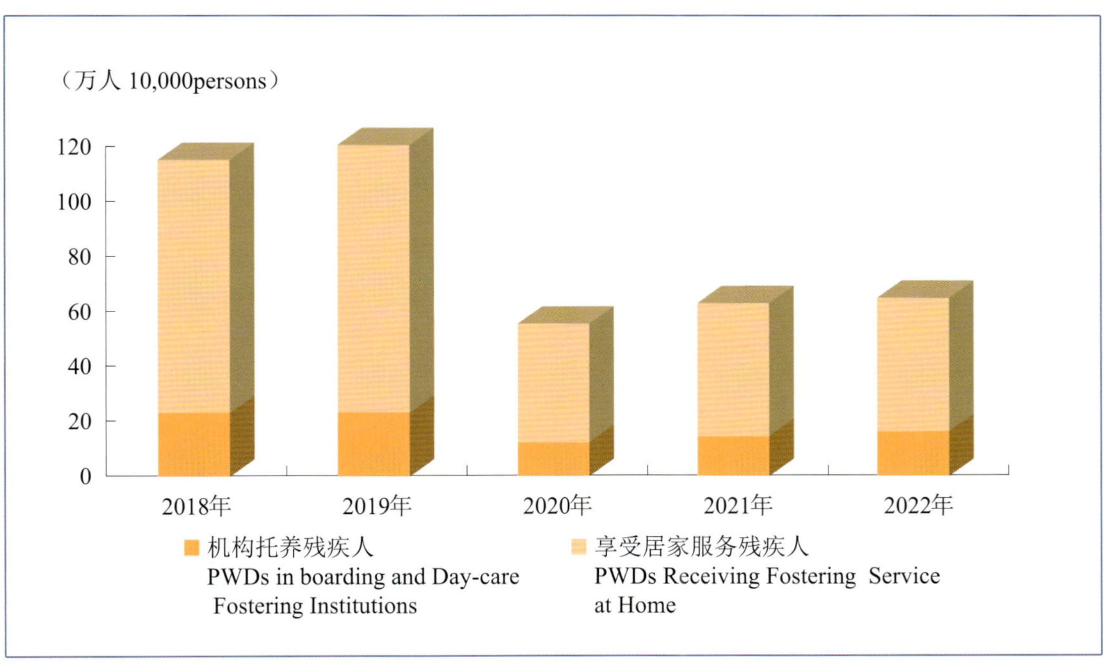

图-6 2018-2022年省、地级电视手语栏目播出情况

Chart 6 Sign Language Displayed In Provincial and Municipal TV Programs during 2018- 2022

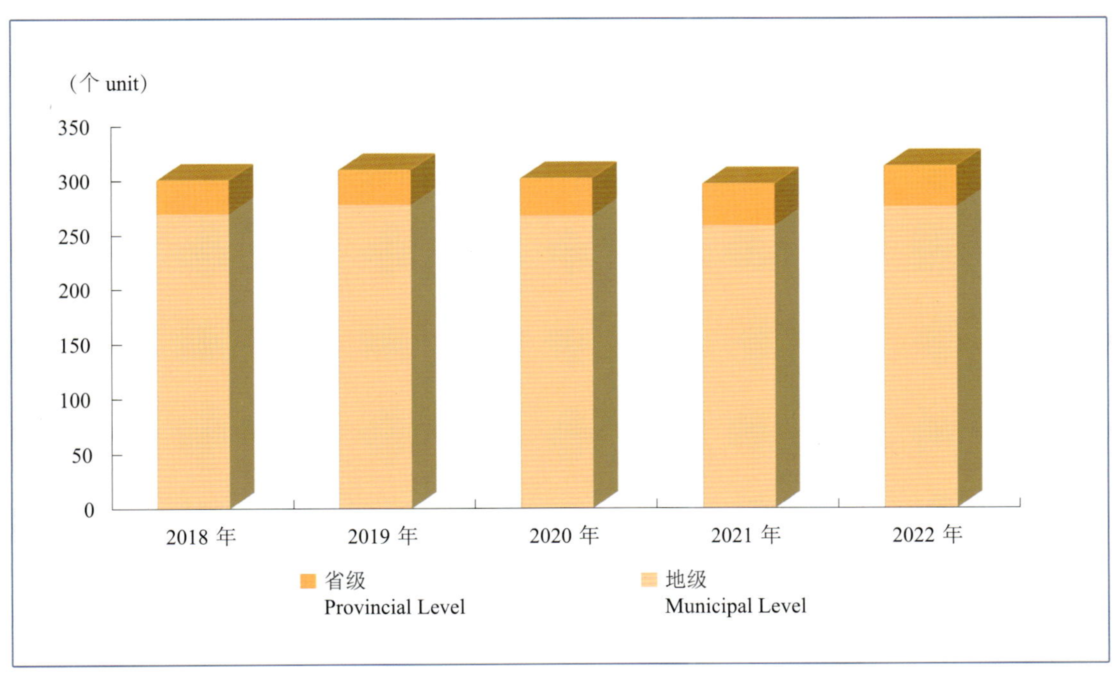

图-7 2018-2022年残疾人群众体育健身活动情况

Chart 7 Fitness Sports Activities for Persons with Disabilities during 2018-2022

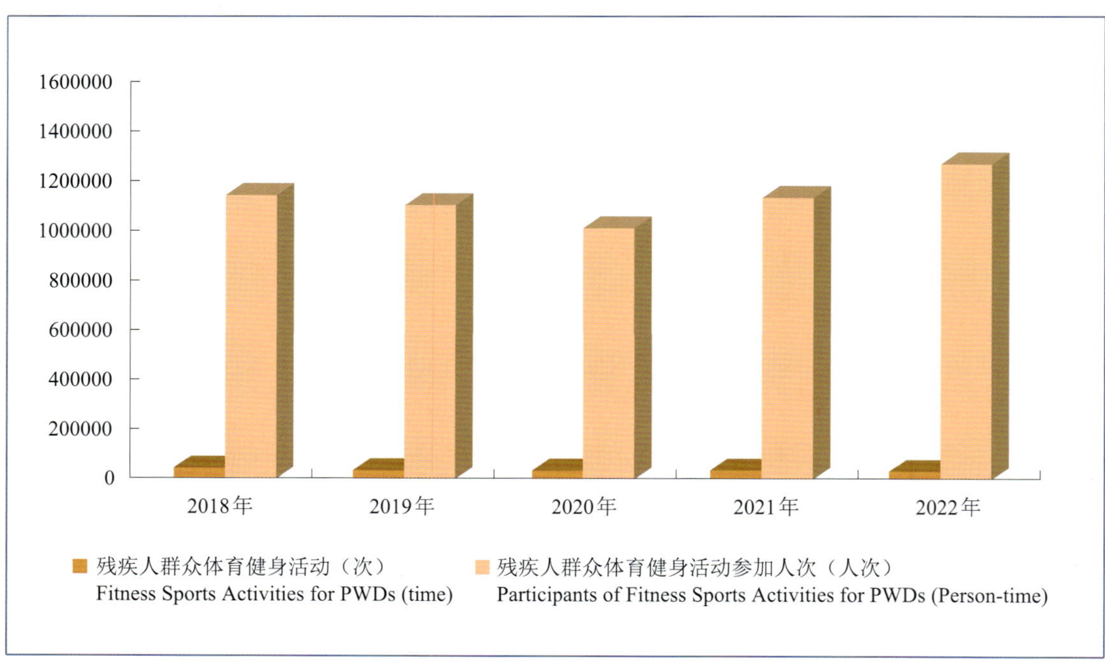

图-8 2018-2022年省级残疾人体育比赛情况

Chart 8 Sports Events for Persons with Disabilities at Provincial Level during 2018-2022

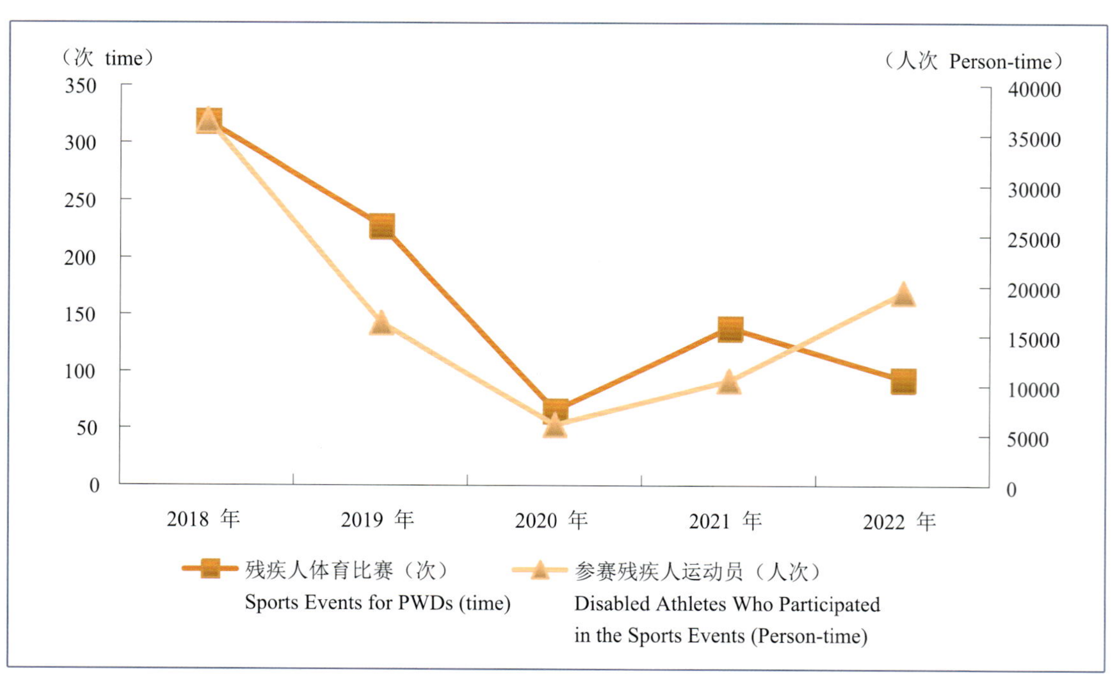

图-9 2018-2022年残疾人专职委员选聘情况

Chart 9 Appointment of Commissioners for Disability Issuses at Grass-roots during 2018-2022

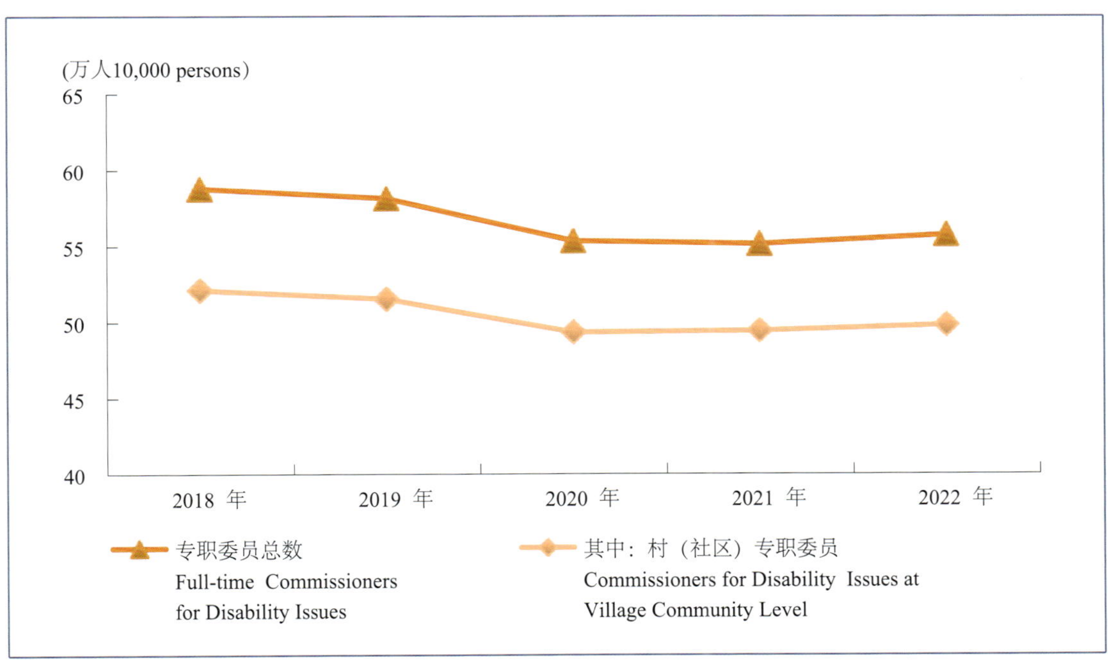

图-10 2022年残疾人服务设施建设情况

Chart 10 Development of Service Facilities for Persons with Disabilities in 2022

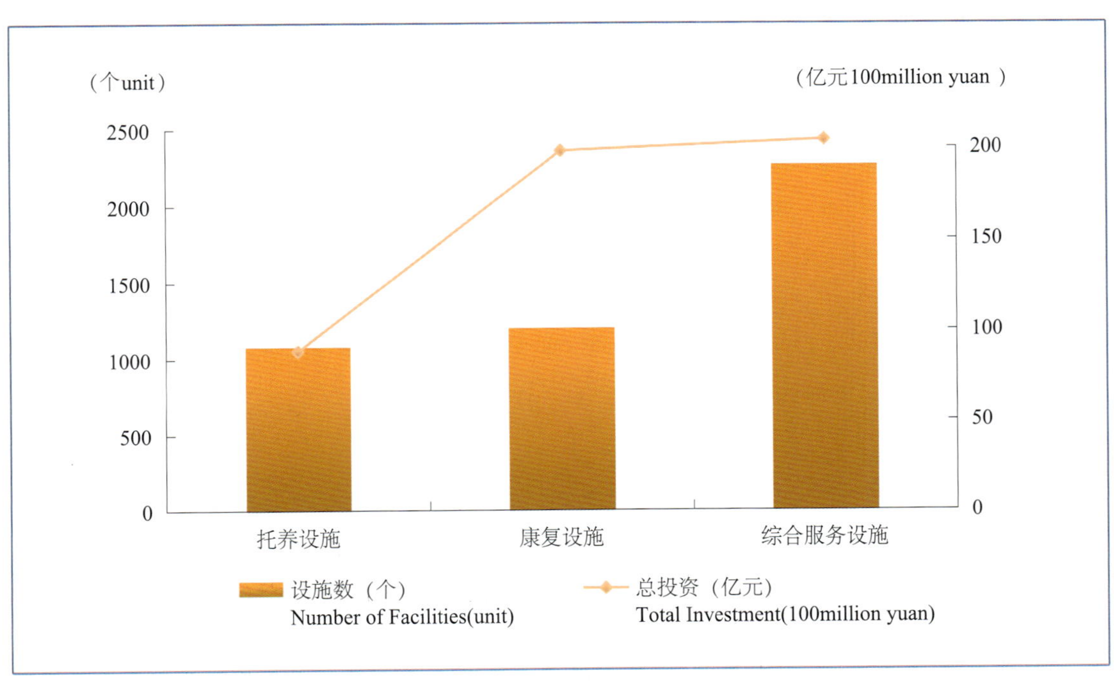

统计公报

Statistical Communique

2022年残疾人事业发展统计公报

2022年，各级残联以习近平新时代中国特色社会主义思想为指导，全面贯彻党的二十大精神，认真贯彻落实习近平总书记关于残疾人工作的重要指示批示精神，深入实施《“十四五”残疾人保障和发展规划》，全面推进残疾人事业高质量发展。

一、康复

贯彻落实《“十四五”残疾人保障和发展规划》、《国家残疾预防行动计划（2021-2025年）》和《“十四五”残疾人康复服务实施方案》，推动“十四五”残疾预防和残疾人康复工作高质量发展。深入贯彻实施《国务院关于建立残疾儿童康复救助制度的意见》，加强和改进残疾儿童康复救助服务，提升残疾儿童家庭获得感，40.7万残疾儿童得到康复救助。以农村低收入残疾人为重点，持续开展残疾人精准康复服务行动，856.7万残疾人得到基本康复服务，164.8万残疾人得到基本辅助器具适配服务。得到康复服务的持证残疾人中，有视力残疾人75.5万、听力残疾人67.4万、言语残疾人5.6万、肢体残疾人414.3万、智力残疾人65.6万、精神残疾人157万、多重残疾人49.7万。积极维护残疾人健康，通过多部门数据比对，核实低收入残疾人参加基本医疗保险、接受家庭医生签约情况，有针对性地帮助残疾人加入基本医疗保险，接受家庭医生签约服务。

加强残疾人康复机构与人才队伍建设，深化社区康复工作。制定《残联系统康复机构业务规范建设评估指南（试行）》，编写全国残联系统康复专业技术人员规范化培训大纲23册，全面推进残联系统康复机构业务规范建设和康复专业技术人员规范化培训。截至2022年底，全国有残疾人康复机构11661个，康复机构在岗人员达32.8万人，其中，管理人员3.4万人，业务人员23.9万人，其他人员5.5万人。全年完成康复专业技术人员规范化培训1.7万人。

二、教育

落实《“十四五”特殊教育发展提升行动计划》，为残疾人教育创造更好的条件和环境。会同教育部印发《辅助器具进校园工程实施方案》，为义务教育阶段有需要的残疾学生提供适配服务；会同教育部、中央编办、财政部等部门修订印发《残疾人中等职业学校设置标准》，加强残疾人中等职业学校基础能力建设和规范化管理；实施彩票公益金助学项目，资助29所残疾人职业学校改善办学条件、加强实训基地建设。实施《第二期国家手语和盲文规范化行动计划（2021-2025年）》，建立健全工作协调机制，与教育部、国家语委牵头建立由中央宣传部等七部门和有关专家组成的工作协调小组、专家组，定期会商调度，共同推动手语和盲文规范化、标准化工作，大力推广国家通用手语和国家通用盲文。《中国少年先锋队队歌、呼号、入队誓词和中国共产主义青年团团歌、入团誓词国家通用手语方案》作为国家语委语言文字规范正式发布实施，国家通用手语和国家通用盲文水平等级标准、手语翻译资格（水平）标准试点工作有序开展，国家通用盲文测试大纲和题库逐步完善。

全国共有特殊教育普通高中（部、班）118个，在校生11431人，其中聋生6506人、盲生1736人、其他3189人。残疾人中等职业学校（班）184个，在校生19014人，毕业生5157人，毕业生中1473人获得职业资格证书。高等教育阶段，招收30035名残疾学生，其中高职（专科）17644人，本科10703人，硕士生1520人，博士生168人。

三、就业

全国城乡新增残疾人就业59.2万人，其中，城镇新增就业14.3万人，农村新增就业44.9万人；全国城乡实名培训残疾人50.2万人。

全国城乡持证残疾人就业人数为905.5万人，其中按比例就业86.7万人，集中就业26.0万人，个体就业64.1万人，公益性岗位就业17.9万人，辅助性就业15.2万人，灵活就业265.6万人，从事农业种养加430.0万人。

开展农村困难残疾人实用技术培训，为28.5万人次残疾人赋能。全国3508个残疾人就业帮扶基地共安置4.5万残疾人就业，带动8万户残疾人家庭增收。

全国共培训盲人保健按摩人员 17639 人次、盲人医疗按摩人员 7298 人次。现有保健按摩机构 16926 个，医疗按摩机构 1041 个。1844 人获得盲人医疗按摩人员初级职务任职资格，500 人获得中级职务任职资格。

四、社会保障

截至 2022 年底，参加城乡居民基本养老保险的残疾人数达 2761.7 万。1209.3 万残疾人领取养老金。60 岁以下参保的残疾人中，692.3 万重度残疾人和 285.5 万非重度残疾得到参保缴费资助。

残疾人托养服务工作稳步推进，开展残疾人托养服务的各级各类机构达 8906 个，其中寄宿制服务机构 1763 个，日间照料机构 4135 个，综合性服务机构 1362 个。15.5 万残疾人通过寄宿制和日间照料服务机构接受托养服务，47.2 万残疾人接受居家服务。

五、宣传文化

以“促进残疾人就业,保障残疾人权益”为主题，组织第三十二次“全国助残日”活动，突出迎接宣传贯彻党的二十大工作主线，围绕北京 2022 年冬残奥会等重大活动、重要节点，组织媒体开展“奋进新征程 建功新时代”、“人民幸福生活是最大的人权”、“奋斗者 正青春”等主题宣传，新华社采写、播发《残疾人也可以活出精彩的人生——以习近平同志为核心的党中央关心残疾人事业纪实》，配合中宣部、国务院新闻办起草并发表《中国残疾人体育事业发展和权利保障》白皮书，央视新闻联播共 57 次报道残疾人事业。创新服务方式，为基层残疾人提供优质文化产品和服务。与中央文明办等 12 部门共同印发《关于进一步推进扶残助残文明实践活动的实施意见》，组织“残疾人心向党、筑梦新时代”第十届全国残疾人艺术汇演汇报演出，以“奋进新征程 喜迎二十大”为主题继续开展 2022 年全国残疾人文化周活动，举办“共享芬芳•共铸美好”巡演展览，全年累计举办 14 场演出展览，推动“光明影院”公益点播专区上线全国有线电视，设立“仁美文艺”公众号，编辑出版《残疾人作家作品集(2021)》，残疾人精神文化生活得到极大丰富。全国共有省级残疾人专题广播节目 24 个、电视手语栏目 37 个，地级残疾人专题广播节目 195 个、电视手语栏目 270 个。全国各级公共图书馆设立盲文及盲文有声读物阅览室 1377 个，开展残疾人文化周活动 10010 场次，全国省地两级残联艺术团 229 个。

六、体育

第 13 届冬残奥会于 2022 年 3 月 4 日至 13 日在北京和张家口举行。中国体育代表团牢记习近平总书记关于北京冬残奥会筹办备赛和残疾人事业的重要指示，按照党中央、国务院决策部署，发扬“使命在肩、奋斗有我”的精神，自强不息、团结拼搏，夺得 18 枚金牌、20 枚银牌、23 枚铜牌，位居金牌榜和奖牌榜榜首，取得了参加冬残奥会的历史最好成绩，实现了冬季项目的历史性跨越，为祖国和人民赢得了荣誉，为成功举办北京冬残奥会作出了重大贡献。配合杭州组委会、协调亚洲残奥委员会做好亚残运会筹办工作，妥善应对延期带来的新问题。启动 2025 年全国第十二届残运会暨第九届特奥会筹办工作。加强残疾人体育技术人才培养，晋升 1637 名裁判员，成立分级委员会。启动 2024 年巴黎残奥会、2026 年米兰-科尔蒂纳丹佩佐冬残奥会新周期备战准备工作。参加法国射击世界杯、韩国举重亚锦赛、印度盲人足球亚锦赛、葡萄牙盲人门球世锦赛等 4 项国际赛事，获得 23 金、9 银、3 铜。实施残疾人康复健身体育行动，开展健身周、特奥日、冰雪季活动，全国残疾人社区文体活动参与率由 2021 年的 23.9%上升至 2022 年的 26.3%。

七、维权

制定或修改关于残疾人的专门法规和规章：省级 6 个、地级 9 个；制定或修改保障残疾人权益的规范性文件：省级 42 个、地级 66 个、县级 185 个。全国县级以上人大开展《中华人民共和国残疾人保障法》执法检查和专题调研 413 次；政协开展视察和专题调研 262 次。全国开展省级普法宣传教育活动 184 次，88 万余人次参加；举办省级法律培训班 39 个，27216 人次参加。全国成立残疾人法律救助工作协调机构 2869 个，建立残疾人法律救助工作站 2633 个。各地残联办理建议、提案 1564 件。

全国共出台了 761 个省、地、县级无障碍环境建设与管理法规、政府令和规范性文件；全国开展无障碍环境建设检查 9996 次，无障碍培训 5.2 万人次。截至 2022 年底，共为 61 万困难重度残疾人家庭实施无障碍改造，为 26.3 万残疾人发放残疾人机动轮椅车燃油补贴。

八、组织建设

全国省地县乡（除新疆生产建设兵团外）共有

残联 4 万个，各省（区、市）、市（地、州、盟）、县（市、区、旗）全部成立残联，98.1%的乡镇（街道）已建立残联；99.1%的社区（村）建立残协，共 58.9 万个。

地方各级残联工作人员 11.1 万人，乡镇（街道）残联、村（社区）残协专职委员总计 55.7 万人。83.9%的省级残联、63.0%的地级残联配备了残疾人领导干部，48.9%的县级残联配备了残疾人干部。

地方各级残疾人专门协会 1.5 万个，其中省、地、县级各类专门协会已建比例分别为 98.8%、97.8%和 92.7%。全国助残社会组织 3131 个。

九、服务设施

残疾人服务设施建设得到全面发展。截至 2022 年底，全国已竣工的各级残疾人综合服务设施 2263 个，总建设规模 611.1 万平方米，总投资 203.8 亿元；已竣工各级残疾人康复设施 1200 个，总建设规模 606.9 万平方米，总投资 197.8 亿元；已竣工的各级残疾人托养服务设施 1076 个，总建设规模 318.0 万平方米，总投资 87.8 亿元。

Statistical Communique on the Undertaking for Persons with Disabilities in 2022

In 2022, Disabled Persons' Federations (hereinafter referred to as "DPFs") at all levels, under the guidance of Xi Jinping Thought on Socialism with Chinese Characteristics for a New Era, studied and followed the guiding principles of the 20th National Congress of the Communist Party of China and the important statements and instructions of President Xi Jinping on the work for persons with disabilities, earnestly implemented the Plan on the Protection and Development of Persons with Disabilities during the 14th Five-Year Plan Period (2021-2025), and advanced the high-quality development of disability-related undertakings in all respects.

I. Rehabilitation

Implementing the Plan on the Protection and Development of Persons with Disabilities during the 14th Five-Year Plan Period (2021-2025), the National Disability Prevention Action Plan (2021-2025) and the Implementation Plan for Rehabilitation Service of Persons with Disabilities during the 14th Five-Year Plan Period (2021-2025), DPFs advanced high-quality development of the work on disability prevention and rehabilitation of persons with disabilities during the 2021-2025 period. The Opinions of the State Council on Establishing Rehabilitation Assistance System for Children with Disabilities was implemented to improve rehabilitation assistance service for children with disabilities and the sense of gaining among families with children with disabilities. A total of 407,000 children have received rehabilitation services. A targeted rehabilitation service campaign was continuously carried out with focus on low-income persons with disabilities in rural areas. 8.57 million persons with disabilities received basic rehabilitation services, and 1.65 million were offered with basic assistive devices. Among those registered persons with disabilities receiving rehabilitation services, 755,000 are with visual impairment, 674,000 with hearing impairment, 56,000 with speech impairment, 4.14 million with physical disabilities, 656,000 with intellectual impairment, 1.57 million with psychosocial disability and 497,000 with multiple disabilities. Active measures were taken to safeguard the health of persons with disabilities. With cross-checked data from different departments, China gained a clear picture of the access to basic health insurance and the signing rate for family doctor service for low-income persons with disabilities, and targeted services had been taken to expand the coverage of basic health insurance and increase the family doctor service signing rate among persons with disabilities.

Efforts were made to build facilities and teams for rehabilitation. Community-based rehabilitation service was advanced. The Guidelines for the Evaluation of Standardized Services Provided by Rehabilitation Facilities Affiliated to DPFs (Trial) was formulated, and 23 syllabuses of standardized training for DPF rehabilitation professionals drafted, to provide guidance for standardized service procedures and personnel training for DPFs. By the end of 2022, there had been 11,661 rehabilitation facilities for persons with disabilities across the country, with 328,000 staff including 34,000 in managerial positions, 239,000 service personnel, and 55,000 in supporting roles. In 2022, 17,000 rehabilitation technical professionals received standardized training.

II. Education

DPFs implemented the Action Plan for Improving Special Education during the 14th Five-Year Plan Period (2021-2025) to create better education conditions and environment for persons with disabilities. Together with the Ministry of Education, China Disabled Persons' Federation (CDPF) released the Implementation Plan for Providing Assistive Devices on Campus, delivering the devices to students in need at the compulsory education stage. Together with the Ministry of Education, the State Commission Office of Public Sectors Reform and the Ministry of Finance, CDPF revised and issued Standards for the Setup of Secondary Vocational Schools for Persons with Disabilities, to enhance basic capacity building and standardized management of secondary vocational schools for persons with disabilities. The program of providing financial support to students with proceeds from lotteries was launched, which provides funds for 29 vocational schools for persons with disabilities in improving their facilities and building training bases. The Second-Phase Action Plan on Standardizing Sign Language and Braille (2021-2025) was implemented to build a sound coordination mechanism. A coordination group and an expert panel were established under the leadership of the Ministry of Education, the State Language Commission and CDPF, with members from seven ministerial departments including the Publicity Department of the CPC Central Committee, who met regularly to promote standardization and use of Chinese national sign language and Braille. The State Language Commission released Chinese National Sign Language for the Anthem, Slogan and Accession Oath of the Chinese Young Pioneers and the Anthem and Accession Oath of the Communist Youth League of China. The pilot work on grading of Chinese national sign language and Braille and accreditation of sign language translation was carried out in an orderly manner. The testing syllabus and database of testing questions for Chinese national Braille had been improved.

There were 118 high school (departments or classes) providing special education across China, enrolling 11,431 students, 6,506 of whom have hearing impairment, 1,736 with visual impairment and 3,189 with other disabilities. There were 184 secondary vocational schools (classes) for persons with disabilities, enrolling 19,014 students. The number of graduates from these vocational schools stood at 5,157, and 1,473 had acquired job qualification certificates. In terms of higher education, 30,035 students with disabilities were enrolled in universities and colleges, including 17,644 enrolled in higher vocational programs, 10,703 in undergraduate programs, 1,520 in graduate programs and 168 in doctoral programs.

III. Employment

A total of 592,000 new jobs were created for persons with disabilities in rural and urban areas across China, including 143,000 in urban areas and 449,000 in rural areas. A total of 502,000 persons with disabilities received real-name training.

The national workforce included 9,055,000 registered persons with disabilities in rural and urban areas. Of them, 867,000 were offered with jobs in government departments, public institutions and other state-funded organizations in accordance with the quota scheme, 260,000 offered with jobs in special organizations delivering services for persons with disabilities, 641,000 were self-employed, 179,000 offered with public-welfare positions, 152,000 offered with jobs under supported employment, 2,656,000 were flexibly employed, and 4.3 million worked in the farming sector.

Skills training programs were launched for persons with disabilities in difficulties in rural areas and had empowered 285,000 of them. 3,508 employment assistance bases for persons with disabilities across the country helped 45,000 persons with disabilities secure a job, and helped 80,000 households with persons with disabilities increase their income.

A total of 17,639 visually impaired people were trained with skills for health-care massage across the country, and 7,298 with massage skills for medical treatment. There were 16,926 health-care massage service providers and 1,041 ones providing massage services as medical treatment. A total of 1,844 visually impaired people received qualifications as junior massage professionals, and 500 granted with intermediate professional title.

IV. Social Security

By the end of 2022, 27,617,000 persons with disabilities were covered by the basic pension scheme for urban and rural residents, with more than 12,093,000 pensioners with disabilities. Among persons with disabilities aged under 60, 6,923,000 with severe disabilities and 2,855,000 with non-severe disabilities received government subsidies for their contribution to the basic pension scheme.

Steady progress was made in caring services for persons with disabilities. There were 8,906 facilities at various levels providing caring services for persons with disabilities. Of them, 1,763 were boarding facilities, 4,135 provided day-time caring services, and

1,362 provided comprehensive services. A total of 155,000 persons with disabilities received services at boarding and day-time caring facilities, and 472,000 received services at their home.

V. Publicity and Culture

With the theme of facilitating employment and safeguarding rights and interests, a special campaign was held to celebrate the 32nd National Day for Assisting Persons with Disabilities. Thematic publicity campaigns, including "Striving on the New Journey, Making Accomplishments in the New Era," "The Most Important Human Rights for People is to Live A Happy Life" and "Young People: Time for Hardworking,", among other key events, were organized to publicize the guiding principles of the 20th CPC National Congress and mark the Beijing 2022 Paralympic Winter Games. Xinhua News Agency published a feature on what the CPC Central Committee with Xi Jinping at the core had done for persons with disabilities. CDPF assisted the Publicity Department of the CPC Central Committee and the State Council Information Office in drafting the white paper entitled China's Parasports: Progress and the Protection of Rights. The prime-time news program of the China Media Group, Xinwen Lianbo, made 57 coverage of the work on disability. New ways of service were introduced to provide high-quality cultural products and services for persons with disabilities at the community level. CDPF, together with 12 ministries and departments including the Office of the Central Commission for Guiding Cultural and Ethical Progress, released Implementation Opinions on Further Promoting Activities of Helping and Supporting Persons with Disabilities. The 10th national art gala of persons with disabilities was organized under the theme of rallying around the CPC and chasing dreams in the new era. The 2022 National Culture Week of Persons with Disabilities was also launched with the theme of striving on the new journey and welcoming the 20th CPC National Congress. A performance and exhibition tour was staged, with a total of 14 performances and exhibitions across the country. A special film-on-demand section targeting persons with disabilities were launched on the national TV cable services. The public account on Weixin, "Ren Mei Wen Yi," was launched to disseminate cultural information to persons with disabilities. The 2021 Collections of Works of Writers with Disabilities was edited and published. All this greatly enriched the cultural life for persons with disabilites. Nationwide, provincial-level DPFs ran 24 special radio programs for persons with disabilities, and 37 sign language TV programs, municipal-level DPFs operated 195 special radio programs and 270 sign language TV programs. Public libraries across the country had set up 1,377 Braille reading rooms and Braille audio rooms. A total of 10,010 Culture Week events for persons with disabilities were organized. There were 229 art troupes of persons with disabilities at the provincial and prefecture levels.

VI. Sports

The 13th Paralympic Winter Games was held in Beijing and Zhangjiakou from March 4 to 13, 2022. The delegation of Chinese Para athletes, keeping in mind of President Xi Jinping's instructions on the preparation for the Beijing 2022 Paralympic Winter Games and the undertaking for persons with disabilities, followed the decisions and arrangements by the CPC Central Committee and the State Council and did their best in the competitions. They claimed 18 gold medals, 20 silver medals and 23 bronze medals, ranking first on both the gold medal and overall medal table, setting a record of Chinese delegation in the history of Winter Paralympics, marking a leapfrog progress in winter sports, and wining honor for the country and the people. They also made important contributions to the success of the Beijing 2022 Paralympic Winter Games. CDPF assisted the Organizing Committee for the Hangzhou 2022 Asian Para Games, coordinated the Asian Paralympic Committee in preparing for the Hangzhou Asian Para Games, and properly tackled problems arising from the postponing of the Games. The preparations for the 12th National Games for Persons with Disabilities and the ninth Special Olympic Games in 2025 were started. Efforts were made to cultivate technical personnel for para sports. A total of 1,637 people were promoted as referees, and classification committees were set up. Preparations for competing in the Paris 2024 Paralympic Summer Games and Milano Cortina 2026 Paralympic Winter Games were started. Chinese para athletes competed in the Paris World Shooting Para

Sport World Cup, the Weightlifting Asian Championships in the Republic of Korea, the IBSA Blind Football Asia-Oceania Championships in India, and the 2022 IBSA Blind Goalball World Championships in Portugal, and claimed 23 gold medals, nine silver medals and three bronze medals. Campaigns for promoting rehabilitation and fitness among persons with disabilities were launched. The Exercise Week, Special Olympics Day, ice and snow season, among other sports events, were organized. The participation rate of persons with disabilities in community-level cultural and sports activities climbed from 23.9 percent in 2021 to 26.3 percent in 2022.

VII. Rights Protection

Six special rules and regulations at the provincial level and nine at the municipal level concerning persons with disabilities were formulated or revised. A total of 42 government documents at the provincial level, 66 at the municipal level and 185 at the county level for the rights and interests protection of persons with disabilities were formulated and revised. People's congresses at the county level and above carried out 413 inspections and surveys on the law enforcement and special issues regarding the rights protection of persons with disabilities, in addition to 262 such inspections and surveys organized by committees of the Chinese People's Political Consultative Conference. A total of 184 provincial-level events for popularizing knowledge of law were organized nationwide, involving more than 880,000 participants. A total of 39 provincial-level training sessions on law were launched, involving 27,216 participants. Nationwide, there were 2,869 institutions providing legal assistance to persons with disabilities, and 2,633 legal aid centers for persons with disabilities. DPFs at all levels handled 1,564 suggestions and proposals.

A total of 761 regulations, government decrees and documents at provincial, municipal and county levels were issued for the building and management of a barrier-free environment. The country made 9,996 inspections on the building of a barrier-free environment, and 52,000 people received training on accessibility. By the end of 2022, home accessibility renovation had been done for 610,000 disadvantaged households with members living with severe disabilities, and 263,000 persons with disabilities were offered with fuel subsidies for automobile wheelchairs.

VIII. Organization Building

There were 40,000 DPFs across China, covering all provinces (autonomous regions and municipalities directly under the central government), prefectures (cities and autonomous prefectures), and counties (districts and autonomous counties), and 98.1percent of townships (sub-districts). In addition, 99.1 percent neighborhoods (villages) had set up their own DPF, amounting to 589,000 in total.

The number of staff of DPFs at all levels reached 111,000. Disability commissioners in township-level and community-level DPFs totaled 557,000. In addition, 83.9 percent of provincial-level DPFs, 63 percent of prefecture-level DPFs, and 48.9 percent of county-level DPFs had appointed persons with disabilities as leading officials.

There were 15,000 specialized associations for persons with disabilities at all levels, covering 98.8 percent, 97.8 percent and 92.7 percent of provincial regions, cities/prefectures and counties, respectively. There were 3,131 civil society organizations dedicated to helping persons with disabilities nationwide.

IX. Service Facilities

The construction of service facilities for persons with disabilities was advanced in a holistic manner. By the end of 2022, a total of 2,263 comprehensive service facilities for persons with disabilities had been completed across the country, with the total construction area of 6,111,000 square meters and the total investment amount of 20.38 billion RMB. A total of 1,200 rehabilitation facilities for persons with disabilities were completed, with the combined construction area of 6,069,000 square meters and total investment of 19.78 billion yuan. In addition, the construction of 1,076 caring service centers for persons with disabilities was completed, with the total construction area of 3,180,000 square meters and total investment amount of 8.78 billion RMB.

3

综合统计资料

Overall Statistics

3-1 中国残疾人事业主要业务进展情况 (2018－2022)

指 标 名 称		Item	
康 复		**Rehabilitation**	
1. 残疾人精准康复服务		**Provision of Targeted Rehabilitation Service**	
视力残疾人	(万人)	Visual Disability	(10,000 persons)
听力残疾人	(万人)	Hearing Disability	(10,000 persons)
言语残疾人	(万人)	Speech Disability	(10,000 persons)
肢体残疾人	(万人)	Physical Disability	(10,000 persons)
智力残疾人	(万人)	Intellectual Disability	(10,000 persons)
精神残疾人	(万人)	Mental Disability	(10,000 persons)
多重残疾人	(万人)	Multiple Disabilities	(10,000 persons)
2. 残疾人辅助器具供应服务		**Provision of Assistive Devices**	
辅助器具供应	(万人)	Assistive Devices Provided	(10,000 persons)
3. 康复机构建设		**Construction of Rehabilitation Institution**	
残疾人康复机构	(个)	Rehabilitation Institutions for PWDs	(unit)
康复机构在岗人员	(万人)	Staff of Rehabilitation Institutions	(10,000 persons)
4. 社区康复		**Community-Based Rehabilitation (CBR)**	
开展社区康复服务的县(市、区)*	(个)	Counties and Districts Providing CBR	(unit)
社区康复协调员	(万人)	CBR Coordinators	(10,000 persons)
教 育		**Education**	
1. 残疾人高级中等教育		**Senior Secondary Education for PWDs**	
特教普通高中	(个)	Special Education Senior High Schools	(unit)
特教普通高中在校学生	(人)	Students in Special Education Senior High Schools	(person)
中等职业教育机构	(个)	Secondary Vocational Schools	(unit)
中等职业教育在校学生	(人)	Students in Secondary Vocational Schools	(person)
2. 残疾人高等教育		**Higher Education for PWDs**	
高校录取残疾考生	(人)	Disabled Students Admitted to Higher Education Institutions	(person)
就 业		**Employment**	
1. 城乡持证残疾人就业状况		**Employment of PWDs in Urban and Rural Areas**	
按比例就业	(万人)	Employed through Quoto Scheme	(10,000 persons)
集中就业	(万人)	Employed through PWDs-Oriented Post	(10,000 persons)
个体就业	(万人)	Self-Employed	(10,000 persons)
公益性岗位就业	(万人)	Employed through Welfare Post	(10,000 persons)

注：*“开展社区康复服务的县(市、区)”包含正式行政区划单位和开发区、管委会等非正式行政区划，以及新疆兵团下属县级单位。
Counties (cities and districts) providing community rehabilitation service include formal administrative divisions and development zones, informal administrative divisions such as management committees, and county-level units subordinate to the Xinjiang Production and Construction Corps .

Summary on the Development of the Work for Persons with Disabilities (2018－2022)

2018－2022年完成情况 Implementation (2018-2022)				
2018	2019	2020	2021	2022
120.5	112.2	114.6	78.4	75.5
66.1	73.1	81.6	65.1	67.4
7.5	4.4	5.1	5.1	5.6
592.3	553.5	542.8	407.0	414.3
83.8	82.3	86.4	68.8	65.6
150.8	161.5	178.4	157.6	157.0
48.2	46.8	54.7	49.8	49.7
319.1	314.5	242.6	177.0	164.8
9036	9775	10440	11260	11661
25.0	26.4	29.5	31.8	32.8
2750	2731	2726	2686	2625
47.8	47.8	47.8	48.1	48.2
102	103	104	117	118
7666	8676	10173	11847	11431
133	145	147	161	184
19475	17319	17877	17934	19014
13027	14415	15804	16861	30035
81.3	74.9	78.4	81.8	86.7
33.1	29.1	27.8	26.8	26.0
71.4	64.2	63.4	63.5	64.1
13.1	14.4	14.7	14.8	17.9

3-1 续表 1

指标名称		Item	
辅助性就业	(万人)	Assistive Employment	(10,000 persons)
灵活就业(含社区就业、居家就业)	(万人)	Flexible Employment	(10,000 persons)
从事农业种养加	(万人)	Engaged in Agricultural Planting, Husbandry and Processing	(10,000 persons)
2. 盲人按摩		**Massage by the Blind**	
按摩人员培训		Massage Training	
保健按摩人员	(人)	Training for Health-Care Masseurs	(person)
医疗按摩人员	(人)	Training for Therapeutical Masseurs	(person)
按摩机构		Institutions of Blind Massage	
医疗按摩机构	(个)	Therapeutical Massage Clinics	(unit)
保健按摩机构	(个)	Health-Care Massage Houses	(unit)
3. 实用技术培训	(万人次)	**Training on Practical Skills and Technologies for PWDs**	(10,000 person-times)
4. 残疾人就业帮扶基地建设		**Poverty Alleviation Bases for PWDs in Rural Areas**	
残疾人就业帮扶基地	(个)	Poverty Alleviation Bases for PWDs	(unit)
安置残疾人就业	(万人)	PWDs Provided with Employment Opportunities	(10,000 persons)
辐射带动残疾人户	(万户)	Benefited PWDs with Financial Difficult	(10,000 households)
社会保障		**Social Security**	
1. 社会保险		**Social Insurance**	
残疾居民参加城乡社会养老保险	(万人)	PWDs Covered by Pension Scheme	(10,000 persons)
2. 托养服务		**Institutional Care Services**	
托养服务机构	(个)	Institutional Care Service Facilities	(unit)
托养残疾人	(万人)	PWDs Receiving Institutional Care Service	(10,000 persons)
宣传文化		**Publicity and Cultural Activities**	
1. 宣传		**Publicity at Provincial and Municipal Level**	
省、地级广播电台残疾人专题节目	(个)	Radio Programs on Disability	(unit)
省、地级电视手语栏目	(个)	TV Programmes with Sign Language	(unit)
2. 文化		**Cultural Activities at Provincial and Municipal Level**	
省、地级盲文及盲人有声读物阅览室	(个)	Reading Rooms with Braille and Audio Reading Materials	(unit)
省、地级残疾人文化周	(场次)	Cultural Week for PWDs	(session)
省、地级残疾人文化艺术类比赛及展览	(次)	Cultural or Artistic Competitions and Exhibitions for PWDs	(time)
体　育			
1. 残疾人群众体育健身活动情况			
残疾人群众体育健身活动	(次)	Fitness Sports Activities for PWDs	(time)
残疾人群众体育健身活动参加人次	(万人次)	Participants of Fitness Sports Activities for PWDs	(person-time)
2. 省级残疾人体育比赛情况			
残疾人体育比赛	(次)	Sports Events for PWDs	(time)
参赛残疾人运动员	(人次)	Disabled Athletes Who Participated in the Sports Events	(person-time)
维　权		**Rights Protection**	
1. 法规体系和政策文件		Legal System	

Continued 1

2018–2022年完成情况 Implementation(2018-2022)				
2018	2019	2020	2021	2022
14.8	14.3	14.3	14.3	15.2
254.6	228.2	238.8	250.3	265.6
480.1	430.1	424.2	430.1	430.1
19732	14678	12761	13483	17639
10160	7318	7820	8372	7298
1126	894	873	1105	1041
16776	13181	17313	17128	16926
58.8	50.9	45.7	42.3	28.5
5490	4662	4581	4362	3508
7	6.2	5.6	5.0	4.5
13.5	10.0	9.6	9.3	8.0
2561.2	2630.7	2699.2	2733.1	2761.7
8435	9941	8370	11278	8906
111.1	116.2	53.7	60.9	62.7
230	244	234	226	219
295	304	296	291	307
301	312	317	319	323
940	1072	1072	1020	1667
663	799	690	721	698
49432	38932	38508	40332	36298
127.8	123.4	113.1	126.7	141.9
319	228	66	139	94
36572	16341	6085	10556	19438

3−1　续表 2

指　标　名　称		Item	
制定或修改关于残疾人的专门法规、规章	(个)	Disability-Specific Laws and Regulations Formulated or Amended	(unit)
制定或修改保障残疾人权益的规范性文件	(个)	Normative Documents on Rights of PWDs Formulated or Amended	(unit)
2. 执法检查		**Inspections on Law Enforcement**	
人大执法检查或专题调研	(次)	Inspections and Researches by People's Congresses	(time)
政协视察或专题调研	(次)	Inspections and Researches by Political Consultative Conferences	(time)
3. 法律救助		**Legal Aid**	
残疾人法律救助工作协调机构	(个)	Coordinating Agency for Legal Assistance Work for PWDs	(unit)
残疾人法律救助工作站	(个)	Legal Assistance Stations for PWDs	(unit)
4. 参政议政		**PWDs Participating in Administration and Discussion of State Affairs**	
办理人大、政协交办的议案、建议、提案	(件)	Suggestions and Proposals Handled by Disabled Persons' Federations	(case)
5. 无障碍环境建设		**Accessible Environments Building**	
无障碍环境建设与管理法规、政府令	(个)	Regulations and Decrees on Accessible Environments Building and Management	(unit)
6. 残疾人机动轮椅车燃油补贴	(万人)	**Gas Subsidy for Motorized Wheelchairs of PWDs**	(10,000 persons)
组织建设		**Organizational Structure**	
1. 省地县乡残联实有人员	(万人)	**Staff of Disabled Persons' Federations at Provincial, Municipal, County and Township Level**	(10,000 persons)
2. 地级残联		**Disabled Persons' Federations at Municipal Level**	
配备残疾人领导干部的残联	(个)	Disabled Persons' Federations Whose Leadership Include PWDs	(unit)
残疾人干部	(人)	Staff with Disability	(person)
3. 县级残联		**Disabled Persons' Federations at County Level**	
配备残疾人干部的残联	(个)	Disabled Persons' Federations Whose Leadership Include PWDs	(unit)
残疾人干部	(人)	Staff with Disability	(person)
4. 乡级残联与村级残疾人协会		**Disabled Persons' Federations in Township (Town, Sub-district) and Villages (Communities)**	
已建乡、镇、街道残联	(万个)	Disabled Persons' Federation Established	(10,000 units)
其中：已配专兼职理事长	(万人)	Disabled Persons' Federation with Full-Time (Part-Time) President	(10,000 persons)

Continued 2

2018–2022年完成情况　Implementation (2018-2022)				
2018	2019	2020	2021	2022
24	21	9	12	15
228	255	249	240	293
294	293	318	341	413
280	229	282	251	262
1988	2201	2881	2862	2869
1814	2021	2795	2620	2633
1081	1113	1109	1187	1564
475	537	674	753	761
65.1	47.4	34.1	29.6	26.3
11.1	11.1	10.8	11.0	11.1
236	240	223	206	213
429	432	491	482	483
1499	1450	1456	1464	1467
2195	2133	2313	2270	2244
3.9	3.8	3.7	3.7	3.7
2.1	2.1	1.9	1.9	1.9

3-1 续表 3

指 标 名 称		Item	
已建村(社区)残疾人协会	(万个)	Associations of Disabled Persons Established in Villages (Communities)	(10,000 units)
选聘残疾人专职委员	(万人)	Full-time Commissioners for Disability Issues	(10,000 persons)
5．省级以下各类专门协会		**Special Associations below Provincial Level**	
盲人协会	(个)	Associations of Persons with Visual Disability	(unit)
聋人协会	(个)	Associations of Persons with Hearing Disability	(unit)
肢残人协会	(个)	Associations of Persons with Physical Disability	(unit)
智力残疾人及亲友协会	(个)	Associations of Persons with Intellectual Disability and Their Relatives and Friends	(unit)
精神残疾人及亲友协会	(个)	Associations of Persons with Psychosocial Disability and Their Relatives and Friends	(unit)
智力残疾人及亲友协会和精神残疾人及亲友协会合一的协会	(个)	Joint Associations of Persons with Intellectual or Psychosocial Disability and Their Relatives and Friends	(unit)
残疾人服务设施建设		**Service Facilities for PWDs**	
1．残疾人综合服务设施		**Comprehensive Service Facilities for PWDs**	
已竣工	(个)	Completed Projects	(unit)
总建设规模	(万平米)	Construction Area	(10,000 sq.m)
2．残疾人康复设施		**Rehabilitation Service Facilities for PWDs**	
已竣工	(个)	Completed Projects	(unit)
总建设规模	(万平米)	Construction Area	(10,000 sq.m)
3．残疾人托养设施		**Institutional Care Service Facilities for PWDs**	
已竣工	(个)	Completed Projects	(unit)
总建设规模	(万平米)	Construction Area	(10,000 sq.m)
信息化建设		**Application of IT**	
1．残疾人人口基础库数据	(万人)	Data of the National Basic Database of Persons with Disabilities	(10,000 persons)
2．省、地、县各级残联网站	(个)	Websites at Provincial, Municipal, and County Levels	(unit)

Continued 3

2018–2022年完成情况 Implementation (2018-2022)				
2018	2019	2020	2021	2022
54.9	54	53.9	56.7	58.9
58.7	58.1	55.3	55.1	55.7
3140	3018	3024	3036	3064
3121	3006	3013	3031	3056
3154	3035	3044	3058	3082
2991	2873	2870	2884	2946
2992	2868	2870	2886	2950
128	128	136	140	107
2364	2341	2318	2290	2263
578.3	584.5	612.3	612.9	611.1
914	1006	1063	1164	1200
344.9	414.2	462.7	550.6	606.9
791	887	1024	1048	1076
214.8	251.3	285.4	303.8	318.0
3566.2	3681.7	3780.7	3804.9	3768.2
1155	1051	1047	1056	1032

3-2 全国残疾人人口基础库主要数据
Statistics of the National Basic Information Database of Persons with Disabilities

单位：人 (截止时间：2022年12月31日) (person)

地 区	Region	已办理残疾人证 Registered Persons with Disabilities	0-15岁 Aged 0-15	16-59岁 Aged 16-59	60岁及以上 Aged 60 and above
全 国	**Nationwide**	**37681660**	**1201979**	**19120885**	**17358796**
北 京	Beijing	563243	7900	205653	349690
天 津	Tianjin	375727	5252	152305	218170
河 北	Hebei	1844425	55530	931678	857217
山 西	Shanxi	1012868	24081	521066	467721
内蒙古	Inner Mongolia	772921	16001	403344	353576
辽 宁	Liaoning	1063776	18540	572846	472390
吉 林	Jilin	835278	14855	453693	366730
黑龙江	Heilongjiang	1014484	15669	583777	415038
上 海	Shanghai	603047	3932	160537	438578
江 苏	Jiangsu	1723025	52065	851527	819433
浙 江	Zhejiang	1412006	33087	592596	786323
安 徽	Anhui	1944084	59484	1001986	882614
福 建	Fujian	886246	39190	428741	418315
江 西	Jiangxi	1259451	52109	740237	467105
山 东	Shandong	2652782	86565	1207936	1358281
河 南	Henan	2924573	104513	1435443	1384617
湖 北	Hubei	1668818	39125	873032	756661
湖 南	Hunan	1962441	61627	1040865	859949
广 东	Guangdong	1846531	102944	955440	788147
广 西	Guangxi	1348208	63589	697394	587225
海 南	Hainan	202337	10154	115058	77125
重 庆	Chongqing	897298	29015	492170	376113
四 川	Sichuan	2855399	77503	1413051	1364845
贵 州	Guizhou	1246641	53340	718036	475265
云 南	Yunnan	1501045	53509	844117	603419
西 藏	Tibet	112935	9619	68195	35121
陕 西	Shaanxi	1299885	26347	584943	688595
甘 肃	Gansu	877051	27996	474952	374103
青 海	Qinghai	176624	9357	105463	61804
宁 夏	Ningxia	228317	8006	123994	96317
新 疆	Xinjiang	505658	39214	325426	141018
新疆兵团	Xinjiang Production and Construction Corps	64536	1861	45384	17291

3-2　续表 1　Continued 1

单位：人 (person)

地　区	Region	已办理证件残疾人 Registered Persons with Disabilities					
		性　别 Gender		残疾等级 Disability Grading			
		男　性 Male	女　性 Female	残疾一级 Grade-1	残疾二级 Grade-2	残疾三级 Grade-3	残疾四级 Grade-4
全　国	**Nationwide**	**21746314**	**15935346**	**4927464**	**12006295**	**9592626**	**11155275**
北　京	Beijing	297750	265493	67819	121121	137229	237074
天　津	Tianjin	200562	175165	35654	111338	102577	126158
河　北	Hebei	1063876	780549	242426	604288	409412	588299
山　西	Shanxi	610737	402131	132282	324866	239679	316041
内蒙古	Inner Mongolia	445594	327327	79568	240447	211200	241706
辽　宁	Liaoning	644707	419069	128089	333971	293200	308516
吉　林	Jilin	497403	337875	91450	287293	227622	228913
黑龙江	Heilongjiang	615408	399076	117388	299632	279442	318022
上　海	Shanghai	302428	300619	76557	110903	145855	269732
江　苏	Jiangsu	942381	780644	205757	571331	497698	448239
浙　江	Zhejiang	805548	606458	185982	284624	421271	520129
安　徽	Anhui	1088325	855759	219725	812951	486648	424760
福　建	Fujian	514527	371719	144883	298572	207062	235729
江　西	Jiangxi	759190	500261	131652	386920	343415	397464
山　东	Shandong	1541222	1111560	387083	946055	632832	686812
河　南	Henan	1655603	1268970	330525	1040609	760763	792676
湖　北	Hubei	969750	699068	238349	600931	400124	429414
湖　南	Hunan	1174588	787853	241410	759479	429892	531660
广　东	Guangdong	1058411	788120	311812	724923	427464	382332
广　西	Guangxi	777596	570612	194132	458854	303118	392104
海　南	Hainan	118409	83928	66311	53582	45276	37168
重　庆	Chongqing	533366	363932	102336	254941	223002	317019
四　川	Sichuan	1646822	1208577	374955	845951	717101	917392
贵　州	Guizhou	765003	481638	164063	264545	303278	514755
云　南	Yunnan	879438	621607	185796	357123	354291	603835
西　藏	Tibet	57290	55645	13572	23398	28327	47638
陕　西	Shaanxi	728561	571324	171692	331871	482151	314171
甘　肃	Gansu	494621	382430	158511	261600	222773	234167
青　海	Qinghai	97145	79479	25852	55951	45854	48967
宁　夏	Ningxia	125392	102925	27252	79851	56522	64692
新　疆	Xinjiang	296208	209450	67081	140077	140540	157960
新疆兵团	Xinjiang Production and Construction Corps	38453	26083	7500	18297	17008	21731

3-2 续表 2 Continued 2

单位：人 (person)

地区	Region	已办理证件残疾人 Registered Persons with Disabilities				
		残疾类别 Disability Category				
		视力残疾人 Persons with Visual Disability	听力残疾人 Persons with Hearing Disability	言语残疾人 Persons with Speech Disability	肢体残疾人 Persons with Physical Disability	智力残疾人 Persons with Intellectual Disability
全 国	**Nationwide**	**4034659**	**3329227**	**597211**	**19934996**	**3454412**
北 京	Beijing	58747	47406	3330	319694	49782
天 津	Tianjin	29868	28147	4267	246975	30296
河 北	Hebei	157981	140047	31323	1094850	171900
山 西	Shanxi	104309	102508	20816	567766	97011
内蒙古	Inner Mongolia	74576	77277	13394	426345	66939
辽 宁	Liaoning	107653	86831	10648	581336	114726
吉 林	Jilin	88321	77897	13236	456163	78062
黑龙江	Heilongjiang	100666	84317	12711	595881	93530
上 海	Shanghai	94507	84552	5490	294066	55806
江 苏	Jiangsu	197864	117606	8880	903198	221512
浙 江	Zhejiang	134288	229605	17045	647893	139059
安 徽	Anhui	205566	134484	27678	989973	185902
福 建	Fujian	79133	134037	12774	399438	101881
江 西	Jiangxi	131235	100009	18364	639655	126570
山 东	Shandong	194182	213439	25604	1534074	234685
河 南	Henan	270682	232620	64216	1662206	299249
湖 北	Hubei	211943	141978	34899	796888	142543
湖 南	Hunan	244155	148025	38256	985936	181412
广 东	Guangdong	140748	174908	30626	799656	205911
广 西	Guangxi	138185	99066	25124	684757	121197
海 南	Hainan	18256	14707	3518	100806	20099
重 庆	Chongqing	128981	64807	15257	460686	86569
四 川	Sichuan	412276	242247	44339	1554174	200373
贵 州	Guizhou	138036	81310	30510	728302	83534
云 南	Yunnan	183682	129980	32590	805164	98779
西 藏	Tibet	17368	13715	5074	57117	2982
陕 西	Shaanxi	152003	130612	17660	662391	87622
甘 肃	Gansu	93547	92541	11593	450490	74807
青 海	Qinghai	23015	24667	3589	91604	15705
宁 夏	Ningxia	28406	23994	3436	119367	20098
新 疆	Xinjiang	66682	50876	10213	246296	39281
新疆兵团	Xinjiang Production and Construction Corps	7798	5012	751	31849	6590

3-2 续表 3 Continued 3

单位：人 (person)

地 区	Region	已办理证件残疾人 Registered Persons with Disabilities			
		残疾类别 Disability Category		户口性质 Registered Permanent Residence	
		精神残疾人 Persons with Mental Disability	多重残疾人 Persons with Multiple Disabilities	农业 Rural	非农业 Urban
全 国	**Nationwide**	**4305926**	**2025229**	**29763449**	**7918211**
北 京	Beijing	53618	30666	212300	350943
天 津	Tianjin	27530	8644	141505	234222
河 北	Hebei	138536	109788	1610667	233758
山 西	Shanxi	73362	47096	817064	195804
内蒙古	Inner Mongolia	74075	40315	540251	232670
辽 宁	Liaoning	118773	43809	597899	465877
吉 林	Jilin	86959	34640	494174	341104
黑龙江	Heilongjiang	95795	31584	535200	479284
上 海	Shanghai	53006	15620	94651	508396
江 苏	Jiangsu	210273	63692	1339911	383114
浙 江	Zhejiang	178799	65317	1120584	291422
安 徽	Anhui	273088	127393	1658828	285256
福 建	Fujian	108468	50515	734325	151921
江 西	Jiangxi	171775	71843	1020192	239259
山 东	Shandong	293143	157655	2338985	313797
河 南	Henan	267103	128497	2617267	307306
湖 北	Hubei	240292	100275	1353632	315186
湖 南	Hunan	262978	101679	1654704	307737
广 东	Guangdong	381669	113013	1378523	468008
广 西	Guangxi	200436	79443	1211485	136723
海 南	Hainan	36112	8839	150578	51759
重 庆	Chongqing	101399	39599	665163	232135
四 川	Sichuan	283768	118222	2396251	459148
贵 州	Guizhou	98195	86754	1120354	126287
云 南	Yunnan	172072	78778	1325525	175520
西 藏	Tibet	6479	10200	103976	8959
陕 西	Shaanxi	138941	110656	1128482	171403
甘 肃	Gansu	79027	75046	752249	124802
青 海	Qinghai	6430	11614	138867	37757
宁 夏	Ningxia	18876	14140	159638	68679
新 疆	Xinjiang	45752	46558	347760	157898
新疆兵团	Xinjiang Production and Construction Corps	9197	3339	2459	62077

3-2 续表 4 Continued 4

单位：人 (person)

地 区	Region	已办理证件残疾人 Registered Persons with Disabilities					
		受教育程度 Education					
		文 盲 Illiterate	小 学 Primary School	初 中 Junior High School	高中及中专 Senior High or Vocational School	大学专科及以上 Junior College and Above	其 他 Others
全 国	**Nationwide**	**6795068**	**14955363**	**11236192**	**3165108**	**780299**	**749630**
北 京	Beijing	54111	95473	218320	127172	60247	7920
天 津	Tianjin	29909	85193	150395	80061	26375	3794
河 北	Hebei	227081	752212	632875	154377	32447	45433
山 西	Shanxi	123437	349247	404887	95839	22771	16687
内蒙古	Inner Mongolia	124933	288237	255020	76220	19427	9084
辽 宁	Liaoning	106753	333741	470945	111070	28777	12490
吉 林	Jilin	95021	269208	331164	116715	17767	5403
黑龙江	Heilongjiang	80774	351281	424848	121094	24641	11846
上 海	Shanghai	41829	113484	254010	142856	50861	7
江 苏	Jiangsu	508755	546935	484101	138594	39482	5158
浙 江	Zhejiang	264080	637009	367713	88863	29637	24704
安 徽	Anhui	576940	748180	467282	92589	26943	32150
福 建	Fujian	140066	418641	215753	60795	14325	36666
江 西	Jiangxi	156132	546155	400311	95506	17384	43963
山 东	Shandong	507016	1001184	810804	223625	42511	67642
河 南	Henan	769899	1010467	838099	204405	37933	63770
湖 北	Hubei	341640	553897	533394	182193	33217	24477
湖 南	Hunan	239742	858321	605720	195244	27489	35925
广 东	Guangdong	245792	781054	542881	157554	38272	80978
广 西	Guangxi	146478	658344	385993	81082	15610	60701
海 南	Hainan	34840	64147	74671	20021	3629	5029
重 庆	Chongqing	86284	460005	254124	58671	13415	24799
四 川	Sichuan	438372	1492426	701072	149680	36826	37023
贵 州	Guizhou	343966	550169	269648	48538	17864	16456
云 南	Yunnan	370502	727843	285164	68664	26516	22356
西 藏	Tibet	65063	38158	5163	1427	1051	2073
陕 西	Shaanxi	253056	478962	415216	115974	23873	12804
甘 肃	Gansu	260160	344108	184433	64320	14795	9235
青 海	Qinghai	44922	86334	26902	10888	4179	3399
宁 夏	Ningxia	55876	85270	58047	18442	7272	3410
新 疆	Xinjiang	57026	211890	141504	51532	20830	22876
新疆兵团	Xinjiang Production and Construction Corps	4613	17788	25733	11097	3933	1372

分省统计资料

Provincial Statistics

一、康复
Rehabilitation

4-1-1 社区康复
Community-Based Rehabilitation(CBR)

地 区	Region	开展社区康复服务的市辖区* Districts Delivering CBR Services	开展社区康复服务的县(市)* Counties Delivering CBR Services	社区康复协调员 CBR Coordinators
		个 unit	个 unit	人 person
全 国	**Nationwide**	**1003**	**1622**	**482255**
北 京	Beijing	16		6098
天 津	Tianjin	16		4420
河 北	Hebei	53	102	46228
山 西	Shanxi	24	84	21191
内蒙古	Inner Mongolia	25	83	12328
辽 宁	Liaoning	64	39	13992
吉 林	Jilin	33	38	11240
黑龙江	Heilongjiang	59	67	7137
上 海	Shanghai	16		4579
江 苏	Jiangsu	63	41	20059
浙 江	Zhejiang	41	53	23450
安 徽	Anhui	51	62	17651
福 建	Fujian	30	55	14522
江 西	Jiangxi	36	73	15808
山 东	Shandong	61	71	46028
河 南	Henan	60	103	46502
湖 北	Hubei	44	51	9847
湖 南	Hunan	35	77	24947
广 东	Guangdong	70	56	24789
广 西	Guangxi	35	52	15510
海 南	Hainan	4	8	2306
重 庆	Chongqing	29	12	11538
四 川	Sichuan	39	84	19092
贵 州	Guizhou	9	65	10731
云 南	Yunnan	13	89	13225
西 藏	Tibet	2	8	803
陕 西	Shaanxi	32	73	14386
甘 肃	Gansu	16	64	13623
青 海	Qinghai	7	37	3669
宁 夏	Ningxia	9	13	2399
新 疆	Xinjiang	11	58	3628
新疆兵团	Xinjiang Production and Construction Corps		4	529

注：*“开展社区康复服务的县(市、区)”包含正式行政区划单位和开发区、管委会等非正式行政区划，以及新疆兵团下属县级单位。

The data in "Counties Delivering CBR Services" covered formal administrative units and informal administrative units such as development zones, as well as county-level units under the jurisdiction of Xinjiang Production and Construction Corps .

4-1-2 残疾人接受基本康复服务总体情况
Basic Rehabilitation Services Received by Persons with Disabilities

地区	Region	合计 Total	其中：0-6岁残疾儿童 Disabled Children Aged 0-6	视力残疾 Persons with Visual Disability	听力残疾 Persons with Hearing Disability	言语残疾 Persons with Speech Disability	肢体残疾 Persons with Physical Disability
		人 person	人 person	人 person	人 person	人 person	人 person
全国	**Nationwide**	**8566562**	**341154**	**754959**	**673620**	**56250**	**4142513**
北京	Beijing	180021	3436	7646	20116	172	74609
天津	Tianjin	51541	3402	3995	3090	56	28271
河北	Hebei	299367	9526	16837	15360	1920	185789
山西	Shanxi	92052	6343	4857	5556	117	52560
内蒙古	Inner Mongolia	64636	4090	4499	5567	222	33859
辽宁	Liaoning	192284	6787	17398	11809	796	97062
吉林	Jilin	133541	3443	11900	9452	532	80481
黑龙江	Heilongjiang	73081	3434	6046	4406	48	46021
上海	Shanghai	130809	1456	20110	14756	902	70307
江苏	Jiangsu	233374	29293	16040	7873	178	90203
浙江	Zhejiang	671221	13235	60325	88807	8669	225046
安徽	Anhui	361032	17534	19785	15471	1416	102734
福建	Fujian	322535	17617	18665	40125	1455	132831
江西	Jiangxi	161553	9572	13263	11056	270	66528
山东	Shandong	1478328	29815	104550	111811	13482	860342
河南	Henan	340672	32359	23378	22499	2688	200508
湖北	Hubei	458819	17298	48932	36969	3413	193212
湖南	Hunan	315762	18884	33291	21232	1386	149429
广东	Guangdong	298843	26911	10793	19104	2318	73078
广西	Guangxi	166445	18135	15318	8499	592	73062
海南	Hainan	27980	4001	636	487	193	5124
重庆	Chongqing	263076	9415	27659	14552	2552	104516
四川	Sichuan	973287	14703	134442	70970	6118	537705
贵州	Guizhou	121705	8199	12903	7798	1362	61464
云南	Yunnan	248081	7088	24112	21125	2453	112216
西藏	Tibet	16502	411	2476	2313	373	9572
陕西	Shaanxi	553463	9789	59756	48713	330	310228
甘肃	Gansu	132890	6176	13107	13097	525	66274
青海	Qinghai	46942	1838	5822	6617	746	24689
宁夏	Ningxia	62686	3215	6250	5874	486	29967
新疆	Xinjiang	87094	3539	9759	8213	473	42396
新疆兵团	Xinjiang Production and Construction Corps	6940	210	409	303	7	2430

4-1-2　续表　Continued

地　区	Region	智力残疾 Persons with Intellectual Disability	精神残疾 Persons with Mental Disability	多重残疾 Persons with Multiple Disabilities	0-17岁未持证残疾儿 Unregistered Disabled Children Aged 0-17
		人 person	人 person	人 person	人 person
全　国	**Nationwide**	**655662**	**1569851**	**496511**	**217198**
北　京	Beijing	7731	53181	14432	2134
天　津	Tianjin	3747	7419	1661	3302
河　北	Hebei	13765	44630	14221	6845
山　西	Shanxi	6233	13461	4935	4333
内蒙古	Inner Mongolia	2218	11706	3403	3162
辽　宁	Liaoning	14135	33059	12579	5447
吉　林	Jilin	7921	14948	5887	2420
黑龙江	Heilongjiang	4034	7457	2263	2806
上　海	Shanghai	9164	9525	4114	1931
江　苏	Jiangsu	17900	68911	8714	23555
浙　江	Zhejiang	93216	148513	40853	5792
安　徽	Anhui	21297	164686	25382	10261
福　建	Fujian	39170	62346	17502	10441
江　西	Jiangxi	9691	46471	9594	4680
山　东	Shandong	128249	154433	93518	11943
河　南	Henan	21162	29974	15811	24652
湖　北	Hubei	36486	99814	26477	13516
湖　南	Hunan	17030	65518	14534	13342
广　东	Guangdong	19847	141156	18541	14007
广　西	Guangxi	14355	30479	10893	13247
海　南	Hainan	1424	16749	1062	2305
重　庆	Chongqing	24161	70661	13346	5629
四　川	Sichuan	61801	116712	39267	6272
贵　州	Guizhou	8777	12515	11736	5150
云　南	Yunnan	15300	54051	15270	3554
西　藏	Tibet	108	228	1426	6
陕　西	Shaanxi	34042	52471	39806	8117
甘　肃	Gansu	8738	15015	11616	4518
青　海	Qinghai	3748	1600	2910	810
宁　夏	Ningxia	4123	9608	4167	2211
新　疆	Xinjiang	5661	9696	10163	733
新疆兵团	Xinjiang Production and Construction Corps	428	2858	428	77

4-1-3 辅助器具适配服务
Provision of Assistive Devices

地 区	Region	接受辅助器具适配服务的残疾人 Persons with Disablities Fitted with Assistive Devices	接受盲杖适配服务 Persons with Disablities Fitted with Tactile Sticks	接受助视器适配服务 Persons with Disablities Fitted with Visual Aids	接受其他视力辅助器具适配服务 Persons with Disablities Fitted with Other Visual Assistive Devices	接受助听器适配服务 Persons with Disablities Fitted with Hearing Aids	接受人工耳蜗适配服务 Persons with Disablities Fitted with Cochlears
		人 person	人 person	人 person	人 person	人 person	人 person
全 国	**Nationwide**	**1647513**	**68396**	**20987**	**108432**	**141092**	**961**
北 京	Beijing	92028	1	2265	2924	7501	61
天 津	Tianjin	14508	521	110	780	747	25
河 北	Hebei	85262	3029	1097	1905	5791	19
山 西	Shanxi	41793	1385	391	1135	3498	
内蒙古	Inner Mongolia	31701	906	323	1865	3607	4
辽 宁	Liaoning	40755	706	193	3927	1599	97
吉 林	Jilin	49891	2454	651	2375	3451	
黑龙江	Heilongjiang	31056	958	504	1611	1265	32
上 海	Shanghai	53670	935	1709	7632	2135	10
江 苏	Jiangsu	58530	3438	416	4008	2538	23
浙 江	Zhejiang	43803	2058	1137	3263	9878	36
安 徽	Anhui	50649	2803	220	2636	1635	35
福 建	Fujian	38205	423	190	1422	15818	32
江 西	Jiangxi	55432	2813	467	4866	5061	73
山 东	Shandong	88446	1174	370	4827	2416	
河 南	Henan	106536	2791	547	4969	6656	54
湖 北	Hubei	82811	4457	1242	8338	5674	
湖 南	Hunan	134560	10990	1042	9115	10401	17
广 东	Guangdong	50686	775	294	2977	8473	54
广 西	Guangxi	36027	1148	315	5034	2214	1
海 南	Hainan	2231	67	3	103	56	
重 庆	Chongqing	44858	3174	628	3133	3122	35
四 川	Sichuan	127066	7538	1503	11824	7046	31
贵 州	Guizhou	35088	2021	657	3280	2790	20
云 南	Yunnan	50295	2623	577	2680	7028	48
西 藏	Tibet	13687	417	658	998	1840	138
陕 西	Shaanxi	67566	1994	1234	2537	4446	2
甘 肃	Gansu	46167	3668	799	1607	6612	5
青 海	Qinghai	23208	1129	600	1672	3316	35
宁 夏	Ningxia	19333	907	507	1378	2031	65
新 疆	Xinjiang	29573	1014	231	3504	2260	8
新疆兵团	Xinjiang Production and Construction Corps	2092	79	107	107	187	1

4-1-3　续表 1　Continued 1

地区	Region	接受助听器辅助材料及其他听力辅助器具适配服务 Persons with Disablities Fitted with Other Hearing Aids	接受轮椅适配服务 Persons with Disablities Fitted with Wheelchairs	接受助行器具适配服务 Persons with Disablities Fitted with Walking Aids	接受站立架适配服务 Persons with Disablities Fitted with Standing Frame	接受坐姿椅适配服务 Persons with Disablities Fitted with Sitting Posture Chair
		人 person	人 person	人 person	人 person	人 person
全　国	**Nationwide**	**32466**	**431720**	**190161**	**8161**	**20726**
北　京	Beijing	17416	12725	10498	10	
天　津	Tianjin	73	5354	2212	34	207
河　北	Hebei	402	31023	9728	543	313
山　西	Shanxi	284	12441	6832	47	486
内蒙古	Inner Mongolia	146	10448	3865	97	439
辽　宁	Liaoning	365	9337	4266	59	528
吉　林	Jilin	660	13998	6266	503	360
黑龙江	Heilongjiang	162	10727	5730	73	428
上　海	Shanghai	316	4818	4437	114	564
江　苏	Jiangsu	340	22843	6772	50	1012
浙　江	Zhejiang	872	12131	2605	26	105
安　徽	Anhui	416	17165	5362	440	466
福　建	Fujian	607	5337	2823	92	170
江　西	Jiangxi	351	13393	5886	943	877
山　东	Shandong	917	25000	14882	98	91
河　南	Henan	394	34682	7436	179	459
湖　北	Hubei	461	15351	8632	419	690
湖　南	Hunan	953	30052	16112	1143	3154
广　东	Guangdong	334	17006	6462	190	605
广　西	Guangxi	207	10601	3985	63	371
海　南	Hainan	8	1079	355	24	28
重　庆	Chongqing	370	9935	6832	93	347
四　川	Sichuan	622	32848	13246	377	1227
贵　州	Guizhou	453	7316	4083	357	500
云　南	Yunnan	1732	12524	6037	278	788
西　藏	Tibet	132	2447	1468	144	606
陕　西	Shaanxi	903	22130	10238	60	1390
甘　肃	Gansu	764	14189	4490	667	599
青　海	Qinghai	387	4993	3113	795	2344
宁　夏	Ningxia	671	4300	3495	158	909
新　疆	Xinjiang	713	4865	1704	68	638
新疆兵团	Xinjiang Production and Construction Corps	35	662	309	17	25

4-1-3 续表 2 Continued 2

地 区	Region	接受其他肢体辅助器具适配服务 Persons with Disablities Fitted with Other Mobility Aids	接受假肢适配服务 Persons with Disablities Fitted with Prosthetics	接受矫形器适配服务 Persons with Disablities Fitted with Orthotics	接受生活自助具适配服务 Persons with Disablities Fitted with Life self-help kit	接受其他辅助器具适配服务 Persons with Disablities Fitted with Other Aids
		人 person	人 person	人 person	人 person	人 person
全 国	**Nationwide**	**453596**	**23034**	**24306**	**154946**	**39015**
北 京	Beijing	38788	357	2874	510	9694
天 津	Tianjin	2195	162	344	1795	46
河 北	Hebei	22049	687	852	8225	116
山 西	Shanxi	12066	227	199	3177	69
内蒙古	Inner Mongolia	7327	255	120	2818	121
辽 宁	Liaoning	15302	726	373	4316	902
吉 林	Jilin	15850	516	191	5731	354
黑龙江	Heilongjiang	6480	329	25	3317	52
上 海	Shanghai	25603	228	603	5091	768
江 苏	Jiangsu	17087	663	1128	6062	315
浙 江	Zhejiang	7206	1057	503	2008	407
安 徽	Anhui	16927	710	2900	3155	402
福 建	Fujian	7012	1761	1495	2742	404
江 西	Jiangxi	16558	1270	298	4726	439
山 东	Shandong	12236	1168	888	15642	7665
河 南	Henan	35585	707	1076	9393	2089
湖 北	Hubei	26237	1629	1168	7240	1413
湖 南	Hunan	36777	1568	537	14765	218
广 东	Guangdong	8020	1105	1299	5251	1674
广 西	Guangxi	6273	416	731	4221	2046
海 南	Hainan	317	39		195	2
重 庆	Chongqing	9333	580	1729	6334	125
四 川	Sichuan	35843	1702	1313	12546	6052
贵 州	Guizhou	9613	1049	636	4504	215
云 南	Yunnan	12057	832	775	4547	334
西 藏	Tibet	4662	524	106	427	318
陕 西	Shaanxi	20340	506	385	4672	385
甘 肃	Gansu	8642	453	592	2430	771
青 海	Qinghai	4002	219	739	2056	141
宁 夏	Ningxia	3299	1385	205	3383	224
新 疆	Xinjiang	9702	134	207	3295	1249
新疆兵团	Xinjiang Production and Construction Corps	208	70	15	372	5

4-1-4 康复机构
Rehabilitation Institutions

地 区	Region	残疾人康复机构 Rehabilitation Institutions for Persons with Disabilities	各类康复机构 Specialized Rehabilitation Institutions		
			视力残疾康复机构 Rehabilitation Institution for Visual Disabilities	听力言语残疾康复机构 Rehabilitation Institutions for Hearing and Speech Disabilities	肢体残疾康复机构 Rehabilitation Institutions for Physical Disabilities
		个 unit	个 unit	个 unit	个 unit
全 国	**Nationwide**	**11661**	**1430**	**1919**	**5512**
北 京	Beijing	173	9	23	67
天 津	Tianjin	99	16	7	16
河 北	Hebei	572	70	94	317
山 西	Shanxi	286	27	37	125
内蒙古	Inner Mongolia	293	61	70	172
辽 宁	Liaoning	462	65	63	221
吉 林	Jilin	243	50	39	152
黑龙江	Heilongjiang	271	44	36	176
上 海	Shanghai	956	68	30	254
江 苏	Jiangsu	530	116	88	173
浙 江	Zhejiang	314	19	55	134
安 徽	Anhui	309	15	73	116
福 建	Fujian	394	21	98	110
江 西	Jiangxi	316	23	82	135
山 东	Shandong	1438	93	92	950
河 南	Henan	546	60	167	335
湖 北	Hubei	273	7	38	110
湖 南	Hunan	497	53	86	140
广 东	Guangdong	1036	162	191	404
广 西	Guangxi	452	51	68	233
海 南	Hainan	62	1	6	22
重 庆	Chongqing	300	68	58	131
四 川	Sichuan	365	58	72	195
贵 州	Guizhou	295	56	62	117
云 南	Yunnan	279	50	80	115
西 藏	Tibet	11	1	5	6
陕 西	Shaanxi	346	56	51	228
甘 肃	Gansu	209	63	69	119
青 海	Qinghai	68	8	13	44
宁 夏	Ningxia	53	8	22	43
新 疆	Xinjiang	178	16	28	123
新疆兵团	Xinjiang Production and Construction Corps	35	15	16	29

4-1-4 续表 Continued

地区	Region	各类康复机构 Specialized Rehabilitation Institutions			
		智力残疾康复机构 Rehabilitation Institutions for Intellectual Disabilities	精神残疾康复机构 Rehabilitation Institutions for Mental Disabilities	孤独症儿童康复机构 Rehabilitation Institutions for Children with Autism	辅助器具服务机构 Assistive Technology Institutions Providing
		个 unit	个 unit	个 unit	个 unit
全 国	**Nationwide**	**4661**	**2078**	**3634**	**2000**
北 京	Beijing	56	29	41	10
天 津	Tianjin	26	8	47	21
河 北	Hebei	207	147	128	52
山 西	Shanxi	150	42	106	57
内蒙古	Inner Mongolia	125	40	88	64
辽 宁	Liaoning	182	95	136	93
吉 林	Jilin	69	56	44	41
黑龙江	Heilongjiang	73	32	63	27
上 海	Shanghai	267	287	28	262
江 苏	Jiangsu	174	54	209	78
浙 江	Zhejiang	173	45	175	45
安 徽	Anhui	172	22	160	45
福 建	Fujian	212	50	219	72
江 西	Jiangxi	148	54	128	28
山 东	Shandong	429	161	361	133
河 南	Henan	291	70	192	92
湖 北	Hubei	86	51	74	59
湖 南	Hunan	179	71	145	141
广 东	Guangdong	459	252	471	136
广 西	Guangxi	269	52	239	73
海 南	Hainan	41	5	44	3
重 庆	Chongqing	147	67	82	30
四 川	Sichuan	161	87	100	66
贵 州	Guizhou	105	99	70	65
云 南	Yunnan	107	68	39	116
西 藏	Tibet	4		3	10
陕 西	Shaanxi	98	59	72	45
甘 肃	Gansu	106	35	81	63
青 海	Qinghai	38	5	29	17
宁 夏	Ningxia	40	8	35	13
新 疆	Xinjiang	55	19	19	38
新疆兵团	Xinjiang Production and Construction Corps	12	8	6	5

4-1-5 康复人才
Rehabilitation Professionals

地 区	Region	康复机构在岗人员 Staff in Rehabilitation Institutions	业务人员 Professionals	管理人员 Managerial Personnel	其他人员 Other Staff
		人 person	人 person	人 person	人 person
全 国	**Nationwide**	**327736**	**239156**	**33833**	**54747**
北 京	Beijing	3617	2776	413	428
天 津	Tianjin	2853	1926	290	637
河 北	Hebei	15398	10746	1846	2806
山 西	Shanxi	9748	6681	1046	2021
内蒙古	Inner Mongolia	7187	5074	682	1431
辽 宁	Liaoning	9943	7160	1151	1632
吉 林	Jilin	8042	5813	1109	1120
黑龙江	Heilongjiang	5240	3701	582	957
上 海	Shanghai	7569	4035	1187	2347
江 苏	Jiangsu	15361	10930	1799	2632
浙 江	Zhejiang	12646	9551	1219	1876
安 徽	Anhui	10877	8651	916	1310
福 建	Fujian	12282	8434	1449	2399
江 西	Jiangxi	8221	5392	949	1880
山 东	Shandong	43692	35369	3235	5088
河 南	Henan	17528	14492	1512	1524
湖 北	Hubei	8944	6360	924	1660
湖 南	Hunan	16458	11939	1918	2601
广 东	Guangdong	31455	22322	2829	6304
广 西	Guangxi	10989	7735	1164	2090
海 南	Hainan	3498	1222	381	1895
重 庆	Chongqing	9650	6729	1100	1821
四 川	Sichuan	13347	10241	1244	1862
贵 州	Guizhou	11022	7636	1225	2161
云 南	Yunnan	10467	7907	1108	1452
西 藏	Tibet	97	40	28	29
陕 西	Shaanxi	10106	7742	1166	1198
甘 肃	Gansu	4423	3439	521	463
青 海	Qinghai	1414	1040	228	146
宁 夏	Ningxia	1751	1297	172	282
新 疆	Xinjiang	2797	2190	311	296
新疆兵团	Xinjiang Production and Construction Corps	1114	586	129	399

4-1-5 续表 1 Continued 1

地 区	Region	康复机构在岗人员 Staff in Rehabilitation Institutions			
		视力残疾康复在岗人员 Staff for Vision Rehabilitation	业务人员 Professionals	管理人员 Managerial Personnels	其他人员 Other Staff
		人 person	人 person	人 person	人 person
全 国	**Nationwide**	**19771**	**12919**	**2718**	**4134**
北 京	Beijing	77	61	11	5
天 津	Tianjin	320	237	43	40
河 北	Hebei	454	198	79	177
山 西	Shanxi	910	608	159	143
内蒙古	Inner Mongolia	798	554	76	168
辽 宁	Liaoning	805	519	104	182
吉 林	Jilin	1303	862	229	212
黑龙江	Heilongjiang	228	165	45	18
上 海	Shanghai	462	253	83	126
江 苏	Jiangsu	1496	987	207	302
浙 江	Zhejiang	131	50	21	60
安 徽	Anhui	400	313	58	29
福 建	Fujian	358	232	51	75
江 西	Jiangxi	177	110	32	35
山 东	Shandong	1467	991	206	270
河 南	Henan	888	655	82	151
湖 北	Hubei	94	75	10	9
湖 南	Hunan	2195	1432	283	480
广 东	Guangdong	1867	1179	177	511
广 西	Guangxi	419	246	55	118
海 南	Hainan	7	5	1	1
重 庆	Chongqing	1242	780	196	266
四 川	Sichuan	850	625	89	136
贵 州	Guizhou	929	589	138	202
云 南	Yunnan	774	451	86	237
西 藏	Tibet	2	1	1	
陕 西	Shaanxi	442	277	87	78
甘 肃	Gansu	368	251	62	55
青 海	Qinghai	62	36	13	13
宁 夏	Ningxia	120	87	13	20
新 疆	Xinjiang	89	64	16	9
新疆兵团	Xinjiang Production and Construction Corps	37	26	5	6

4-1-5　续表 2　Continued 2

地　区	Region	康复机构在岗人员 Staff in Rehabilitation Institutions			
		听力言语康复在岗人员 Staff for Hearing and Speech Rehabilitation	业务人员 Professionals	管理人员 Managerial Personnel	其他人员 Other Staff
		人 person	人 person	人 person	人 person
全　国	**Nationwide**	**17758**	**11378**	**2212**	**4168**
北　京	Beijing	373	255	53	65
天　津	Tianjin	56	38	4	14
河　北	Hebei	968	693	132	143
山　西	Shanxi	384	258	59	67
内蒙古	Inner Mongolia	865	221	56	588
辽　宁	Liaoning	561	356	66	139
吉　林	Jilin	318	220	65	33
黑龙江	Heilongjiang	187	131	28	28
上　海	Shanghai	277	55	43	179
江　苏	Jiangsu	770	576	84	110
浙　江	Zhejiang	545	384	63	98
安　徽	Anhui	663	506	85	72
福　建	Fujian	750	489	106	155
江　西	Jiangxi	843	426	103	314
山　东	Shandong	978	691	112	175
河　南	Henan	1680	1303	179	198
湖　北	Hubei	597	429	67	101
湖　南	Hunan	757	530	98	129
广　东	Guangdong	1739	1032	172	535
广　西	Guangxi	518	332	79	107
海　南	Hainan	68	49	8	11
重　庆	Chongqing	428	253	80	95
四　川	Sichuan	727	499	81	147
贵　州	Guizhou	640	364	71	205
云　南	Yunnan	631	300	89	242
西　藏	Tibet	15	6	3	6
陕　西	Shaanxi	412	283	62	67
甘　肃	Gansu	519	348	80	91
青　海	Qinghai	131	100	19	12
宁　夏	Ningxia	123	96	14	13
新　疆	Xinjiang	199	135	38	26
新疆兵团	Xinjiang Production and Construction Corps	36	20	13	3

4−1−5　续表 3　Continued 3

地　区	Region	康复机构在岗人员 Staff in Rehabilitation Institutions			
		肢体残疾康复在岗人员 Staff for Physical Rehabilitation	业务人员 Professionals	管理人员 Managerial Personnel	其他人员 Other Staff
		人 person	人 person	人 person	人 person
全　国	**Nationwide**	**98246**	**79881**	**7257**	**11108**
北　京	Beijing	942	739	85	118
天　津	Tianjin	498	342	26	130
河　北	Hebei	5268	3727	487	1054
山　西	Shanxi	2438	1987	180	271
内蒙古	Inner Mongolia	2303	1875	199	229
辽　宁	Liaoning	2839	2340	234	265
吉　林	Jilin	2505	2030	333	142
黑龙江	Heilongjiang	2125	1662	165	298
上　海	Shanghai	2885	1674	213	998
江　苏	Jiangsu	3488	2839	226	423
浙　江	Zhejiang	3620	2930	273	417
安　徽	Anhui	2829	2458	171	200
福　建	Fujian	2061	1646	183	232
江　西	Jiangxi	1972	1533	179	260
山　东	Shandong	19732	16975	1071	1686
河　南	Henan	6184	5542	411	231
湖　北	Hubei	2501	1911	202	388
湖　南	Hunan	3347	2790	297	260
广　东	Guangdong	7072	5474	533	1065
广　西	Guangxi	2843	2259	239	345
海　南	Hainan	349	264	48	37
重　庆	Chongqing	2192	1687	176	329
四　川	Sichuan	4557	3937	230	390
贵　州	Guizhou	3145	2623	238	284
云　南	Yunnan	2569	2182	132	255
西　藏	Tibet	31	12	3	16
陕　西	Shaanxi	3608	3039	323	246
甘　肃	Gansu	1320	1126	128	66
青　海	Qinghai	547	426	76	45
宁　夏	Ningxia	567	440	54	73
新　疆	Xinjiang	1353	1139	127	87
新疆兵团	Xinjiang Production and Construction Corps	556	273	15	268

4-1-5 续表 4 Continued 4

地 区	Region	康复机构在岗人员 Staff in Rehabilitation Institutions			
		智力残疾康复在岗人员 Staff for Intellectual Rehabilitation	业务人员 Professionals	管理人员 Managerial Personnel	其他人员 Other Staff
		人 person	人 person	人 person	人 person
全 国	**Nationwide**	**61031**	**45966**	**5824**	**9241**
北 京	Beijing	745	547	113	85
天 津	Tianjin	419	327	38	54
河 北	Hebei	2560	1889	278	393
山 西	Shanxi	1866	1371	188	307
内蒙古	Inner Mongolia	1269	1010	124	135
辽 宁	Liaoning	1806	1340	195	271
吉 林	Jilin	752	631	49	72
黑龙江	Heilongjiang	1007	709	100	198
上 海	Shanghai	1530	630	277	623
江 苏	Jiangsu	2359	1642	214	503
浙 江	Zhejiang	1845	1393	208	244
安 徽	Anhui	2642	2075	213	354
福 建	Fujian	2676	1748	359	569
江 西	Jiangxi	1840	1287	177	376
山 东	Shandong	7006	5798	517	691
河 南	Henan	4468	3928	315	225
湖 北	Hubei	1405	1038	111	256
湖 南	Hunan	2810	2234	339	237
广 东	Guangdong	5108	3795	425	888
广 西	Guangxi	3261	2460	298	503
海 南	Hainan	1479	330	117	1032
重 庆	Chongqing	1672	1144	199	329
四 川	Sichuan	2123	1775	160	188
贵 州	Guizhou	1543	1249	158	136
云 南	Yunnan	2567	2163	230	174
西 藏	Tibet	8	3	4	1
陕 西	Shaanxi	1616	1348	148	120
甘 肃	Gansu	1000	841	91	68
青 海	Qinghai	409	299	66	44
宁 夏	Ningxia	397	309	36	52
新 疆	Xinjiang	543	470	41	32
新疆兵团	Xinjiang Production and Construction Corps	300	183	36	81

4-1-5 续表 5 Continued 5

地 区	Region	康复机构在岗人员 Staff in Rehabilitation Institutions			
		精神残疾康复在岗人员 Staff for Mental Rehabilitation	业务人员 Professionals	管理人员 Managerial Personnel	其他人员 Other Staff
		人 person	人 person	人 person	人 person
全 国	**Nationwide**	**71784**	**49208**	**7803**	**14773**
北 京	Beijing	758	643	66	49
天 津	Tianjin	603	289	40	274
河 北	Hebei	4620	3224	624	772
山 西	Shanxi	2849	1787	274	788
内蒙古	Inner Mongolia	1018	765	78	175
辽 宁	Liaoning	2287	1533	317	437
吉 林	Jilin	2451	1579	342	530
黑龙江	Heilongjiang	681	373	102	206
上 海	Shanghai	1542	973	297	272
江 苏	Jiangsu	2951	1869	314	768
浙 江	Zhejiang	4101	3014	350	737
安 徽	Anhui	1440	1240	111	89
福 建	Fujian	2308	1414	301	593
江 西	Jiangxi	1520	1005	238	277
山 东	Shandong	7084	5354	627	1103
河 南	Henan	1958	1448	194	316
湖 北	Hubei	2693	1754	310	629
湖 南	Hunan	4337	3127	462	748
广 东	Guangdong	7707	5036	591	2080
广 西	Guangxi	772	477	92	203
海 南	Hainan	141	22	11	108
重 庆	Chongqing	2848	2056	270	522
四 川	Sichuan	3834	2602	471	761
贵 州	Guizhou	3459	2030	380	1049
云 南	Yunnan	3489	2612	425	452
西 藏	Tibet				
陕 西	Shaanxi	2950	2050	353	547
甘 肃	Gansu	613	459	49	105
青 海	Qinghai	90	70	20	
宁 夏	Ningxia	193	115	13	65
新 疆	Xinjiang	352	218	38	96
新疆兵团	Xinjiang Production and Construction Corps	135	70	43	22

4-1-5　续表 6　Continued 6

地　区	Region	康复机构在岗人员 Staff in Rehabilitation Institutions			
		孤独症儿童康复在岗人员 Staff for Rehabilitation of Children with Autism	业务人员 Professionals	管理人员 Managerial Personnel	其他人员 Other Staff
		人 person	人 person	人 person	人 person
全　国	**Nationwide**	**47108**	**33532**	**5451**	**8125**
北　京	Beijing	588	422	75	91
天　津	Tianjin	861	655	114	92
河　北	Hebei	1270	887	189	194
山　西	Shanxi	799	561	111	127
内蒙古	Inner Mongolia	723	558	93	72
辽　宁	Liaoning	1334	955	141	238
吉　林	Jilin	605	429	62	114
黑龙江	Heilongjiang	931	628	117	186
上　海	Shanghai	250	203	29	18
江　苏	Jiangsu	3322	2570	352	400
浙　江	Zhejiang	2293	1727	268	298
安　徽	Anhui	2751	1988	226	537
福　建	Fujian	2520	1616	355	549
江　西	Jiangxi	1778	1013	189	576
山　东	Shandong	5881	4300	572	1009
河　南	Henan	1763	1312	239	212
湖　北	Hubei	1393	1033	138	222
湖　南	Hunan	2038	1456	241	341
广　东	Guangdong	7345	5470	786	1089
广　西	Guangxi	2342	1783	279	280
海　南	Hainan	1423	540	193	690
重　庆	Chongqing	1024	696	118	210
四　川	Sichuan	942	648	131	163
贵　州	Guizhou	957	649	139	169
云　南	Yunnan	170	119	34	17
西　藏	Tibet	6	2	1	3
陕　西	Shaanxi	785	576	113	96
甘　肃	Gansu	462	346	63	53
青　海	Qinghai	115	66	25	24
宁　夏	Ningxia	238	177	25	36
新　疆	Xinjiang	166	133	23	10
新疆兵团	Xinjiang Production and Construction Corps	33	14	10	9

4-1-5 续表 7 Continued 7

地 区	Region	康复机构在岗人员 Staff in Rehabilitation Institutions				培训康复管理人员 Rehabilitation Managerial Staff Trained	培训康复业务人员 Rehabilitation Professionals Trained
		辅助器具残疾康复在岗人员 Staff for Rehabilitation with Assistive Devices	业务人员 Professionals	管理人员 Managerial Personnel	其他人员 Other Staff		
		人 person	人 person	人 person	人 person	人次 person-time	人次 person-time
全 国	**Nationwide**	**12038**	**6272**	**2568**	**3198**	**109533**	**550271**
北 京	Beijing	134	109	10	15	3012	27006
天 津	Tianjin	96	38	25	33	584	4560
河 北	Hebei	258	128	57	73	2761	9388
山 西	Shanxi	502	109	75	318	3429	26312
内蒙古	Inner Mongolia	211	91	56	64	1150	5082
辽 宁	Liaoning	311	117	94	100	3958	20064
吉 林	Jilin	108	62	29	17	2148	9110
黑龙江	Heilongjiang	81	33	25	23	676	2304
上 海	Shanghai	623	247	245	131	2857	14876
江 苏	Jiangsu	975	447	402	126	5097	25512
浙 江	Zhejiang	111	53	36	22	7154	38616
安 徽	Anhui	152	71	52	29	1999	13389
福 建	Fujian	1609	1289	94	226	9492	32870
江 西	Jiangxi	91	18	31	42	6266	8753
山 东	Shandong	1544	1260	130	154	9776	67523
河 南	Henan	587	304	92	191	3813	21131
湖 北	Hubei	261	120	86	55	4450	25806
湖 南	Hunan	974	370	198	406	5379	26089
广 东	Guangdong	617	336	145	136	8699	64006
广 西	Guangxi	834	178	122	534	2481	15179
海 南	Hainan	31	12	3	16	462	3262
重 庆	Chongqing	244	113	61	70	3408	18001
四 川	Sichuan	314	155	82	77	7478	21163
贵 州	Guizhou	349	132	101	116	3429	9732
云 南	Yunnan	267	80	112	75	3496	16231
西 藏	Tibet	35	16	16	3		110
陕 西	Shaanxi	293	169	80	44	3260	13370
甘 肃	Gansu	141	68	48	25	941	3309
青 海	Qinghai	60	43	9	8	353	1292
宁 夏	Ningxia	113	73	17	23	563	2366
新 疆	Xinjiang	95	31	28	36	813	3327
新疆兵团	Xinjiang Production and Construction Corps	17		7	10	149	532

二、教育
Education

4-2-1 高中教育阶段
Senior High Education

地 区	Region	特殊教育普通高中学校(班) Special Education Senior High Schools/ Classes	盲普通高中 Senior High Schools for Blind Students	聋普通高中 Senior High Schools for Deaf Students	其他 Others	学生 Students 招生 Newly Enrolled Students with Disabilities	盲 Students with Visual Disability	聋 Students with Hearing Disability
		个 unit	个 unit	个 unit	个 unit	人 person	人 person	人 person
全 国	**Nationwide**	**118**	**11**	**39**	**68**	**2721**	**443**	**2278**
北 京	Beijing	2	1	1		39	14	25
天 津	Tianjin	2	1	1		42	7	35
河 北	Hebei	10	1	5	4	509	34	475
山 西	Shanxi	9	1	4	4	108	11	97
内蒙古	Inner Mongolia	4		1	3	10		10
辽 宁	Liaoning	5		1	4	15	4	11
吉 林	Jilin	5		2	3	34		34
黑龙江	Heilongjiang							
上 海	Shanghai	1	1			33	33	
江 苏	Jiangsu	4		1	3	177	9	168
浙 江	Zhejiang	6	1	1	4	82	42	40
安 徽	Anhui	2			2	88	25	63
福 建	Fujian	5			5	129	23	106
江 西	Jiangxi	1			1	8		8
山 东	Shandong	7	2	2	3	101	28	73
河 南	Henan	8		3	5	169	21	148
湖 北	Hubei	7	1	2	4	138	17	121
湖 南	Hunan	7		1	6	56		56
广 东	Guangdong	7	1	3	3	146	20	126
广 西	Guangxi	4		2	2	115	8	107
海 南	Hainan							
重 庆	Chongqing	2	1	1		71	38	33
四 川	Sichuan	9		2	7	224	65	159
贵 州	Guizhou	6		4	2	265	30	235
云 南	Yunnan							
西 藏	Tibet							
陕 西	Shaanxi							
甘 肃	Gansu	1			1	6	1	5
青 海	Qinghai	1		1		4		4
宁 夏	Ningxia	1			1	80	13	67
新 疆	Xinjiang	2		1	1	72		72
新疆兵团	Xinjiang Production and Construction Corps							

4-2-1 续表 1 Continued 1

地区	Region	学生 Students					
		在校生 Students in School	盲 Students with Visual Disability	聋 Students with Hearing Disability	毕业生 Graduates	盲 Students with Visual Disability	聋 Students with Hearing Disability
		人 person	人 person	人 person	人 person	人 person	人 person
全 国	**Nationwide**	**11431**	**1736**	**6506**	**3650**	**886**	**2119**
北 京	Beijing	157	37	120	42	7	35
天 津	Tianjin	114	27	87	30	8	22
河 北	Hebei	846	101	646	181	53	101
山 西	Shanxi	695	44	374	197	13	110
内蒙古	Inner Mongolia	492		112	65		18
辽 宁	Liaoning	291	4	117	60	14	15
吉 林	Jilin	210		84	98		82
黑龙江	Heilongjiang						
上 海	Shanghai	122	122		34	34	
江 苏	Jiangsu	573	27	454	155	9	136
浙 江	Zhejiang	709	305	227	172	40	79
安 徽	Anhui	503	152	350	125	30	95
福 建	Fujian	827	58	232	209	18	45
江 西	Jiangxi	32	6	26	8		8
山 东	Shandong	915	247	390	229	111	83
河 南	Henan	740	88	457	81	8	73
湖 北	Hubei	314	28	236	98	16	65
湖 南	Hunan	462	42	171	90		51
广 东	Guangdong	607	71	372	194	19	121
广 西	Guangxi	360	43	262	87	6	67
海 南	Hainan						
重 庆	Chongqing	190	106	84	70	35	35
四 川	Sichuan	923	139	585	1159	425	668
贵 州	Guizhou	708	78	630	184	37	146
云 南	Yunnan						
西 藏	Tibet						
陕 西	Shaanxi						
甘 肃	Gansu	165	3	51	27	1	13
青 海	Qinghai	140		140	22		22
宁 夏	Ningxia	70	8	62	30	2	28
新 疆	Xinjiang	266		237	3		1
新疆兵团	Xinjiang Production and Construction Corps						

4-2-1 续表 2 Continued 2

地 区	Region	残疾人中等职业学校(班) Secondary Vocational Schools/Classes for PWDs	教育部门办 Supervised by Educational Departments	残联部门办 Supervised by Disabled Persons' Federations	其他 Others
		个 unit	个 unit	个 unit	个 unit
全 国	**Nationwide**	**184**	**171**	**9**	**4**
北 京	Beijing	3	3		
天 津	Tianjin				
河 北	Hebei	4	3		1
山 西	Shanxi	2	2		
内蒙古	Inner Mongolia	4	3	1	
辽 宁	Liaoning	15	15		
吉 林	Jilin	2	1	1	
黑龙江	Heilongjiang	5	5		
上 海	Shanghai	17	17		
江 苏	Jiangsu	11	10	1	
浙 江	Zhejiang	30	29		1
安 徽	Anhui	7	5	1	1
福 建	Fujian	16	16		
江 西	Jiangxi	8	7		1
山 东	Shandong	10	10		
河 南	Henan	4	4		
湖 北	Hubei	3	3		
湖 南	Hunan	3	2	1	
广 东	Guangdong	9	9		
广 西	Guangxi	1	1		
海 南	Hainan	1	1		
重 庆	Chongqing	3	3		
四 川	Sichuan	7	7		
贵 州	Guizhou	1		1	
云 南	Yunnan	5	5		
西 藏	Tibet				
陕 西	Shaanxi	6	5	1	
甘 肃	Gansu	2	2		
青 海	Qinghai	2	1	1	
宁 夏	Ningxia	1	1		
新 疆	Xinjiang	2	1	1	
新疆兵团	Xinjiang Production and Construction Corps				

4-2-1 续表 3 Continued 3

地 区	Region	残疾人中等职业学校(班)学生 Students of Secondary Vocational Schools/Classes for PWDs						
		招生 Newly Enrolled Students	残疾学生 Disabled Students	盲 Students with Visual Disability	聋 Students with Hearing Disability	肢残 Students with Physical Disability	其他 Others	非残疾学生 Non-disabled Students
		人 person	人 person	人 person	人 person	人 person	人 person	人 person
全 国	**Nationwide**	**7074**	**7018**	**1032**	**2017**	**1240**	**2729**	**56**
北 京	Beijing	112	112		14		98	
天 津	Tianjin							
河 北	Hebei	851	851	50	85	600	116	
山 西	Shanxi	85	85	1	32	4	48	
内蒙古	Inner Mongolia	62	62	11	15	12	24	
辽 宁	Liaoning	225	225	57	35	9	124	
吉 林	Jilin	102	94	10	22	41	21	8
黑龙江	Heilongjiang	117	117	16	48		53	
上 海	Shanghai	319	305		15	20	270	14
江 苏	Jiangsu	383	375	106	147	19	103	8
浙 江	Zhejiang	628	623	2	57	12	552	5
安 徽	Anhui	335	335	93	104	44	94	
福 建	Fujian	176	175	32	51	2	90	1
江 西	Jiangxi	394	394	30	197	40	127	
山 东	Shandong	268	268	63	89	22	94	
河 南	Henan	189	189	78	111			
湖 北	Hubei	142	142	1	85		56	
湖 南	Hunan	247	229	63	81	50	35	18
广 东	Guangdong	571	571	79	124	35	333	
广 西	Guangxi	82	82	2	18	19	43	
海 南	Hainan	46	46	6	32		8	
重 庆	Chongqing	95	95		45	4	46	
四 川	Sichuan	148	148	3	24	30	91	
贵 州	Guizhou	562	560	112	265	32	151	2
云 南	Yunnan	218	218	53	121	3	41	
西 藏	Tibet							
陕 西	Shaanxi	414	414	126	93	164	31	
甘 肃	Gansu	81	81	15	47		19	
青 海	Qinghai	88	88	12	27	20	29	
宁 夏	Ningxia	20	20		6	1	13	
新 疆	Xinjiang	114	114	11	27	57	19	
新疆兵团	Xinjiang Production and Construction Corps							

4-2-1　续表 4　Continued 4

地　区	Region	残疾人中等职业学校(班)学生 Students of Secondary Vocational Schools/Classes for PWDs						
		在校学生 Students in Schools	残疾学生 Disabled Students	盲 Students with Visual Disability	聋 Students with Hearing Disability	肢残 Students with Physical Disability	其他 Others	非残疾学生 Non-disabled Students
		人 person	人 person	人 person	人 person	人 person	人 person	人 person
全　国	**Nationwide**	**19014**	**18911**	**3063**	**5509**	**1975**	**8364**	**103**
北　京	Beijing	308	308		54		254	
天　津	Tianjin							
河　北	Hebei	327	327	6	64	200	57	
山　西	Shanxi	449	449	22	103	57	267	
内蒙古	Inner Mongolia	235	235	43	24	23	145	
辽　宁	Liaoning	1002	1002	213	186	58	545	
吉　林	Jilin	371	371	28	71	118	154	
黑龙江	Heilongjiang	359	359	54	131		174	
上　海	Shanghai	1061	1020		61	55	904	41
江　苏	Jiangsu	1368	1358	540	492	49	277	10
浙　江	Zhejiang	1977	1965	2	151	35	1777	12
安　徽	Anhui	1049	1049	246	312	127	364	
福　建	Fujian	523	521	98	179	5	239	2
江　西	Jiangxi	888	888	81	338	91	378	
山　东	Shandong	1006	1006	222	287	120	377	
河　南	Henan	670	670	238	432			
湖　北	Hubei	481	481	15	209		257	
湖　南	Hunan	662	624	166	190	165	103	38
广　东	Guangdong	1811	1811	256	461	115	979	
广　西	Guangxi	216	216	5	48	58	105	
海　南	Hainan	133	133	13	96		24	
重　庆	Chongqing	170	170	4	108	3	55	
四　川	Sichuan	370	370	24	63	33	250	
贵　州	Guizhou	615	615	119	265	72	159	
云　南	Yunnan	643	643	166	367	10	100	
西　藏	Tibet							
陕　西	Shaanxi	1312	1312	391	429	397	95	
甘　肃	Gansu	336	336	33	197		106	
青　海	Qinghai	253	253	2	113	20	118	
宁　夏	Ningxia	24	24		4	2	18	
新　疆	Xinjiang	395	395	76	74	162	83	
新疆兵团	Xinjiang Production and Construction Corps							

4-2-1 续表 5 Continued 5

地区	Region	残疾人中等职业学校(班)学生 Students of Secondary Vocational Schools/Classes for PWDs						
		毕业生 Graduates	残疾学生 Disabled Students	盲 Students with Visual Disability	聋 Students with Hearing Disability	肢残 Students with Physical Disability	其他 Others	非残疾学生 Non-disabled Students
		人 person	人 person	人 person	人 person	人 person	人 person	人 person
全 国	**Nationwide**	**5157**	**5124**	**1068**	**1696**	**596**	**1764**	**33**
北 京	Beijing	99	99		16		83	
天 津	Tianjin							
河 北	Hebei	214	212	31	46	120	15	2
山 西	Shanxi	70	70		36		34	
内蒙古	Inner Mongolia	39	39	2	13	2	22	
辽 宁	Liaoning	222	222	61	64	3	94	
吉 林	Jilin	71	67	11	13	41	2	4
黑龙江	Heilongjiang	73	73	10	33		30	
上 海	Shanghai	169	161		19	5	137	8
江 苏	Jiangsu	399	399	102	129	23	145	
浙 江	Zhejiang	542	537	5	44	11	477	5
安 徽	Anhui	304	304	100	121	47	36	
福 建	Fujian	155	155	34	52	1	68	
江 西	Jiangxi	283	283	28	150	22	83	
山 东	Shandong	421	421	148	215	33	25	
河 南	Henan	231	231	94	137			
湖 北	Hubei	80	80		48		32	
湖 南	Hunan	207	196	56	87	53		11
广 东	Guangdong	446	446	98	109	38	201	
广 西	Guangxi	86	86	2	18	18	48	
海 南	Hainan	36	36		28		8	
重 庆	Chongqing	44	44		34		10	
四 川	Sichuan	35	35	10	2	1	22	
贵 州	Guizhou	203	200	82	94	15	9	3
云 南	Yunnan	116	116	46	58		12	
西 藏	Tibet							
陕 西	Shaanxi	375	375	106	61	108	100	
甘 肃	Gansu	71	71	25	42		4	
青 海	Qinghai	29	29		15		14	
宁 夏	Ningxia	14	14			1	13	
新 疆	Xinjiang	123	123	17	12	54	40	
新疆兵团	Xinjiang Production and Construction Corps							

4-2-1 续表 6 Continued 6

地 区	Region	残疾人中等职业学校(班)学生 Students of Secondary Vocational Schools/Classes for PWDs						
		毕业生获得职业资格证书 Graduates Granted Professional Qualification Certificates	残疾学生 Disabled Students	盲 Students with Visual Disability	聋 Students with Hearing Disability	肢残 Students with Physical Disability	其他 Others	非残疾学生 Non-disabled Students
		人 person	人 person	人 person	人 person	人 person	人 person	人 person
全 国	**Nationwide**	**1473**	**1470**	**328**	**429**	**309**	**404**	**3**
北 京	Beijing	31	31				31	
天 津	Tianjin							
河 北	Hebei	148	148	30	13	104	1	
山 西	Shanxi	17	17		17			
内蒙古	Inner Mongolia	1	1		1			
辽 宁	Liaoning							
吉 林	Jilin							
黑龙江	Heilongjiang							
上 海	Shanghai	19	19		2	1	16	
江 苏	Jiangsu	79	79	8	50	10	11	
浙 江	Zhejiang	145	145		17		128	
安 徽	Anhui	288	288	95	112	47	34	
福 建	Fujian	60	60	6	28		26	
江 西	Jiangxi	92	92		71	11	10	
山 东	Shandong	126	126	55	46	1	24	
河 南	Henan	10	10		10			
湖 北	Hubei							
湖 南	Hunan	14	14		14			
广 东	Guangdong	69	69		29	27	13	
广 西	Guangxi	4	4		4			
海 南	Hainan							
重 庆	Chongqing	10	10				10	
四 川	Sichuan							
贵 州	Guizhou	15	12	12				3
云 南	Yunnan							
西 藏	Tibet							
陕 西	Shaanxi	316	316	93	15	108	100	
甘 肃	Gansu	12	12	12				
青 海	Qinghai							
宁 夏	Ningxia							
新 疆	Xinjiang	17	17	17				
新疆兵团	Xinjiang Production and Construction Corps							

4-2-2 高等教育
Higher Education

地区	Region	高等院校 Higher Education Institutions					
		2022年残疾考生入学人数 Disabled Students Enrolled in 2022	博士研究生 Doctoral candidate	视力残疾 Students with Visual Disability	听力残疾 Students with Hearing Disability	肢体残疾 Students with Physical Disability	其他残疾 Students with Other Disability
		人 person	人 person	人 person	人 person	人 person	人 person
全 国	**Nationwide**	**30035**	**168**	**19**	**25**	**122**	**2**
北 京	Beijing	217	6	1		4	1
天 津	Tianjin	149	1			1	
河 北	Hebei	1561	9	1	2	6	
山 西	Shanxi	1269	8	1	1	5	1
内蒙古	Inner Mongolia	715	3			3	
辽 宁	Liaoning	517	4			4	
吉 林	Jilin	559	3	1		2	
黑龙江	Heilongjiang	646	6	1		5	
上 海	Shanghai	114	2		1	1	
江 苏	Jiangsu	971	7		1	6	
浙 江	Zhejiang	610	7		2	5	
安 徽	Anhui	1661	11	2	1	8	
福 建	Fujian	645	3		1	2	
江 西	Jiangxi	1398	8		2	6	
山 东	Shandong	1763	12	1	4	7	
河 南	Henan	2742	24	3	3	18	
湖 北	Hubei	986	3			3	
湖 南	Hunan	1276	6			6	
广 东	Guangdong	1038	4	1		3	
广 西	Guangxi	1116	6			6	
海 南	Hainan	127					
重 庆	Chongqing	989	3			3	
四 川	Sichuan	2321	11	2	1	8	
贵 州	Guizhou	1678	2	1	1		
云 南	Yunnan	1611	3	1		2	
西 藏	Tibet	220					
陕 西	Shaanxi	825	5		2	3	
甘 肃	Gansu	772	2	1		1	
青 海	Qinghai	351					
宁 夏	Ningxia	346	3	1	1	1	
新 疆	Xinjiang	775	6	1	2	3	
新疆兵团	Xinjiang Production and Construction Corps	67					

注："2022年残疾考生入学人数"为中国残联和教育部有关部门比对结果。
Disabled Students enrolled in 2022，comparison result between the China Disabled Persons' Federation and the Ministry of Education of the People's Republic of China.

4-2-2 续表 1 Continued 1

地 区	Region	高等院校 Higher Education Institutions				
		硕士研究生 Postgraduates	视力残疾 Students with Visual Disability	听力残疾 Students with Hearing Disability	肢体残疾 Students with Physical Disability	其他残疾 Students with Other Disability
		人 person	人 person	人 person	人 person	人 person
全 国	**Nationwide**	**1520**	**207**	**240**	**981**	**92**
北 京	Beijing	27	3	10	13	1
天 津	Tianjin	17		8	7	2
河 北	Hebei	94	8	15	64	7
山 西	Shanxi	72	10	8	50	4
内蒙古	Inner Mongolia	45		6	37	2
辽 宁	Liaoning	41	2	13	24	2
吉 林	Jilin	31	4	11	15	1
黑龙江	Heilongjiang	40	2	7	28	3
上 海	Shanghai	6		1	5	
江 苏	Jiangsu	69	9	16	42	2
浙 江	Zhejiang	32	3	11	14	4
安 徽	Anhui	113	10	12	87	4
福 建	Fujian	30	3	7	19	1
江 西	Jiangxi	67	9	9	44	5
山 东	Shandong	126	21	15	82	8
河 南	Henan	163	24	13	114	12
湖 北	Hubei	66	11	13	38	4
湖 南	Hunan	47	8	11	25	3
广 东	Guangdong	35	3	5	25	2
广 西	Guangxi	21	4	4	13	
海 南	Hainan	2			1	1
重 庆	Chongqing	40	10	6	23	1
四 川	Sichuan	123	25	15	77	6
贵 州	Guizhou	62	13	6	39	4
云 南	Yunnan	43	8		33	2
西 藏	Tibet	1			1	
陕 西	Shaanxi	39	4	9	22	4
甘 肃	Gansu	38	9	5	19	5
青 海	Qinghai	3			3	
宁 夏	Ningxia	12	1	3	8	
新 疆	Xinjiang	12	3	1	6	2
新疆兵团	Xinjiang Production and Construction Corps	3			3	

4-2-2 续表 2 Continued 2

地 区	Region	高等院校 Higher Education Institutions				
		本科生 Undergraduates	视力残疾 Students with Visual Disability	听力残疾 Students with Hearing Disability	肢体残疾 Students with Physical Disability	其他残疾 Students with Other Disability
		人 person	人 person	人 person	人 person	人 person
全 国	**Nationwide**	**10703**	**1398**	**1975**	**6257**	**1073**
北 京	Beijing	84	13	25	37	9
天 津	Tianjin	63	2	22	35	4
河 北	Hebei	522	59	117	281	65
山 西	Shanxi	460	38	85	294	43
内蒙古	Inner Mongolia	274	34	41	174	25
辽 宁	Liaoning	236	20	49	147	20
吉 林	Jilin	210	31	50	110	19
黑龙江	Heilongjiang	234	28	57	130	19
上 海	Shanghai	56	10	20	26	
江 苏	Jiangsu	364	46	117	164	37
浙 江	Zhejiang	281	42	96	133	10
安 徽	Anhui	586	63	108	344	71
福 建	Fujian	238	31	50	132	25
江 西	Jiangxi	462	78	63	265	56
山 东	Shandong	575	68	145	306	56
河 南	Henan	982	135	117	637	93
湖 北	Hubei	305	46	72	161	26
湖 南	Hunan	450	65	100	235	50
广 东	Guangdong	409	47	106	213	43
广 西	Guangxi	326	40	45	216	25
海 南	Hainan	42	6	7	27	2
重 庆	Chongqing	368	50	52	216	50
四 川	Sichuan	685	110	121	381	73
贵 州	Guizhou	614	88	49	433	44
云 南	Yunnan	639	89	60	441	49
西 藏	Tibet	76	9	13	49	5
陕 西	Shaanxi	408	48	90	218	52
甘 肃	Gansu	290	31	48	158	53
青 海	Qinghai	94	12	9	64	9
宁 夏	Ningxia	138	22	14	82	20
新 疆	Xinjiang	197	32	24	124	17
新疆兵团	Xinjiang Production and Construction Corps	35	5	3	24	3

4-2-2　续表 3　Continued 3

地　区	Region	高等院校 Higher Education Institutions				
		专科(高职) Students of Vocational College	视力残疾 Students with Visual Disability	听力残疾 Students with Hearing Disability	肢体残疾 Students with Physical Disability	其他残疾 Students with Other Disability
		人 person	人 person	人 person	人 person	人 person
全　国	**Nationwide**	**17644**	**2074**	**2550**	**10089**	**2931**
北　京	Beijing	100	9	13	50	28
天　津	Tianjin	68	8	16	36	8
河　北	Hebei	936	83	155	561	137
山　西	Shanxi	729	87	124	397	121
内蒙古	Inner Mongolia	393	33	56	203	101
辽　宁	Liaoning	236	14	47	134	41
吉　林	Jilin	315	28	47	181	59
黑龙江	Heilongjiang	366	49	69	189	59
上　海	Shanghai	50	5	13	24	8
江　苏	Jiangsu	531	36	114	301	80
浙　江	Zhejiang	290	56	106	100	28
安　徽	Anhui	951	81	141	526	203
福　建	Fujian	374	38	73	182	81
江　西	Jiangxi	861	119	111	468	163
山　东	Shandong	1050	102	189	628	131
河　南	Henan	1573	163	222	1006	182
湖　北	Hubei	612	62	112	329	109
湖　南	Hunan	773	99	92	458	124
广　东	Guangdong	590	95	70	334	91
广　西	Guangxi	763	89	75	456	143
海　南	Hainan	83	17	15	34	17
重　庆	Chongqing	578	70	57	321	130
四　川	Sichuan	1502	187	193	857	265
贵　州	Guizhou	1000	135	74	670	121
云　南	Yunnan	926	121	107	569	129
西　藏	Tibet	143	26	15	80	22
陕　西	Shaanxi	373	55	48	186	84
甘　肃	Gansu	442	41	63	242	96
青　海	Qinghai	254	55	30	119	50
宁　夏	Ningxia	193	28	26	95	44
新　疆	Xinjiang	560	80	66	341	73
新疆兵团	Xinjiang Production and Construction Corps	29	3	11	12	3

4-2-2 续表 4 Continued 4

地区	Region	高等特殊教育学院 Special Higher Education Institutions				
		机构 Institutions	录取残疾考生 Newly Enrolled Students	研究生 Postgraduates	盲 Students with Visual Disability	聋 Students with Hearing Disability
		个 unit	人 person	人 person	人 person	人 person
全 国	**Nationwide**	**22**	**2317**	**44**	**18**	**19**
北 京	Beijing	1	101	6	6	
天 津	Tianjin	1	135	14		10
河 北	Hebei					
山 西	Shanxi					
内蒙古	Inner Mongolia					
辽 宁	Liaoning	1	49			
吉 林	Jilin	1	235	24	12	9
黑龙江	Heilongjiang	1	100			
上 海	Shanghai	1	6			
江 苏	Jiangsu	2	70			
浙 江	Zhejiang	1	454			
安 徽	Anhui					
福 建	Fujian	1	40			
江 西	Jiangxi					
山 东	Shandong	2	439			
河 南	Henan	3	317			
湖 北	Hubei					
湖 南	Hunan	1	99			
广 东	Guangdong	2	106			
广 西	Guangxi					
海 南	Hainan					
重 庆	Chongqing	1	23			
四 川	Sichuan	1	42			
贵 州	Guizhou					
云 南	Yunnan	1	101			
西 藏	Tibet					
陕 西	Shaanxi	1				
甘 肃	Gansu					
青 海	Qinghai					
宁 夏	Ningxia					
新 疆	Xinjiang					
新疆兵团	Xinjiang Production and Construction Corps					

4-2-2　续表 5　Continued 5

地区	Region	高等特殊教育学院 Special Higher Education Institutions					
		本科 Undergraduates	盲 Students with Visual Disability	聋 Students with Hearing Disability	专科(高职) Students of Vocational College	盲 Students with Visual Disability	聋 Students with Hearing Disability
		人 person	人 person	人 person	人 person	人 person	人 person
全　国	**Nationwide**	**846**	**192**	**328**	**1427**	**284**	**489**
北　京	Beijing	95	34	29			
天　津	Tianjin	121		68			
河　北	Hebei						
山　西	Shanxi						
内蒙古	Inner Mongolia						
辽　宁	Liaoning				49	6	15
吉　林	Jilin	211	90	60			
黑龙江	Heilongjiang	100		38			
上　海	Shanghai	6		6			
江　苏	Jiangsu	70	24	27			
浙　江	Zhejiang				454	79	184
安　徽	Anhui						
福　建	Fujian				40		15
江　西	Jiangxi						
山　东	Shandong	67	44	14	372	64	118
河　南	Henan	132		54	185	105	39
湖　北	Hubei						
湖　南	Hunan				99		40
广　东	Guangdong				106	21	36
广　西	Guangxi						
海　南	Hainan						
重　庆	Chongqing	23		19			
四　川	Sichuan	21		13	21		19
贵　州	Guizhou						
云　南	Yunnan				101	9	23
西　藏	Tibet						
陕　西	Shaanxi						
甘　肃	Gansu						
青　海	Qinghai						
宁　夏	Ningxia						
新　疆	Xinjiang						
新疆兵团	Xinjiang Production and Construction Corps						

4-2-2 续表 6 Continued 6

地区	Region	高等特殊教育学院 Special Higher Education Institutions				
		机构 Institutions	录取残疾考生 Newly Enrolled Students	研究生 Postgraduates	盲 Students with Visual Disability	聋 Students with Hearing Disability
		个 unit	人 person	人 person	人 person	人 person
全 国	**Nationwide**	**22**	**2317**	**44**	**18**	**19**
北 京	Beijing	1	101	6	6	
天 津	Tianjin	1	135	14		10
河 北	Hebei					
山 西	Shanxi					
内蒙古	Inner Mongolia					
辽 宁	Liaoning	1	49			
吉 林	Jilin	1	235	24	12	9
黑龙江	Heilongjiang	1	100			
上 海	Shanghai	1	6			
江 苏	Jiangsu	2	70			
浙 江	Zhejiang	1	454			
安 徽	Anhui					
福 建	Fujian	1	40			
江 西	Jiangxi					
山 东	Shandong	2	439			
河 南	Henan	3	317			
湖 北	Hubei					
湖 南	Hunan	1	99			
广 东	Guangdong	2	106			
广 西	Guangxi					
海 南	Hainan					
重 庆	Chongqing	1	23			
四 川	Sichuan	1	42			
贵 州	Guizhou					
云 南	Yunnan	1	101			
西 藏	Tibet					
陕 西	Shaanxi	1				
甘 肃	Gansu					
青 海	Qinghai					
宁 夏	Ningxia					
新 疆	Xinjiang					
新疆兵团	Xinjiang Production and Construction Corps					

三、就业
Employment

4-3-1　残疾人就业状况
Employment of Persons with Disabilities

地　区	Region	就业合计 Employed PWDs	按比例就业 Employed through Quoto Scheme	集中就业 Employed through PWDs-Oriented Post	个体就业 Self-Employed
		人 person	人 person	人 person	人 person
全　国	**Nationwide**	**9055417**	**866580**	**259613**	**641280**
北　京	Beijing	108582	68390	1853	11354
天　津	Tianjin	63486	43924	420	4301
河　北	Hebei	419612	19693	3976	12602
山　西	Shanxi	251758	6970	5977	13412
内蒙古	Inner Mongolia	191498	11000	4683	17025
辽　宁	Liaoning	241716	34273	11330	18271
吉　林	Jilin	181033	8688	4181	15670
黑龙江	Heilongjiang	214332	15102	4040	23146
上　海	Shanghai	67135	45839	7751	380
江　苏	Jiangsu	372867	91061	41855	25623
浙　江	Zhejiang	329179	94040	33967	32567
安　徽	Anhui	513280	12889	6835	43178
福　建	Fujian	221435	14076	3934	17680
江　西	Jiangxi	398195	13032	17971	40255
山　东	Shandong	558879	71323	15833	30379
河　南	Henan	536025	23867	11271	80696
湖　北	Hubei	392645	31859	16423	24921
湖　南	Hunan	429492	23782	12390	31133
广　东	Guangdong	409891	83372	7142	16900
广　西	Guangxi	326932	18442	1656	12162
海　南	Hainan	40451	4484	452	1077
重　庆	Chongqing	240755	19253	7902	18886
四　川	Sichuan	854215	24481	10438	50108
贵　州	Guizhou	399947	10885	6836	22835
云　南	Yunnan	426341	18100	6828	17429
西　藏	Tibet	19184	1316	455	747
陕　西	Shaanxi	260845	10637	4013	16453
甘　肃	Gansu	263522	6549	1791	14561
青　海	Qinghai	49509	2700	1466	2633
宁　夏	Ningxia	68954	6092	1294	4414
新　疆	Xinjiang	183301	22524	3916	18265
新疆兵团	Xinjiang Production and Construction Corps	20421	7937	734	2217

4-3-1 续表 Continued

地 区	Region	公益性岗位就业 Employed through Welfare Post	辅助性就业 Assistive Employment	灵活就业（含社区、居家就业） Flexible Employment	从事农村种养加 Engaged in Agricultural Planting, Husbandry and Processing
		人 person	人 person	人 person	人 person
全 国	**Nationwide**	**179289**	**151636**	**2656438**	**4300581**
北 京	Beijing	1141	1180	16427	8237
天 津	Tianjin	954	101	1972	11814
河 北	Hebei	2575	1981	70482	308303
山 西	Shanxi	1165	1047	57866	165321
内蒙古	Inner Mongolia	1886	1054	54771	101079
辽 宁	Liaoning	5973	5208	41484	125177
吉 林	Jilin	2855	1078	45852	102709
黑龙江	Heilongjiang	5402	1227	74355	91060
上 海	Shanghai	2195	3902	6087	981
江 苏	Jiangsu	39325	18048	69843	87112
浙 江	Zhejiang	5100	18434	97885	47186
安 徽	Anhui	3405	4740	161810	280423
福 建	Fujian	2409	2532	79387	101417
江 西	Jiangxi	11485	7249	187420	120783
山 东	Shandong	31134	4374	121383	284453
河 南	Henan	6873	15039	135775	262504
湖 北	Hubei	4543	5784	126035	183080
湖 南	Hunan	3042	6425	145325	207395
广 东	Guangdong	6131	14120	122991	159235
广 西	Guangxi	3680	2543	69962	218487
海 南	Hainan	530	194	7930	25784
重 庆	Chongqing	2668	2336	79724	109986
四 川	Sichuan	6696	14686	376908	370898
贵 州	Guizhou	5231	2887	143284	207989
云 南	Yunnan	3492	3734	102106	274652
西 藏	Tibet	312	268	10353	5733
陕 西	Shaanxi	5081	4133	78384	142144
甘 肃	Gansu	3082	3069	72675	161795
青 海	Qinghai	1588	671	19249	21202
宁 夏	Ningxia	1828	1240	23470	30616
新 疆	Xinjiang	6928	2176	49077	80415
新疆兵团	Xinjiang Production and Construction Corps	580	176	6166	2611

4-3-2 农村困难残疾人实用技术培训及就业帮扶基地建设
Training on Practical Skills and Technologies for PWDs in Rual Areas

地 区	Region	困难残疾人实用技术培训 Training on Practical Skills and Technologies for PWDs		残疾人就业帮扶基地建设 Poverty Alleviation Bases for PWDs		
		本年度培训残疾人 Training on Practical Skills and Technologies for PWDs in 2022	本年度培训投入经费 Fund for Training on Practical Skills and Technologies for PWDs in 2022	残疾人就业帮扶基地 Poverty Alleviation Bases for PWDs	安置残疾人就业 PWDs Provided with Employment Opportunities	辐射带动残疾人 Benefited PWDs
		人次 person-times	万元 10,000 yuan	个 unit	人 person	户 household
全 国	**Nationwide**	**285181**	**25308.4**	**3508**	**44677**	**80390**
北 京	Beijing	1590				
天 津	Tianjin	244	39.2	9	121	58
河 北	Hebei	6963	1014.6	129	1995	2045
山 西	Shanxi	1803	263.1	21	584	546
内蒙古	Inner Mongolia	9033	619.1	105	660	648
辽 宁	Liaoning	4497	333.0	41	443	1375
吉 林	Jilin	6751	336.8	161	966	1818
黑龙江	Heilongjiang	3815	103.6	50	751	527
上 海	Shanghai	868	74.1	182	2443	1326
江 苏	Jiangsu	8484	211.5	108	1210	1266
浙 江	Zhejiang	3559	149.9	220	938	2366
安 徽	Anhui	13166	985.0	110	1470	956
福 建	Fujian	8727	356.0	38	511	414
江 西	Jiangxi	5024	592.4	80	944	790
山 东	Shandong	19607	764.9	157	5058	2614
河 南	Henan	20941	2816.9	64	3917	4026
湖 北	Hubei	9139	823.9	96	1547	2797
湖 南	Hunan	12323	2265.9	455	6546	9537
广 东	Guangdong	9360	394.8	37	880	523
广 西	Guangxi	22371	1209.6	148	636	17412
海 南	Hainan	4345	492.1	14	204	276
重 庆	Chongqing	11936	585.2	112	654	1153
四 川	Sichuan	47586	5193.8	161	2150	3657
贵 州	Guizhou	4531	511.2	135	1071	2075
云 南	Yunnan	8454	1193.7	311	2332	11088
西 藏	Tibet	940	119.5	4	12	9
陕 西	Shaanxi	18777	2285.4	149	2237	3926
甘 肃	Gansu	11237	765.3	182	2127	3941
青 海	Qinghai	2085	174.1	48	712	465
宁 夏	Ningxia	2733	288.3	64	929	1977
新 疆	Xinjiang	1791	268.7	88	467	678
新疆兵团	Xinjiang Production and Construction Corps	2501	76.7	29	162	101

四、社会保障
Social Security

4-4-1 残疾人参加社会保险情况
Social Insurance Coverage of Persons with Disabilities

地 区	Region	残疾居民参加城乡社会养老保险 Residents with Disabilities Covered by Pension Insurance	享受养老保金 PWDs Drawing Pension	重度残疾人 Persons with Severe Disability
		万人 10,000 persons	万人 10,000 persons	万人 10,000 persons
全 国	**Nationwide**	**2761.7**	**1209.3**	**531.8**
北 京	Beijing	13.6	9.2	3.0
天 津	Tianjin	8.1	5.3	2.3
河 北	Hebei	154.8	62.0	28.6
山 西	Shanxi	87.1	36.8	15.1
内蒙古	Inner Mongolia	53.7	26.0	10.5
辽 宁	Liaoning	51.9	23.2	10.9
吉 林	Jilin	55.7	22.6	10.8
黑龙江	Heilongjiang	47.8	19.4	7.1
上 海	Shanghai	9.7	4.6	1.4
江 苏	Jiangsu	126.2	57.7	26.6
浙 江	Zhejiang	81.7	44.7	16.7
安 徽	Anhui	162.5	65.7	34.1
福 建	Fujian	72.9	35.5	16.3
江 西	Jiangxi	98.0	36.4	15.0
山 东	Shandong	192.4	96.5	49.0
河 南	Henan	269.4	129.8	45.3
湖 北	Hubei	123.5	52.2	28.4
湖 南	Hunan	159.5	67.5	33.1
广 东	Guangdong	110.1	39.8	26.8
广 西	Guangxi	99.6	43.7	21.8
海 南	Hainan	15.9	6.5	4.3
重 庆	Chongqing	56.0	24.3	10.7
四 川	Sichuan	232.0	102.8	45.4
贵 州	Guizhou	96.6	40.4	12.9
云 南	Yunnan	120.1	49.2	18.3
西 藏	Tibet	10.2	3.0	1.0
陕 西	Shaanxi	94.6	42.4	13.3
甘 肃	Gansu	96.5	40.6	13.5
青 海	Qinghai	12.6	4.8	2.2
宁 夏	Ningxia	13.1	6.1	3.0
新 疆	Xinjiang	33.7	10.1	4.2
新疆兵团	Xinjiang Production and Construction Corps	2.3	0.5	0.3

4-4-1 续表 Continued

地 区	Region	残疾居民参加城乡社会养老保险 Residents with Disabilities Covered by Pension Insurance				
		60周岁以下参保残疾人 PWDs under 60	重度残疾人 Persons with Severe Disability	全部或部分代缴 PWDs Whose Pension Premium Were Fully or Partially Covered by Government	其他残疾人 Other PWDs	全部或部分代缴 PWDs Whose Pension Premium Were Fully or Partially Covered by Government
		万人 10,000 persons	万人 10,000 persons	万人 10,000 persons	万人 10,000 persons	万人 10,000 persons
全 国	**Nationwide**	**1552.5**	**714.9**	**692.3**	**837.6**	**285.5**
北 京	Beijing	4.5	2.8	2.8	1.7	1.7
天 津	Tianjin	2.7	2.3	2.3	0.4	0.4
河 北	Hebei	92.7	37.6	36.0	55.1	13.2
山 西	Shanxi	50.3	21.4	20.5	28.9	7.5
内蒙古	Inner Mongolia	27.7	13.1	12.5	14.6	5.4
辽 宁	Liaoning	28.7	13.1	12.8	15.6	3.7
吉 林	Jilin	33.1	17.1	16.6	16.0	5.7
黑龙江	Heilongjiang	28.4	10.6	9.7	17.7	4.4
上 海	Shanghai	5.1	4.1	4.1	0.9	0.2
江 苏	Jiangsu	68.5	31.3	31.0	37.2	20.2
浙 江	Zhejiang	37.0	14.4	14.3	22.6	20.8
安 徽	Anhui	96.8	48.3	47.4	48.5	7.0
福 建	Fujian	37.3	20.6	20.5	16.7	15.7
江 西	Jiangxi	61.7	25.7	25.0	35.9	16.2
山 东	Shandong	96.0	47.2	46.4	48.8	8.6
河 南	Henan	139.6	52.0	49.2	87.6	6.7
湖 北	Hubei	71.3	39.8	36.6	31.4	8.9
湖 南	Hunan	92.0	48.1	47.5	43.9	16.7
广 东	Guangdong	70.3	47.9	46.9	22.4	13.9
广 西	Guangxi	55.9	31.3	31.0	24.6	11.2
海 南	Hainan	9.4	5.7	5.4	3.7	1.1
重 庆	Chongqing	31.6	14.8	14.7	16.8	4.9
四 川	Sichuan	129.2	54.8	52.8	74.5	22.8
贵 州	Guizhou	56.3	22.4	21.5	33.8	6.8
云 南	Yunnan	70.9	27.0	26.8	43.9	24.3
西 藏	Tibet	7.2	2.1	1.9	5.2	0.9
陕 西	Shaanxi	52.2	18.0	17.7	34.2	18.3
甘 肃	Gansu	55.9	23.1	22.1	32.7	8.5
青 海	Qinghai	7.8	3.9	3.6	4.0	3.1
宁 夏	Ningxia	7.0	3.9	3.9	3.1	0.6
新 疆	Xinjiang	23.6	9.5	8.2	14.1	5.7
新疆兵团	Xinjiang Production and Construction Corps	1.8	0.8	0.8	0.9	0.2

4-4-2 托养服务
Institutional Care Services

地 区	Region	提供托养服务的机构合计 Institutions Providing Care Services	提供寄宿制托养服务的机构 Boarding Institutions Providing Care Services	提供日间照料托养服务的机构 Institutions Providing Day-Care Services	提供综合托养服务的机构 Institutions Providing Combined Care Services
		个 unit	个 unit	个 unit	个 unit
全 国	**Nationwide**	**8906**	**1763**	**4135**	**1362**
北 京	Beijing	732	305	427	
天 津	Tianjin	29	7	21	1
河 北	Hebei	313	60	5	73
山 西	Shanxi	95	5	1	24
内蒙古	Inner Mongolia	145	58	4	35
辽 宁	Liaoning	155	67	25	27
吉 林	Jilin	165	89	6	37
黑龙江	Heilongjiang	70	3	2	7
上 海	Shanghai				
江 苏	Jiangsu	379	12	272	66
浙 江	Zhejiang	1494	215	1127	152
安 徽	Anhui	332	153	33	86
福 建	Fujian	99	47	39	9
江 西	Jiangxi	260	16	17	56
山 东	Shandong	682	90	392	132
河 南	Henan	397	198	26	122
湖 北	Hubei	232	39	49	47
湖 南	Hunan	264	44	72	56
广 东	Guangdong	1393	31	1344	15
广 西	Guangxi	170	16	2	30
海 南	Hainan	38	11		
重 庆	Chongqing	141	21	55	29
四 川	Sichuan	260	42	35	61
贵 州	Guizhou	135	9		42
云 南	Yunnan	187	34	17	41
西 藏	Tibet	5	1		
陕 西	Shaanxi	197	40	19	58
甘 肃	Gansu	162	14	32	82
青 海	Qinghai	72	19	14	29
宁 夏	Ningxia	94	23	22	9
新 疆	Xinjiang	180	73	77	29
新疆兵团	Xinjiang Production and Construction Corps	29	21		7

4-4-2　续表 1　Continued 1

地　区	Region	获得托养服务的残疾人　PWDs in the Institutions			
		获得寄宿制托养服务的残疾人 PWDs in Boarding Institu-tions	智　力残疾人 Persons with Intellectual Disability	精　神残疾人 Persons with Mental Disability	重度肢体残疾人 Persons with Severe Physical Disability
		人 person	人 person	人 person	人 person
全　国	**Nationwide**	**60582**	**11369**	**32810**	**9916**
北　京	Beijing	1551			
天　津	Tianjin	73	60	5	5
河　北	Hebei	2766	325	2165	114
山　西	Shanxi	307	97	33	149
内蒙古	Inner Mongolia	839	232	348	196
辽　宁	Liaoning	3162	512	2267	218
吉　林	Jilin	1692	362	916	277
黑龙江	Heilongjiang	92	21	53	13
上　海	Shanghai				
江　苏	Jiangsu	493	216	192	66
浙　江	Zhejiang	6312	1156	2177	2252
安　徽	Anhui	2536	563	1342	428
福　建	Fujian	1224	290	452	364
江　西	Jiangxi	740	122	443	101
山　东	Shandong	4411	1025	2390	615
河　南	Henan	8077	1451	3833	2141
湖　北	Hubei	2908	395	2244	142
湖　南	Hunan	2764	1186	699	617
广　东	Guangdong	1649	614	657	182
广　西	Guangxi	2485	171	2066	61
海　南	Hainan	712	39	654	
重　庆	Chongqing	963	166	609	112
四　川	Sichuan	3090	640	1817	451
贵　州	Guizhou	1061	82	796	47
云　南	Yunnan	2508	177	2084	100
西　藏	Tibet	9	2		4
陕　西	Shaanxi	3599	559	2183	496
甘　肃	Gansu	691	136	398	81
青　海	Qinghai	591	215	145	151
宁　夏	Ningxia	891	233	368	185
新　疆	Xinjiang	2158	300	1303	322
新疆兵团	Xinjiang Production and Construction Corps	228	22	171	26

4-4-2 续表 2 Continued 2

地 区	Region	获得托养服务的残疾人 PWDs in the Institutions					
		获得日间照料托养服务的残疾人 PWDs Receiving Day Care	智 力 残疾人 Persons with Intellectual Disability	精 神 残疾人 Persons with Mental Disability	重度肢体残疾人 Persons with Severe Physical Disability	获得居家托养服务残疾人 PWDs Recieving Care Service at Home	获得托养服务的残疾人 PWDs Receiving Care Services
		人 person	人 person	人 person	人 person	人 person	人 person
全 国	**Nationwide**	**94301**	**37390**	**28320**	**18542**	**471991**	**626874**
北 京	Beijing	8832	5581	2057	463	34869	45252
天 津	Tianjin	125	110	5	2	59544	59742
河 北	Hebei	385	148	54	145	19217	22368
山 西	Shanxi	32	9	6	16	4037	4376
内蒙古	Inner Mongolia	133	37	74	18	4417	5389
辽 宁	Liaoning	601	364	126	67	15423	19186
吉 林	Jilin	199	54	35	88	6920	8811
黑龙江	Heilongjiang	60	10	8	37	4593	4745
上 海	Shanghai						
江 苏	Jiangsu	4287	1924	1112	1115	6928	11708
浙 江	Zhejiang	24094	11135	7527	2428	212	30618
安 徽	Anhui	1230	342	578	235	19133	22899
福 建	Fujian	646	359	146	35	17753	19623
江 西	Jiangxi	1940	598	678	514	14065	16745
山 东	Shandong	5977	1777	1886	1829	12748	23136
河 南	Henan	3184	563	1181	1285	5731	16992
湖 北	Hubei	2581	804	882	772	13874	19363
湖 南	Hunan	3739	1740	1090	582	16277	22780
广 东	Guangdong	22267	8236	6971	4087	1841	25757
广 西	Guangxi	329	109	66	125	37177	39991
海 南	Hainan					22358	23070
重 庆	Chongqing	1226	364	477	321	21265	23454
四 川	Sichuan	2173	705	681	617	70362	75625
贵 州	Guizhou	138	27	19	71	9581	10780
云 南	Yunnan	1278	235	538	379	18096	21882
西 藏	Tibet					211	220
陕 西	Shaanxi	1321	281	376	528	15388	20308
甘 肃	Gansu	5132	1114	1272	1879	10317	16140
青 海	Qinghai	1026	356	122	450	2837	4454
宁 夏	Ningxia	420	106	165	118	6758	8069
新 疆	Xinjiang	946	302	188	336	22	3126
新疆兵团	Xinjiang Production and Construction Corps					37	265

五、专门协会
Specialized Associations

4-5-1　省(自治区、直辖市)专门协会建立情况
Establishment of Special Associations at Provincial Level

地　区	Region	盲人协会 Associations of Persons with Visual Disability	聋人协会 Associations of Persons with Hearing Disability	肢残人协会 Associations of Persons with Physical Disability	智力残疾人及亲友协会 Associations of Persons with Intellectual Disability and Their Relatives and Friends	精神残疾人及亲友协会 Associations of Persons with Psychosocial Disability and Their Relatives and Friends
		个 unit	个 unit	个 unit	个 unit	个 unit
全　国	**Nationwide**	**32**	**32**	**32**	**31**	**31**
北　京	Beijing	1	1	1	1	1
天　津	Tianjin	1	1	1	1	1
河　北	Hebei	1	1	1	1	1
山　西	Shanxi	1	1	1	1	1
内蒙古	Inner Mongolia	1	1	1	1	1
辽　宁	Liaoning	1	1	1	1	1
吉　林	Jilin	1	1	1	1	1
黑龙江	Heilongjiang	1	1	1	1	1
上　海	Shanghai	1	1	1	1	1
江　苏	Jiangsu	1	1	1	1	1
浙　江	Zhejiang	1	1	1	1	1
安　徽	Anhui	1	1	1	1	1
福　建	Fujian	1	1	1	1	1
江　西	Jiangxi	1	1	1	1	1
山　东	Shandong	1	1	1	1	1
河　南	Henan	1	1	1	1	1
湖　北	Hubei	1	1	1	1	1
湖　南	Hunan	1	1	1	1	1
广　东	Guangdong	1	1	1	1	1
广　西	Guangxi	1	1	1	1	1
海　南	Hainan	1	1	1	1	1
重　庆	Chongqing	1	1	1	1	1
四　川	Sichuan	1	1	1	1	1
贵　州	Guizhou	1	1	1	1	1
云　南	Yunnan	1	1	1	1	1
西　藏	Tibet	1	1	1		
陕　西	Shaanxi	1	1	1	1	1
甘　肃	Gansu	1	1	1	1	1
青　海	Qinghai	1	1	1	1	1
宁　夏	Ningxia	1	1	1	1	1
新　疆	Xinjiang	1	1	1	1	1
新疆兵团	Xinjiang Production and Construction Corps	1	1	1	1	1

4-5-2 市(地、州、盟)专门协会建立情况
Establishment of Specialized Associations at Municipal Level

地 区	Region	盲人协会 Associations of Persons with Visual Disability	聋人协会 Associations of Persons with Hearing Disability	肢残人协会 Associations of Persons with Physical Disability	智力残疾人及亲友协会 Associations of Persons with Intellectual Disability and Their Relatives and Friends	精神残疾人及亲友协会 Associations of Persons with Psychosocial Disability and Their Relatives and Friends	智力残疾人及亲友协会和精神残疾人及亲友协会合一的协会 Associations of Persons with Intellectual Disability and Psychosocial Disability and Their Relatives and Friends
		个 unit	个 unit	个 unit	个 unit	个 unit	个 unit
全 国	**Nationwide**	**332**	**330**	**335**	**326**	**325**	**5**
北 京	Beijing						
天 津	Tianjin						
河 北	Hebei	11	11	11	11	11	
山 西	Shanxi	11	11	11	11	11	
内蒙古	Inner Mongolia	12	12	12	12	12	
辽 宁	Liaoning	14	14	14	14	14	
吉 林	Jilin	10	10	10	10	10	
黑龙江	Heilongjiang	13	13	13	13	13	
上 海	Shanghai						
江 苏	Jiangsu	13	13	13	13	13	
浙 江	Zhejiang	11	11	11	11	11	
安 徽	Anhui	16	16	16	16	16	
福 建	Fujian	9	9	9	9	9	
江 西	Jiangxi	11	11	11	11	11	
山 东	Shandong	16	16	16	16	16	
河 南	Henan	18	18	18	18	18	
湖 北	Hubei	13	13	13	13	13	
湖 南	Hunan	14	14	14	14	14	
广 东	Guangdong	21	21	21	21	21	
广 西	Guangxi	14	14	14	14	14	
海 南	Hainan	3	3	3	3	3	
重 庆	Chongqing						
四 川	Sichuan	20	20	20	20	20	
贵 州	Guizhou	9	9	9	9	9	
云 南	Yunnan	16	15	16	15	15	1
西 藏	Tibet	2	2	5			1
陕 西	Shaanxi	10	10	10	10	10	
甘 肃	Gansu	16	15	16	15	15	1
青 海	Qinghai	8	8	8	8	8	
宁 夏	Ningxia	5	5	5	5	5	
新 疆	Xinjiang	14	14	14	13	12	1
新疆兵团	Xinjiang Production and Construction Corps	2	2	2	1	1	1

4-5-3　县(县级市、市辖区)专门协会建立情况
Establishment of Specialized Associations at County/District Level

地　区	Region	盲人协会 Associations of Persons with Visual Disability	聋人协会 Associations of Persons with Hearing Disability	肢残人协会 Associations of Persons with Physical Disability	智力残疾人及亲友协会 Associations of Persons with Intellectual Disability and Their Relatives and Friends	精神残疾人及亲友协会 Associations of Persons with Psychosocial Disability and Their Relatives and Friends	智力残疾人及亲友协会和精神残疾人及亲友协会合一的协会 Associations of Persons with Intellectual Disability and Psychosocial Disability and Their Relatives and Friends
		个 unit	个 unit	个 unit	个 unit	个 unit	个 unit
全　国	**Nationwide**	**2732**	**2726**	**2747**	**2620**	**2625**	**102**
北　京	Beijing	16	16	16	16	16	
天　津	Tianjin	16	16	16	16	16	
河　北	Hebei	169	169	169	166	165	3
山　西	Shanxi	118	118	118	113	112	9
内蒙古	Inner Mongolia	103	103	103	90	90	13
辽　宁	Liaoning	105	105	105	105	105	
吉　林	Jilin	64	63	64	61	61	1
黑龙江	Heilongjiang	124	124	124	124	124	
上　海	Shanghai	16	16	16	16	16	
江　苏	Jiangsu	99	99	99	91	92	6
浙　江	Zhejiang	90	90	90	77	77	13
安　徽	Anhui	102	103	103	96	95	6
福　建	Fujian	83	81	83	74	74	9
江　西	Jiangxi	87	87	90	86	87	
山　东	Shandong	138	137	137	136	136	1
河　南	Henan	160	159	160	158	158	1
湖　北	Hubei	97	97	100	96	96	2
湖　南	Hunan	123	123	124	115	115	7
广　东	Guangdong	118	118	119	114	115	3
广　西	Guangxi	111	111	111	109	109	2
海　南	Hainan	19	19	19	18	20	
重　庆	Chongqing	39	39	39	39	39	
四　川	Sichuan	173	171	177	171	168	2
贵　州	Guizhou	82	82	82	79	81	2
云　南	Yunnan	128	128	128	118	119	9
西　藏	Tibet						
陕　西	Shaanxi	105	104	106	102	104	1
甘　肃	Gansu	86	86	86	86	86	
青　海	Qinghai	45	45	45	45	45	
宁　夏	Ningxia	21	21	21	21	21	
新　疆	Xinjiang	85	86	87	76	75	10
新疆兵团	Xinjiang Production and Construction Corps	10	10	10	6	8	2

六、盲人按摩
Massage by the Blind

4-6-1 盲人按摩
Massage by the Blind

地 区	Region	保健按摩人员本年度培训 Blind Health-Care Masseurs Trained in 2022	医疗按摩人员本年度培养 Blind Therapeutical Masseurs Trained in 2022	按摩机构 Institutions of Blind Massage	
				医疗按摩机构 Therapeutical Massage Institrations	保健按摩机构 Health-Care Massage Institrations
		人 person	人 person	人 person	人 person
全 国	**Nationwide**	**17639**	**7298**	**1041**	**16926**
北 京	Beijing	51	163	3	400
天 津	Tianjin	30	111	2	143
河 北	Hebei	349	510	47	546
山 西	Shanxi	386	775	30	617
内蒙古	Inner Mongolia	45	470	146	410
辽 宁	Liaoning	254	106	40	655
吉 林	Jilin	158	225	38	351
黑龙江	Heilongjiang	480	140	36	219
上 海	Shanghai	1800	100	2	310
江 苏	Jiangsu	486	108	70	1048
浙 江	Zhejiang	518	165	83	1105
安 徽	Anhui	247	202	95	277
福 建	Fujian	166	6	8	71
江 西	Jiangxi	528	62	9	180
山 东	Shandong	507	700	109	1431
河 南	Henan	750	600	43	1401
湖 北	Hubei	421	139	47	1101
湖 南	Hunan	669	366	19	668
广 东	Guangdong	368	336	12	1227
广 西	Guangxi	489	131	4	414
海 南	Hainan	131	16		174
重 庆	Chongqing	6002	215	17	500
四 川	Sichuan	98	7	56	967
贵 州	Guizhou	554	199	14	352
云 南	Yunnan	1339	458	16	1139
西 藏	Tibet	14	10		33
陕 西	Shaanxi	102	245	17	323
甘 肃	Gansu	402	190	40	400
青 海	Qinghai	60	110	10	85
宁 夏	Ningxia	190	182	14	232
新 疆	Xinjiang	34	216	13	129
新疆兵团	Xinjiang Production and Construction Corps	11	35	1	18

4-6-1　续表　Continued

地　区	Region	盲人医疗按摩人员专业技术职务任职资格评审 Vocational Qualification Appraisal for Blind Therapeutical Masseurs		盲人保健按摩人员就业 Employed Blind Health-Care Masseurs	盲人医疗按摩人员就业 Employed Blind Therapeutical Masseurs
		中级 Middle-Level Blind Therapeutical Masseurs	初级 Junior-Level Blind Therapeutical Masseurs		
		人 person	人 person	人 person	人 person
全　国	**Nationwide**	**500**	**1844**	**4671**	**1255**
北　京	Beijing	5	11	420	120
天　津	Tianjin		9	8	9
河　北	Hebei	172	989	1802	614
山　西	Shanxi	7	8	57	6
内蒙古	Inner Mongolia	1	5	134	58
辽　宁	Liaoning	1	4	28	10
吉　林	Jilin			1	
黑龙江	Heilongjiang	25	130	41	5
上　海	Shanghai	142	20	175	106
江　苏	Jiangsu		10	337	64
浙　江	Zhejiang	3	69	55	22
安　徽	Anhui	67	390	5	39
福　建	Fujian			3	
江　西	Jiangxi			51	3
山　东	Shandong	4	9	149	28
河　南	Henan	7		180	50
湖　北	Hubei			177	14
湖　南	Hunan	11	36	119	15
广　东	Guangdong			100	9
广　西	Guangxi			60	5
海　南	Hainan			20	1
重　庆	Chongqing			103	16
四　川	Sichuan		1	4	2
贵　州	Guizhou	34	143	174	26
云　南	Yunnan		10	241	5
西　藏	Tibet			8	2
陕　西	Shaanxi			57	7
甘　肃	Gansu	21		109	6
青　海	Qinghai			6	
宁　夏	Ningxia				
新　疆	Xinjiang			44	13
新疆兵团	Xinjiang Production and Construction Corps			3	

七、宣传文化
Publicity and Cultural Activities

4-7-1 宣传文化
Publicity and Cultural Activities

地区	Region	宣传 Publicity		
		省级 At Provincial Level		
		组织新闻发布会 Press Conferences about Disability	广播电台残疾人专题栏目 Radio Programs on Disability	电视手语栏目 TV Programmes with Sign Language
		次 time	个 unit	个 unit
全 国	**Nationwide**	**29**	**24**	**37**
北 京	Beijing			1
天 津	Tianjin		1	1
河 北	Hebei	2	1	1
山 西	Shanxi		1	1
内蒙古	Inner Mongolia	2		2
辽 宁	Liaoning	1	1	1
吉 林	Jilin		1	1
黑龙江	Heilongjiang		1	2
上 海	Shanghai	10		1
江 苏	Jiangsu	1	1	1
浙 江	Zhejiang	3	1	3
安 徽	Anhui		1	1
福 建	Fujian			2
江 西	Jiangxi	1	2	2
山 东	Shandong	2	1	1
河 南	Henan	1	1	1
湖 北	Hubei		1	1
湖 南	Hunan	1	1	1
广 东	Guangdong	1	1	1
广 西	Guangxi	1	1	1
海 南	Hainan			1
重 庆	Chongqing			1
四 川	Sichuan		1	1
贵 州	Guizhou		1	1
云 南	Yunnan	1	1	1
西 藏	Tibet			
陕 西	Shaanxi		1	1
甘 肃	Gansu		1	1
青 海	Qinghai		1	1
宁 夏	Ningxia	2	1	1
新 疆	Xinjiang			1
新疆兵团	Xinjiang Production and Construction Corps			1

4-7-1　续表 1　Continued 1

地　区	Region	宣传 Publicity			
		省级 At Provincial Level			
		新促会 Disability Affairs Publicity Commissions	官方微博 Official Blog	官方微信 Official WeChat	入驻政务客户端平台 Government Administrative Platforms Incorporated with Disability Affairs
		个 unit	个 unit	个 unit	个 unit
全　国	**Nationwide**	**9**	**8**	**30**	**18**
北　京	Beijing		1	1	3
天　津	Tianjin		1	1	1
河　北	Hebei			1	
山　西	Shanxi			1	
内蒙古	Inner Mongolia				
辽　宁	Liaoning			1	
吉　林	Jilin	1	1	1	3
黑龙江	Heilongjiang			1	
上　海	Shanghai		1	1	1
江　苏	Jiangsu	1		1	
浙　江	Zhejiang	1	1	1	
安　徽	Anhui			1	
福　建	Fujian			1	
江　西	Jiangxi			1	1
山　东	Shandong			1	
河　南	Henan	1		1	
湖　北	Hubei			1	1
湖　南	Hunan		1	1	
广　东	Guangdong	1		1	5
广　西	Guangxi			1	
海　南	Hainan	1		1	1
重　庆	Chongqing			1	
四　川	Sichuan		1	1	1
贵　州	Guizhou	1		1	
云　南	Yunnan			1	1
西　藏	Tibet		1	1	
陕　西	Shaanxi			1	
甘　肃	Gansu			1	
青　海	Qinghai			1	
宁　夏	Ningxia	1		1	
新　疆	Xinjiang	1		1	
新疆兵团	Xinjiang Production and Construction Corps				

4-7-1 续表 2 Continued 2

地 区	Region	宣传 Publicity 地级 At Municipal Level 组织新闻发布会 Press Conferences about Disability (次 time)	广播电台残疾人专题栏目 Radio Programs on Disability (个 unit)	电视手语栏目 TV Programmes with Sign Language (个 unit)	新促会 Societies for Promoting News Relating to PWDs (个 unit)
全 国	**Nationwide**	**60**	**195**	**270**	**67**
北 京	Beijing			3	1
天 津	Tianjin		1	3	1
河 北	Hebei	4	7	10	5
山 西	Shanxi		6	6	2
内蒙古	Inner Mongolia		3	6	
辽 宁	Liaoning	1	6	11	3
吉 林	Jilin	1		5	5
黑龙江	Heilongjiang		5	5	3
上 海	Shanghai	3	3	12	2
江 苏	Jiangsu	8	12	16	4
浙 江	Zhejiang	3	12	12	2
安 徽	Anhui	4	16	15	3
福 建	Fujian		4	9	
江 西	Jiangxi	3	6	7	
山 东	Shandong	12	12	8	3
河 南	Henan		11	8	11
湖 北	Hubei	2	10	7	
湖 南	Hunan	1	8	5	2
广 东	Guangdong	2	20	20	6
广 西	Guangxi		1	6	1
海 南	Hainan			2	
重 庆	Chongqing	8	9	36	2
四 川	Sichuan		8	13	
贵 州	Guizhou	5	3	7	1
云 南	Yunnan	2	5	7	3
西 藏	Tibet				
陕 西	Shaanxi		1	2	1
甘 肃	Gansu	1	23	10	6
青 海	Qinghai			9	
宁 夏	Ningxia		1	6	
新 疆	Xinjiang		1	2	
新疆兵团	Xinjiang Production and Construction Corps		1	2	

4-7-1 续表 3 Continued 3

地区	Region	文化 Cultural Activities				
		省级 At Provincial Level				
		公共图书馆盲文及盲人有声读物图书室 Reading Rooms with Braille and Audio Reading Materials in Public Library	残疾人文化周 Cultural Week for PWDs	残疾人文化活动参加人 Participants of Cultural Activities for PWDs	残疾人文化艺术类比赛及展览 Cultural or Artistic Competitions and Exhibitions of PWDs	残疾人艺术团 Arts Groups of PWDs
		个 unit	场次 time	人次 person-time	次 time	个 unit
全 国	**Nationwide**	**32**	**160**	**1038719**	**249**	**23**
北 京	Beijing		1	2884	6	
天 津	Tianjin	1	1	5000	2	4
河 北	Hebei	1	7	1000	9	
山 西	Shanxi	1	1	100	1	
内蒙古	Inner Mongolia	1	1	200	3	
辽 宁	Liaoning	1	3	550	2	
吉 林	Jilin	2	5	85200	3	1
黑龙江	Heilongjiang	1	2	150		1
上 海	Shanghai	1	23	70352	1	1
江 苏	Jiangsu	2	2	220428	2	
浙 江	Zhejiang	1	1	677	143	1
安 徽	Anhui	1	3	1545	2	
福 建	Fujian	2	3	3000	2	1
江 西	Jiangxi	1	9	600	3	
山 东	Shandong	1	2	320	2	1
河 南	Henan	1	2	486		1
湖 北	Hubei	1	5	1668	4	1
湖 南	Hunan		1	1055	1	
广 东	Guangdong	1	1	300	1	1
广 西	Guangxi	1	7	4200	1	1
海 南	Hainan	1	3	350	1	2
重 庆	Chongqing	1	24	12460	13	1
四 川	Sichuan	1	12	8073	35	2
贵 州	Guizhou	1	10	2000		
云 南	Yunnan	1	1	321		
西 藏	Tibet	1	1	200	2	
陕 西	Shaanxi	1	5	600000	1	1
甘 肃	Gansu	1	21	8700	1	
青 海	Qinghai	1	2	900	1	1
宁 夏	Ningxia	1	1	6000	7	1
新 疆	Xinjiang	1				1
新疆兵团	Xinjiang Production and Construction Corps					

4-7-1 续表 4 Continued 4

地 区	Region	文化 Cultural Activities				
		地级 At Municipal Level				
		公共图书馆盲文及盲人有声读物图书室 Reading Rooms with Braille and Audio Reading Materials in Public Library	残疾人文化周 Cultural Week for PWDs	残疾人文化活动参加人 Participants of Cultural Activities for PWDs	残疾人文化艺术类比赛及展览 Cultural or Artistic Competitions and Exhibitions of PWDs	残疾人艺术团 Arts Groups of PWDs
		个 unit	场次 time	人次 person-time	次 time	个 unit
全 国	**Nationwide**	**291**	**1507**	**617955**	**449**	**206**
北 京	Beijing					
天 津	Tianjin					
河 北	Hebei	15	702	35608	28	7
山 西	Shanxi	7	14	2300	6	7
内蒙古	Inner Mongolia	10	18	3171	6	2
辽 宁	Liaoning	16	38	11349	18	15
吉 林	Jilin	8	20	332924	15	11
黑龙江	Heilongjiang	11	45	3761	28	11
上 海	Shanghai					
江 苏	Jiangsu	18	87	66662	57	9
浙 江	Zhejiang	11	16	18177	31	16
安 徽	Anhui	14	43	3014	14	9
福 建	Fujian	6	16	1460	5	1
江 西	Jiangxi	9	35	6051	35	5
山 东	Shandong	16	45	5990	19	21
河 南	Henan	17	51	3230	11	5
湖 北	Hubei	10	60	13140	18	4
湖 南	Hunan	9	17	2349	21	28
广 东	Guangdong	20	87	21151	38	12
广 西	Guangxi	11	51	24176	6	5
海 南	Hainan	2	4	238		1
重 庆	Chongqing					
四 川	Sichuan	23	24	31489	35	6
贵 州	Guizhou	5	2	3650	1	5
云 南	Yunnan	15	12	3096	9	6
西 藏	Tibet	2	1	60		
陕 西	Shaanxi	7	8	2566	5	7
甘 肃	Gansu	15	28	2522	16	7
青 海	Qinghai	5	13	928	6	1
宁 夏	Ningxia	5	46	16980	18	2
新 疆	Xinjiang	4	12	913	2	2
新疆兵团	Xinjiang Production and Construction Corps		12	1000	1	1

4-7-1 续表 5 Continued 5

地区	Region	文化 Cultural Activities 县级 At County Level 公共图书馆盲文及盲人有声读物图书室 Reading Rooms with Braille and Audio Reading Materials in Public Library	残疾人文化周 Cultural Week for PWDs	残疾人文化活动参加人 Participants of Cultural Activities for PWDs
		个 unit	场次 time	人次 person-time
全　国	**Nationwide**	**1054**	**8343**	**858255**
北　京	Beijing	8	391	53751
天　津	Tianjin	6	113	14142
河　北	Hebei	17	462	29251
山　西	Shanxi	13	82	3855
内蒙古	Inner Mongolia	47	195	8039
辽　宁	Liaoning	40	137	8222
吉　林	Jilin	41	163	21310
黑龙江	Heilongjiang	38	164	10538
上　海	Shanghai	37	485	52576
江　苏	Jiangsu	65	1054	159807
浙　江	Zhejiang	76	807	137881
安　徽	Anhui	47	255	24645
福　建	Fujian	41	309	16871
江　西	Jiangxi	24	179	11134
山　东	Shandong	60	269	16992
河　南	Henan	59	194	9523
湖　北	Hubei	27	261	23890
湖　南	Hunan	22	140	6743
广　东	Guangdong	47	401	12090
广　西	Guangxi	19	244	11183
海　南	Hainan	1	19	740
重　庆	Chongqing	40	371	50251
四　川	Sichuan	81	573	91025
贵　州	Guizhou	24	90	6129
云　南	Yunnan	39	164	10753
西　藏	Tibet	1	1	12
陕　西	Shaanxi	47	81	5873
甘　肃	Gansu	42	235	14325
青　海	Qinghai	10	67	3096
宁　夏	Ningxia	23	179	23297
新　疆	Xinjiang	10	90	14804
新疆兵团	Xinjiang Production and Construction Corps	2	168	5507

八、体育
Sports

4-8-1 体 育
Sports

地 区	Region	省级 At Provincial Level					
		残疾人群众体育健身活动 Fitness Sports Activities for PWDs	残疾人群众体育健身活动参加人次 Participants of Fitness Sports Activities for PWDs	残疾人体育比赛 Sports Events for PWDs	参赛残疾人运动员 Disabled Athletes Who Participated in the Sports Events	残疾人体育训练基地 Sports Training Bases for PWDs	聘任教练员 Contracted Coaches
		次 time	人次 person-time	次 time	人次 person-time	个 unit	人 person
全 国	**Nationwide**	**296**	**423051**	**94**	**19438**	**241**	**749**
北 京	Beijing	42	12680	1	273	6	52
天 津	Tianjin	3	2650			6	16
河 北	Hebei	49	19150	15	9000	13	30
山 西	Shanxi	2	150	8	226	5	15
内蒙古	Inner Mongolia	5	190			2	3
辽 宁	Liaoning	6	860	3	19	9	28
吉 林	Jilin	3	5000	3	400	16	28
黑龙江	Heilongjiang	1	80	1	30	6	6
上 海	Shanghai	3	2456	3	586	4	36
江 苏	Jiangsu	2	4400	1	1005	2	13
浙 江	Zhejiang	5	1500	9	527	9	56
安 徽	Anhui	2	160	1	504	6	4
福 建	Fujian	113	9223			19	32
江 西	Jiangxi	3	505	6	796	14	39
山 东	Shandong	2	270	1	1500	12	57
河 南	Henan	1	86			6	55
湖 北	Hubei	2	400	3	535	4	8
湖 南	Hunan	1	4503	1	586	5	15
广 东	Guangdong	5	300	1	100	8	50
广 西	Guangxi	4	860	1	35		15
海 南	Hainan	1	50			12	35
重 庆	Chongqing	4	351000	2	236	24	24
四 川	Sichuan	5	470	10		19	45
贵 州	Guizhou	3	500			6	11
云 南	Yunnan	3	280	1	982	7	18
西 藏	Tibet	4	183	2			2
陕 西	Shaanxi	6	810	7	2	5	9
甘 肃	Gansu	6	615	2	953	7	14
青 海	Qinghai	5	2400	9	750	1	2
宁 夏	Ningxia	5	1320	3	393	2	25
新 疆	Xinjiang					6	6
新疆兵团	Xinjiang Production and Construction Corps						

4-8-1　续表　Continued

地　区	Region	地级 At Municipal Level		县级 At County Level	
		残疾人群众体育健身活动 Fitness Sports Activities for PWDs	残疾人群众体育健身活动参加人数 Participants of Fitness Sports Activities for PWDs	残疾人群众体育健身活动 Fitness Sports Activities for PWDs	残疾人群众体育健身活动参加人数 Participants of Fitness Sports Activities for PWDs
		次 time	人次 person-time	次 time	人次 person-time
全　国	**Nationwide**	**3995**	**166489**	**32007**	**829114**
北　京	Beijing			525	24096
天　津	Tianjin			90	33745
河　北	Hebei	3022	81046	15309	260491
山　西	Shanxi	15	1085	186	5317
内蒙古	Inner Mongolia	6	548	218	3100
辽　宁	Liaoning	25	1552	258	6258
吉　林	Jilin	39	10415	562	27113
黑龙江	Heilongjiang	11	646	75	3235
上　海	Shanghai			1873	66963
江　苏	Jiangsu	204	13441	924	52056
浙　江	Zhejiang	30	4208	804	56174
安　徽	Anhui	40	1987	224	10415
福　建	Fujian	13	1255	183	9975
江　西	Jiangxi	29	2570	137	7549
山　东	Shandong	56	5808	228	8448
河　南	Henan	30	1545	170	4458
湖　北	Hubei	49	12810	651	27325
湖　南	Hunan	14	1200	221	5485
广　东	Guangdong	202	11479	1626	57654
广　西	Guangxi	31	2628	128	5255
海　南	Hainan			10	285
重　庆	Chongqing			557	33201
四　川	Sichuan	30	1446	579	43413
贵　州	Guizhou	2	118	102	2646
云　南	Yunnan	45	3544	5617	36433
西　藏	Tibet			3	1
陕　西	Shaanxi	9	1357	215	5046
甘　肃	Gansu	33	1558	207	16290
青　海	Qinghai	17	1153	53	1928
宁　夏	Ningxia	23	2400	161	10046
新　疆	Xinjiang	2	90	4	220
新疆兵团	Xinjiang Production and Construction Corps	18	600	107	4493

九、维权
Rights Protection

4-9-1 法规体系
Legal System

地 区	Region	制定或修改关于残疾人的专门法规、规章 Disability-specific Laws and Regulations Enacted or Reviewed for PWDs	省级 At Provincial Level	地级 At Municipal Level	制定或修改保障残疾人权益的规范性文件 Polices Enacted or Reviewed for PWDs	省级 At Provincial Level	地级 At Municipal Level	县级 At County Level
		个 unit	个 unit	个 unit	个 unit	个 unit	个 unit	个 unit
全 国	**Nationwide**	**15**	**6**	**9**	**293**	**42**	**66**	**185**
北 京	Beijing	1	1		1	1		
天 津	Tianjin				3	2		1
河 北	Hebei				13		1	12
山 西	Shanxi				1			1
内蒙古	Inner Mongolia				6		2	4
辽 宁	Liaoning				1			1
吉 林	Jilin				2	1		1
黑龙江	Heilongjiang				3		2	1
上 海	Shanghai				6	5		1
江 苏	Jiangsu	1		1	7	1	4	2
浙 江	Zhejiang	2		2	30	8	7	15
安 徽	Anhui				11		4	7
福 建	Fujian				5	2		3
江 西	Jiangxi				44	2	10	32
山 东	Shandong	1	1		23		6	17
河 南	Henan				6		2	4
湖 北	Hubei				5			5
湖 南	Hunan	1		1	18	7	5	6
广 东	Guangdong	3		3	20		13	7
广 西	Guangxi							
海 南	Hainan				5	4		1
重 庆	Chongqing				1			1
四 川	Sichuan	1	1		27		1	26
贵 州	Guizhou				4		1	3
云 南	Yunnan	1		1	11	2	2	7
西 藏	Tibet							
陕 西	Shaanxi				8		2	6
甘 肃	Gansu	1	1		20	2	3	15
青 海	Qinghai	3	2	1	4	2	1	1
宁 夏	Ningxia				6	3		3
新 疆	Xinjiang				2			2
新疆兵团	Xinjiang Production and Construction Corps							

4-9-2 执法检查
Law Enforcement Inspection

地 区	Region	人大执法检查或专题调研 Inspections and Researches by People's Congresses	省级 At Provincial Level	地级 At Municipal Level	县级 At County Level
		次 time	次 time	次 time	次 time
全 国	**Nationwide**	**413**	**12**	**86**	**315**
北 京	Beijing	1			1
天 津	Tianjin	1			1
河 北	Hebei	15		2	13
山 西	Shanxi	10	1	1	8
内蒙古	Inner Mongolia	8		2	6
辽 宁	Liaoning	1		1	
吉 林	Jilin	2		1	1
黑龙江	Heilongjiang	3			3
上 海	Shanghai	4			4
江 苏	Jiangsu	35	1	7	27
浙 江	Zhejiang	52	1	10	41
安 徽	Anhui	4			4
福 建	Fujian	6			6
江 西	Jiangxi	20		3	17
山 东	Shandong	56	1	11	44
河 南	Henan	23	1	10	12
湖 北	Hubei	7		3	4
湖 南	Hunan	44	1	13	30
广 东	Guangdong	21	1	7	13
广 西	Guangxi	3		1	2
海 南	Hainan				
重 庆	Chongqing	19	1		18
四 川	Sichuan	40	1	8	31
贵 州	Guizhou	3			3
云 南	Yunnan	11		3	8
西 藏	Tibet	1	1		
陕 西	Shaanxi	2			2
甘 肃	Gansu	16		2	14
青 海	Qinghai	2	1		1
宁 夏	Ningxia	1			1
新 疆	Xinjiang	2	1	1	
新疆兵团	Xinjiang Production and Construction Corps				

4-9-2 续表 Continued

地 区	Region	政协视察或专题调研 Inspections and Researches by People's Political Consultative Conferences	省级 At Provincial Level	地级 At Municipal Level	县级 At County Level
		次 time	次 time	次 time	次 time
全 国	**Nationwide**	**262**	**4**	**62**	**196**
北 京	Beijing	1			1
天 津	Tianjin				
河 北	Hebei	16		5	11
山 西	Shanxi	5		1	4
内蒙古	Inner Mongolia	2		1	1
辽 宁	Liaoning				
吉 林	Jilin	2		1	1
黑龙江	Heilongjiang	6		2	4
上 海	Shanghai	2			2
江 苏	Jiangsu	22		5	17
浙 江	Zhejiang	49	1	7	41
安 徽	Anhui	5			5
福 建	Fujian	3			3
江 西	Jiangxi	21		5	16
山 东	Shandong	20	2	1	17
河 南	Henan	7		2	5
湖 北	Hubei	8		4	4
湖 南	Hunan	21		8	13
广 东	Guangdong	9		7	2
广 西	Guangxi				
海 南	Hainan				
重 庆	Chongqing	8			8
四 川	Sichuan	23		7	16
贵 州	Guizhou	1			1
云 南	Yunnan	11		3	8
西 藏	Tibet				
陕 西	Shaanxi	5		2	3
甘 肃	Gansu	11			11
青 海	Qinghai	2	1		1
宁 夏	Ningxia	1			1
新 疆	Xinjiang	1		1	
新疆兵团	Xinjiang Production and Construction Corps				

4–9–3　法治宣传
Publicity on Laws

地　区	Region	省级 At Provincial Level			
		普法宣传教育活动 Activities for Law Publicity and Education	普法宣传教育活动参加人 Participants of Activities for Law Publicity and Education	残疾人工作者法律培训班 Law Trainings for Staff Working for PWDs	法律培训班参加人 Trainees of Law Trainings
		次 time	人次 person-time	个 unit	人次 person-time
全　国	**Nationwide**	**184**	**880361**	**39**	**27216**
北　京	Beijing	50	3500	1	80
天　津	Tianjin	1	50	1	18
河　北	Hebei	2	200	1	100
山　西	Shanxi	2	630	1	85
内蒙古	Inner Mongolia	6	1700	2	89
辽　宁	Liaoning	7	900	2	300
吉　林	Jilin	1	269	3	120
黑龙江	Heilongjiang	5	40000		
上　海	Shanghai	3	52700	1	75
江　苏	Jiangsu	6	2600	1	80
浙　江	Zhejiang	4	18306	3	4200
安　徽	Anhui	1	60	1	50
福　建	Fujian	9	20308		
江　西	Jiangxi	32	1850	1	340
山　东	Shandong	4	3275	2	1067
河　南	Henan	1	72	1	72
湖　北	Hubei	3	692000	1	200
湖　南	Hunan	3	120	1	80
广　东	Guangdong	4	8320	1	64
广　西	Guangxi	3	300		
海　南	Hainan	8	654	5	608
重　庆	Chongqing	6	500		
四　川	Sichuan	2	1000	1	70
贵　州	Guizhou	2	300	1	200
云　南	Yunnan	2	812	1	604
西　藏	Tibet	4	1235		
陕　西	Shaanxi	4	2500	1	70
甘　肃	Gansu	4	4100	3	18000
青　海	Qinghai	2	4000	1	30
宁　夏	Ningxia	2	18000	2	614
新　疆	Xinjiang	1	100		
新疆兵团	Xinjiang Production and Construction Corps				

4-9-4 法律救助
Legal Aid

地 区	Region	建立残疾人法律救助协调组织 Legal Assistance and Coordination Organization for PWDs			
		建立残疾人法律救助工作协调机构 Legal Assistance and Coordination Organization for PWDs	省级 At Provincial Level	地级 At Municipal Level	县级 At County Level
		个 unit	个 unit	个 unit	个 unit
全 国	**Nationwide**	**2869**	**31**	**330**	**2508**
北 京	Beijing	13	1		12
天 津	Tianjin	18	1	2	15
河 北	Hebei	182	1	11	170
山 西	Shanxi	88	1	8	79
内蒙古	Inner Mongolia	115	1	12	102
辽 宁	Liaoning	102	1	14	87
吉 林	Jilin	74	1	10	63
黑龙江	Heilongjiang	92	1	13	78
上 海	Shanghai	18	1		17
江 苏	Jiangsu	112	1	13	98
浙 江	Zhejiang	101	1	10	90
安 徽	Anhui	128	1	16	111
福 建	Fujian	95	1	14	80
江 西	Jiangxi	114	1	11	102
山 东	Shandong	121	1	14	106
河 南	Henan	174	1	18	155
湖 北	Hubei	85	1	11	73
湖 南	Hunan	133	1	14	118
广 东	Guangdong	121	1	20	100
广 西	Guangxi	122	1	14	107
海 南	Hainan	24	1	3	20
重 庆	Chongqing	43	1		42
四 川	Sichuan	143	1	18	124
贵 州	Guizhou	77	1	7	69
云 南	Yunnan	101	1	14	86
西 藏	Tibet	84	1	7	76
陕 西	Shaanxi	121	1	11	109
甘 肃	Gansu	103	1	15	87
青 海	Qinghai	47	1	6	40
宁 夏	Ningxia	27	1	5	21
新 疆	Xinjiang	74	1	9	64
新疆兵团	Xinjiang Production and Construction Corps	17		10	7

4-9-4　续表 1　Continued 1

地　区	Region	残疾人法律救助工作站 Legal Assistance Stations for PWDs			
		残疾人法律救助工作站 Legal Assistance Stations for PWDs	省级 At Provincial Level	地级 At Municipal Level	县级 At County Level
		个 unit	个 unit	个 unit	个 unit
全　国	**Nationwide**	**2633**	**27**	**311**	**2295**
北　京	Beijing	4			4
天　津	Tianjin	17	1		16
河　北	Hebei	179	1	11	167
山　西	Shanxi	79		7	72
内蒙古	Inner Mongolia	114	1	12	101
辽　宁	Liaoning	92	1	14	77
吉　林	Jilin	71	1	10	60
黑龙江	Heilongjiang	89	1	11	77
上　海	Shanghai	17	1		16
江　苏	Jiangsu	111	1	13	97
浙　江	Zhejiang	101	1	11	89
安　徽	Anhui	127		16	111
福　建	Fujian	82	1	10	71
江　西	Jiangxi	102	1	11	90
山　东	Shandong	118	1	14	103
河　南	Henan	157	1	17	139
湖　北	Hubei	78	1	12	65
湖　南	Hunan	120	1	14	105
广　东	Guangdong	104	1	17	86
广　西	Guangxi	121	1	14	106
海　南	Hainan	23		3	20
重　庆	Chongqing	42	1		41
四　川	Sichuan	126	1	16	109
贵　州	Guizhou	67	1	3	63
云　南	Yunnan	85	1	12	72
西　藏	Tibet	30	1	7	22
陕　西	Shaanxi	120	1	11	108
甘　肃	Gansu	104	1	16	87
青　海	Qinghai	43	1	6	36
宁　夏	Ningxia	27	1	5	21
新　疆	Xinjiang	65	1	8	56
新疆兵团	Xinjiang Production and Construction Corps	18		10	8

4-9-5 参政议政
Participation of Persons with Disabilities in Administration and Discussion of State Affairs

地 区	Region	残联办理人大建议 Suggestions of People's Congresses Handled by Disabled Persons' Federations	省级 At Provincial Level	地级 At Municipal Level	县级 At County Level
		件 case	件 case	件 case	件 case
全 国	**Nationwide**	**553**	**145**	**205**	**203**
北 京	Beijing	4	1		3
天 津	Tianjin	6	6		
河 北	Hebei	16	5	8	3
山 西	Shanxi	16	10	2	4
内蒙古	Inner Mongolia	7	2	4	1
辽 宁	Liaoning	15	3	10	2
吉 林	Jilin	6	2		4
黑龙江	Heilongjiang	7	2	3	2
上 海	Shanghai	23	13		10
江 苏	Jiangsu	50	12	24	14
浙 江	Zhejiang	81	3	45	33
安 徽	Anhui	33	18	9	6
福 建	Fujian	21	12	4	5
江 西	Jiangxi	22	2	12	8
山 东	Shandong	37	13	16	8
河 南	Henan	5		2	3
湖 北	Hubei	21	2	5	14
湖 南	Hunan	20	6	3	11
广 东	Guangdong	58	6	33	19
广 西	Guangxi	9	5		4
海 南	Hainan	8	6	2	
重 庆	Chongqing	21	4		17
四 川	Sichuan	34	8	11	15
贵 州	Guizhou	3		2	1
云 南	Yunnan	11	2	2	7
西 藏	Tibet				
陕 西	Shaanxi	8		6	2
甘 肃	Gansu	5		2	3
青 海	Qinghai	2	1		1
宁 夏	Ningxia	3	1		2
新 疆	Xinjiang	1			1
新疆兵团	Xinjiang Production and Construction Corps				

4−9−5　续表 Continued

地　区	Region	残联办理政协提案 Proposals of People's Political Consultative Conferences Handled by Disabled Persons' Federations	省级 At Provincial Level	地级 At Municipal Level	县级 At County Level
		件 case	件 case	件 case	件 case
全　国	**Nationwide**	**1011**	**128**	**385**	**498**
北　京	Beijing	18	6		12
天　津	Tianjin	6	3		3
河　北	Hebei	21	3	12	6
山　西	Shanxi	29	5	16	8
内蒙古	Inner Mongolia	22	4	13	5
辽　宁	Liaoning	25	3	18	4
吉　林	Jilin	14	2	4	8
黑龙江	Heilongjiang	14	1	10	3
上　海	Shanghai	30	21		9
江　苏	Jiangsu	72	4	28	40
浙　江	Zhejiang	165	7	70	88
安　徽	Anhui	40	4	11	25
福　建	Fujian	26	5	10	11
江　西	Jiangxi	39	4	16	19
山　东	Shandong	91	7	34	50
河　南	Henan	18		13	5
湖　北	Hubei	39	2	20	17
湖　南	Hunan	37	4	13	20
广　东	Guangdong	85	8	44	33
广　西	Guangxi	11	4	1	6
海　南	Hainan	7	3	1	3
重　庆	Chongqing	35	5		30
四　川	Sichuan	66	7	9	50
贵　州	Guizhou	15	5	8	2
云　南	Yunnan	23	1	11	11
西　藏	Tibet	1	1		
陕　西	Shaanxi	24	4	9	11
甘　肃	Gansu	13		8	5
青　海	Qinghai	3	1		2
宁　夏	Ningxia	15	4	4	7
新　疆	Xinjiang	7		2	5
新疆兵团	Xinjiang Production and Construction Corps				

4−9−6 无障碍环境建设与残疾人机动轮椅车燃油补贴
Promotion of Accessible Environments and Gas Subsidy for Motorized Wheelchairs

地区	Region	无障碍建设与管理法规、政府令 Regulations and Decrees on Accessible Environments Building and Management	无障碍建设领导协调组织 Leading and Coordinating Bodies for Building Accessible Environments	困难重度残疾人家庭无障碍改造 Accessibility Renovation for Homes of Severe PWDs	无障碍建设检查 Inspections on Accessibility	无障碍培训 Trainings on Accessibility	残疾人机动轮椅车燃油补贴 Subsidy for Gas Used by Motorized Wheelchairs of PWDs
		个 unit	个 unit	人 person	次 time	人次 person-time	人 person
全　国	**Nationwide**	**761**	**1627**	**609760**	**9996**	**51638**	**262661**
北　京	Beijing	37	85	8902	1693	7560	25134
天　津	Tianjin	4	17	13936	75	543	12116
河　北	Hebei	50	134	25450	200	744	4573
山　西	Shanxi	19	49	4496	33	290	4376
内蒙古	Inner Mongolia	21	32	22946	71	133	1209
辽　宁	Liaoning	6	54	17575	103	1975	8151
吉　林	Jilin	17	31	7066	13	468	5122
黑龙江	Heilongjiang	1	12	24822	9	665	4059
上　海	Shanghai	5	16	4086	932	665	29566
江　苏	Jiangsu	34	85	14962	336	4112	10853
浙　江	Zhejiang	67	106	15696	746	9984	13589
安　徽	Anhui	10	34	25038	115	261	7834
福　建	Fujian	24	60	5782	199	3094	2078
江　西	Jiangxi	28	44	28890	161	1165	17586
山　东	Shandong	56	109	50692	251	1833	756
河　南	Henan	102	54	48413	58	660	10529
湖　北	Hubei	19	43	60438	84	789	6912
湖　南	Hunan	34	71	27114	165	3764	34078
广　东	Guangdong	36	48	26917	2190	1141	10474
广　西	Guangxi	5	126	19812	62	981	4070
海　南	Hainan	11	12	9220	262	1449	3353
重　庆	Chongqing	12	36	24447	52	1880	2724
四　川	Sichuan	38	71	37649	1480	3184	6887
贵　州	Guizhou	5	24	17514	254	385	1132
云　南	Yunnan	25	74	15761	184	930	13159
西　藏	Tibet		1	2274	1	132	5552
陕　西	Shaanxi	30	39	15273	68	908	8347
甘　肃	Gansu	47	68	12487	56	1343	3834
青　海	Qinghai	5	39	2987	34	10	4488
宁　夏	Ningxia	9	23	9142	68	418	120
新　疆	Xinjiang	4	28	6861	40	134	
新疆兵团	Xinjiang Production and Construction Corps		2	3112	1	38	

4-9-7　残疾人信访
Petitions from Persons with Disabilities

地　区	Region	来信 Petition Letters					
		总计 Subtotal	涉法涉诉类 Regarding Legal Lawsuits	医疗康复类 Medical Rehabilitation	教育类 Education	就业帮扶类 Employment and Poverty Alleviation	社会保障类 Social Security
		件 case	件 case	件 case	件 case	件 case	件 case
全　国	**Nationwide**	**22875**	**864**	**3728**	**890**	**3298**	**4705**
北　京	Beijing	129	39	17	1	4	26
天　津	Tianjin	436	38	65	2	20	96
河　北	Hebei	211	3	7	24	43	73
山　西	Shanxi	811	25	323	27	69	144
内蒙古	Inner Mongolia	745	3	10	6	132	68
辽　宁	Liaoning	420	36	21	11	62	112
吉　林	Jilin	529	28	60	6	39	124
黑龙江	Heilongjiang	270	19	54	28	46	50
上　海	Shanghai	835	31	81	19	58	163
江　苏	Jiangsu	735	16	83	21	98	122
浙　江	Zhejiang	1625	77	138	75	225	330
安　徽	Anhui	519	28	177	2	74	110
福　建	Fujian	651	46	173	14	71	83
江　西	Jiangxi	758	7	317	10	125	225
山　东	Shandong	657	18	101	30	78	86
河　南	Henan	323	29	55	17	47	82
湖　北	Hubei	903	22	87	22	137	301
湖　南	Hunan	1996	76	253	72	263	681
广　东	Guangdong	3266	125	379	166	637	374
广　西	Guangxi	31	4	1		2	8
海　南	Hainan	215	2	17	12	10	103
重　庆	Chongqing	586	24	59	48	50	188
四　川	Sichuan	1699	34	224	57	153	256
贵　州	Guizhou	429	40	29	13	25	104
云　南	Yunnan	2040	35	535	111	475	344
西　藏	Tibet						
陕　西	Shaanxi	1042	11	221	50	170	186
甘　肃	Gansu	518	2	161	39	41	152
青　海	Qinghai	28					2
宁　夏	Ningxia	371	46	40	6	136	71
新　疆	Xinjiang	95		40		8	41
新疆兵团	Xinjiang Production and Construction Corps	2			1		

4-9-7 续表 1 Continued 1

地区	Region	来信 Petition Letters				
		权益保障类 Rights and Interest Protection	控告检举类 Accusation and Disclosure	意见建议类 Opinions and Suggestions	非残类 Unrelated with Disability	其他类 Others
		件 case	件 case	件 case	件 case	件 case
全国	**Nationwide**	**2441**	**689**	**803**	**756**	**4701**
北京	Beijing	9	3	4	1	25
天津	Tianjin	27	121			67
河北	Hebei	33	3	7	2	16
山西	Shanxi	96	2	38	62	25
内蒙古	Inner Mongolia	3	4	2		517
辽宁	Liaoning	53	3	14	24	84
吉林	Jilin	82	33	26	53	78
黑龙江	Heilongjiang	60	2	2		9
上海	Shanghai	138	38	77	29	201
江苏	Jiangsu	150	36	22	17	170
浙江	Zhejiang	204	64	96	10	406
安徽	Anhui	13	2	12	3	98
福建	Fujian	78	15	10		161
江西	Jiangxi	49	4	3	6	12
山东	Shandong	139	2		8	195
河南	Henan	51	6	13	1	22
湖北	Hubei	50	10	38	2	234
湖南	Hunan	187	12	126	9	317
广东	Guangdong	152	13	109	50	1261
广西	Guangxi	5	4	2		5
海南	Hainan	2	9	6		54
重庆	Chongqing	120		46	5	46
四川	Sichuan	131	14	83	468	279
贵州	Guizhou	208		3	1	6
云南	Yunnan	203	7	13	2	315
西藏	Tibet					
陕西	Shaanxi	65	281	10	2	46
甘肃	Gansu	77		41		5
青海	Qinghai	8	1			17
宁夏	Ningxia	43			1	28
新疆	Xinjiang	5				1
新疆兵团	Xinjiang Production and Construction Corps					1

4-9-7 续表 2 Continued 2

地 区	Region	来访 Petition Visits					
		总计 Subtotal	涉法涉诉类 Regarding Legal Lawsuits	医疗康复类 Medical Rehabilitation	教育类 Education	就业帮扶类 Employment and Poverty Alleviation	社会保障类 Social Security
		人次 person-time	人次 person-time	人次 person-time	人次 person-time	人次 person-time	人次 person-time
全 国	**Nationwide**	**91888**	**4955**	**23310**	**4740**	**12257**	**21981**
北 京	Beijing	1480	629	142	58	58	228
天 津	Tianjin	1925	301	114	27	127	371
河 北	Hebei	2485	107	544	149	660	652
山 西	Shanxi	5284	114	2115	166	952	1325
内蒙古	Inner Mongolia	1999	598	244	61	191	444
辽 宁	Liaoning	3636	405	336	188	312	1143
吉 林	Jilin	1241	78	144	57	173	298
黑龙江	Heilongjiang	694	24	30	5	82	148
上 海	Shanghai	2334	152	256	91	548	434
江 苏	Jiangsu	4264	123	1243	186	587	815
浙 江	Zhejiang	2797	301	363	119	351	659
安 徽	Anhui	2239	47	555	122	396	465
福 建	Fujian	954	53	307	71	135	162
江 西	Jiangxi	2990	41	1081	98	552	812
山 东	Shandong	2065	113	173	58	138	468
河 南	Henan	1283	59	172	57	198	292
湖 北	Hubei	3721	222	247	50	320	1406
湖 南	Hunan	7197	516	873	383	1134	2226
广 东	Guangdong	5757	244	1204	413	539	978
广 西	Guangxi	109	17	16	4	13	18
海 南	Hainan	291	6	45	14	16	77
重 庆	Chongqing	2354	272	212	67	487	722
四 川	Sichuan	13681	127	3299	720	2049	3106
贵 州	Guizhou	4235	33	1340	584	264	1527
云 南	Yunnan	4224	87	945	393	431	1400
西 藏	Tibet	12		8		4	
陕 西	Shaanxi	2642	127	713	243	533	782
甘 肃	Gansu	636	8	292	47	80	154
青 海	Qinghai	326	14	12	3	3	11
宁 夏	Ningxia	7335	131	5653	214	708	321
新 疆	Xinjiang	622	6	218	31	126	75
新疆兵团	Xinjiang Production and Construction Corps	1076		414	61	90	462

4-9-7 续表 3 Continued 3

地　区	Region	来访 Petition Visits				
		权益保障类 Rights and Interest Protection	控告检举类 Accusation and Disclosure	意见建议类 Opinions and Suggestions	非残类 Unrelated with Disability	其他类 Others
		人次 person-time	人次 person-time	人次 person-time	人次 person-time	人次 person-time
全　国	**Nationwide**	**8992**	**634**	**1668**	**1747**	**11604**
北　京	Beijing	270	23	43		29
天　津	Tianjin	444	14	44	9	474
河　北	Hebei	230	3	21	27	92
山　西	Shanxi	114	6	15	49	428
内蒙古	Inner Mongolia	70	1	38	237	115
辽　宁	Liaoning	314	40	57	290	551
吉　林	Jilin	238	34	14	10	195
黑龙江	Heilongjiang	223	7	19	4	152
上　海	Shanghai	263	70	199	88	233
江　苏	Jiangsu	652	70	66	45	477
浙　江	Zhejiang	288	98	103	72	443
安　徽	Anhui	137	5	45	4	463
福　建	Fujian	100	23	6	2	95
江　西	Jiangxi	164	24	57	9	152
山　东	Shandong	558	13	7	17	520
河　南	Henan	250	4	35	6	210
湖　北	Hubei	988	67	64	4	353
湖　南	Hunan	968	43	81	75	898
广　东	Guangdong	546	20	93	110	1610
广　西	Guangxi	9	2	6	1	23
海　南	Hainan	43	10	4	4	72
重　庆	Chongqing	306	2	38	3	245
四　川	Sichuan	604	32	412	566	2766
贵　州	Guizhou	376	3	93	1	14
云　南	Yunnan	392	9	18	25	524
西　藏	Tibet					
陕　西	Shaanxi	103	4	19	1	117
甘　肃	Gansu	16		23	2	14
青　海	Qinghai	18			65	200
宁　夏	Ningxia	180	6	34	7	81
新　疆	Xinjiang	94	1	14	14	43
新疆兵团	Xinjiang Production and Construction Corps	34				15

十、组织建设
Disabled Persons' Organizations

4-10-1　省(自治区、直辖市)级残联
Disabled Persons' Federations at Provincial Level

地　区	Region	省市县乡残联实有人员 Staff of Disabled Persons' Federations at Provincial, Municipal, County and Township Level	省级残联机关 Disabled Persons' Federations at Provincial Level		省级残联事业单位 Affiliated Institutions at Provincial Level		
			实有人员 Staff	残疾人干部 Staff with Disability	单位 Affiliated Institutions	实有人员 Total Staff	残疾人 Staff with Disability
		人 person	人 person	人 person	个 unit	人 person	人 person
全　国	**Nationwide**	**110769**	**1586**	**156**	**127**	**7323**	**242**
北　京	Beijing	1305	77	11	7	256	21
天　津	Tianjin	882	49	5	4	143	21
河　北	Hebei	5384	50	3	4	150	9
山　西	Shanxi	4242	54	4	4	173	7
内蒙古	Inner Mongolia	3044	31	3	3	162	8
辽　宁	Liaoning	3048	43	5	1	227	8
吉　林	Jilin	2713	43	6	4	96	
黑龙江	Heilongjiang	2626	47	5	1	49	2
上　海	Shanghai	1257	48	3	5	406	11
江　苏	Jiangsu	4711	65	7	4	112	6
浙　江	Zhejiang	5405	44	5	5	695	12
安　徽	Anhui	3674	48	6	4	180	11
福　建	Fujian	2758	36	1	4	165	6
江　西	Jiangxi	3967	33	2	3	107	
山　东	Shandong	6368	45	7	4	403	9
河　南	Henan	7588	55	6	2	124	6
湖　北	Hubei	3622	54	3	6	80	7
湖　南	Hunan	4942	46	5	6	212	10
广　东	Guangdong	7714	52	3	3	122	5
广　西	Guangxi	3512	45	5	6	256	8
海　南	Hainan	732	67	4	2	82	9
重　庆	Chongqing	2162	40	3	3	131	6
四　川	Sichuan	7075	54	8	3	207	
贵　州	Guizhou	3641	51	6	4	321	15
云　南	Yunnan	3898	65	7	7	187	13
西　藏	Tibet	404	24	2	2	75	6
陕　西	Shaanxi	5104	71	4	7	1515	7
甘　肃	Gansu	4432	83	7	9	447	
青　海	Qinghai	1169	40	6	2	30	1
宁　夏	Ningxia	790	56	7	2	54	2
新　疆	Xinjiang	2459	57	5	5	142	16
新疆兵团	Xinjiang Production and Construction Corps	141	13	2	1	14	

4-10-1 续表 Continued

地 区	Region	干部队伍综合培训情况 Training of Staff						志愿者助残情况 Volunteers	
		省级举办综合培训班 Provincial-level General Trainings	参加省级综合培训人次 Trainees on Provincial-level Trainings	省级举办残疾人干部培训班 Provincial-level Trainings for Staff with Disability	参加省级残疾人干部培训人次 Trainees on Provincial-level Trainings for Staff with Disability	参加全国培训人次 Trainees on State-level Trainings	参加全国残疾人干部培训人次 Trainees on State-level Trainings for Staff with Disability	志愿者登记在册 Registered Volunteers	受助残疾人 PWDs Helped by Volunteers
		期 session	人次 person-time	期 session	人次 person-time	人次 person-time	人次 person-time	人 person	人次 person-time
全 国	**Nationwide**	**281**	**8593**	**12**	**2398**	**47**	**9**	**1892**	**67308**
北 京	Beijing	6	200	1	11	5	2	49	1380
天 津	Tianjin	12	850						
河 北	Hebei	1	400	1	1000	2	6	194	1595
山 西	Shanxi	1	90					116	4317
内蒙古	Inner Mongolia	4	550					82	6640
辽 宁	Liaoning	8	300					59	11372
吉 林	Jilin	16	1960	1	5			323	3126
黑龙江	Heilongjiang	1	450						
上 海	Shanghai							272	10973
江 苏	Jiangsu								
浙 江	Zhejiang	1	100			40	1	1	120
安 徽	Anhui	3	640						
福 建	Fujian	1	80	1	120				
江 西	Jiangxi	2	40						
山 东	Shandong	1	76	1	37			420	1352
河 南	Henan	12	180					97	5314
湖 北	Hubei	1	60					148	15118
湖 南	Hunan	1	78						
广 东	Guangdong							100	1000
广 西	Guangxi								
海 南	Hainan	1	298						
重 庆	Chongqing								
四 川	Sichuan	200	1500						
贵 州	Guizhou	3	282						
云 南	Yunnan								
西 藏	Tibet							17	3400
陕 西	Shaanxi	1	47					10	1071
甘 肃	Gansu								
青 海	Qinghai	1	138	6	1200				
宁 夏	Ningxia	1	49						
新 疆	Xinjiang	2	200						
新疆兵团	Xinjiang Production and Construction Corps	1	25	1	25			4	530

4-10-2 地级残联
Disabled Persons'Federations at Municipal Level

地区	Region	残联 Disabled Persons' Federations	残联机关 Disabled Persons' Federations			
			配备了残疾人领导干部的残联 Disabled Persons' Federations Whose Leadership Include PWDs	实有人员 Staff	残疾人领导干部 Leaders with Disability	残疾人干部 Ordinary Staff with Disability
		个 unit	个 unit	人 person	人 person	人 person
全 国	**Nationwide**	**338**	**213**	**5013**	**234**	**483**
北 京	Beijing					
天 津	Tianjin					
河 北	Hebei	12	7	227	7	15
山 西	Shanxi	11	4	164	4	10
内蒙古	Inner Mongolia	12	10	190	11	21
辽 宁	Liaoning	14	11	306	13	38
吉 林	Jilin	10	4	148	4	16
黑龙江	Heilongjiang	13	7	178	7	14
上 海	Shanghai					
江 苏	Jiangsu	13	9	294	10	20
浙 江	Zhejiang	11	9	172	9	21
安 徽	Anhui	16	10	189	11	17
福 建	Fujian	9	8	125	8	15
江 西	Jiangxi	11	10	130	10	13
山 东	Shandong	16	10	285	11	23
河 南	Henan	18	6	277	7	16
湖 北	Hubei	13	4	141	4	10
湖 南	Hunan	14	7	196	8	13
广 东	Guangdong	21	15	348	16	32
广 西	Guangxi	15	11	159	11	17
海 南	Hainan	3	1	51	2	6
重 庆	Chongqing					
四 川	Sichuan	21	12	260	16	26
贵 州	Guizhou	9	7	156	9	22
云 南	Yunnan	16	12	214	12	30
西 藏	Tibet	7	3	94	3	7
陕 西	Shaanxi	10	7	144	8	14
甘 肃	Gansu	16	13	231	15	33
青 海	Qinghai	8	5	106	6	9
宁 夏	Ningxia	5	4	48	4	6
新 疆	Xinjiang	14	7	180	8	19
新疆兵团	Xinjiang Production and Construction Corps					

4-10-2 续表 Continued

地 区	Region	事业单位 Affiliated Institutions			干部队伍综合培训情况 Training of Staff				志愿者助残情况 Volunteers	
		单位 Institutions	实有人员 Total Staff	残疾人 Staff with Disability	地级举办综合培训班 City-level General Trainings	参加地市级培训人次 Trainees on City-level General Trainings	地级举办残疾人干部培训班 City-level Trainings for Staff with Disability	参加地级残疾人干部培训人次 Trainees on City-level Trainings for Staff with Disability	志愿者登记在册 Registered Volunteers	受助残疾人 PWDs Helped by Volunteers
		个 unit	人 person	人 person	期 session	人次 person-time	期 session	人次 person-time	人 person	人次 person-time
全 国	**Nationwide**	**632**	**10524**	**490**	**355**	**14493**	**148**	**6002**	**36100**	**630626**
北 京	Beijing									
天 津	Tianjin									
河 北	Hebei	22	349	10	19	749	5	100	285	15207
山 西	Shanxi	21	718	55	8	363	4	240	84	13832
内蒙古	Inner Mongolia	16	221	11	11	717	1	67	129	3721
辽 宁	Liaoning	14	294	27	5	233	6	286	5234	19459
吉 林	Jilin	23	313	14	6	101	3	9	305	5960
黑龙江	Heilongjiang	16	147	3	15	512	5	101	90	1473
上 海	Shanghai									
江 苏	Jiangsu	30	522	32	12	794	4	326	2074	50114
浙 江	Zhejiang	24	790	30	12	542	12	310	2325	96632
安 徽	Anhui	29	172	9	14	754	6	152	347	19173
福 建	Fujian	24	273	17	8	400	3	313	1713	18030
江 西	Jiangxi	13	104	4	12	297	7	148	111	4833
山 东	Shandong	33	613	55	17	715	3	175	510	20720
河 南	Henan	48	821	19	22	492	11	468	14327	77237
湖 北	Hubei	29	234	17	13	357	4	180	213	8706
湖 南	Hunan	27	157	8	18	905	9	452	307	10537
广 东	Guangdong	63	2650	78	33	1459	6	483	2502	37971
广 西	Guangxi	34	407	12	10	281	2	132	412	105147
海 南	Hainan	4	36	3	1	165			396	12008
重 庆	Chongqing									
四 川	Sichuan	35	361	20	63	1472	20	691	450	23711
贵 州	Guizhou	16	108	1	3	167	1	30	44	2180
云 南	Yunnan	28	148	13	7	176	4	246	195	4543
西 藏	Tibet	10	49	1	1	14				
陕 西	Shaanxi	17	164	7	17	671	12	352	161	4292
甘 肃	Gansu	24	619	22	9	582	7	469	3248	59102
青 海	Qinghai	7	49		7	322	2	32	48	1441
宁 夏	Ningxia	6	103	13	8	160	9	140	165	2986
新 疆	Xinjiang	17	98	9	4	1093	2	100	25	1369
新疆兵团	Xinjiang Production and Construction Corps	2	4						400	10242

4−10−3　县(县级市、市辖区)级残联
Disabled Persons' Federations at County/District Level

地　区	Region	残　联 Disabled Persons' Federations	配备了残疾人干部的残联 Disabled Persons' Federations with Disabled Staff	残联机关 Disabled Persons' Federations 实有人员 Staff	残疾人干部 Staff with Disability
		个 unit	个 unit	人 person	人 person
全　国	**Nationwide**	**3001**	**1467**	**27375**	**2244**
北　京	Beijing	16	12	172	25
天　津	Tianjin	16	13	183	22
河　北	Hebei	174	101	1465	133
山　西	Shanxi	118	72	1167	102
内蒙古	Inner Mongolia	103	52	922	81
辽　宁	Liaoning	105	41	613	55
吉　林	Jilin	71	25	716	38
黑龙江	Heilongjiang	126	33	537	36
上　海	Shanghai	16	10	139	14
江　苏	Jiangsu	105	47	1285	61
浙　江	Zhejiang	93	64	1233	90
安　徽	Anhui	117	51	929	78
福　建	Fujian	90	30	608	38
江　西	Jiangxi	112	57	943	94
山　东	Shandong	161	87	1824	143
河　南	Henan	174	89	2101	141
湖　北	Hubei	108	39	957	54
湖　南	Hunan	129	66	1374	93
广　东	Guangdong	133	35	1196	44
广　西	Guangxi	111	38	803	45
海　南	Hainan	19	7	191	7
重　庆	Chongqing	41	20	386	26
四　川	Sichuan	190	93	1741	128
贵　州	Guizhou	91	65	910	101
云　南	Yunnan	132	101	1330	176
西　藏	Tibet	74	9	156	9
陕　西	Shaanxi	113	64	1139	115
甘　肃	Gansu	86	77	1045	193
青　海	Qinghai	45	14	341	24
宁　夏	Ningxia	21	10	181	14
新　疆	Xinjiang	97	42	747	61
新疆兵团	Xinjiang Production and Construction Corps	14	3	41	3

4-10-3 续表 Continued

地区	Region	事业单位 Affiliated Institutions			干部队伍综合培训情况 Training of Staff		志愿者助残情况 Volunteers	
		单位 Institutions	实有人员 Total Staff	残疾人 Staff with Disability	县级举办综合培训班 County-level General Trainings	参加县级培训 Trainees on County-level General Trainings	志愿者登记在册 Registered Volunteers	受助残疾人 PWDs Helped by Volunteers
		个 unit	人 person	人 person	期 session	人次 person-time	人 person	万人次 10,000 person-times
全　国	**Nationwide**	**2472**	**15727**	**901**	**206449**	**152707**	**544731**	**769.5**
北　京	Beijing	34	406	30	49	3531	692	2.6
天　津	Tianjin	22	140	3	19	1412	7869	6.2
河　北	Hebei	89	771	36	249	9291	44669	17.8
山　西	Shanxi	87	610	27	111	2719	2163	15.3
内蒙古	Inner Mongolia	44	279	24	97	2522	2869	3.8
辽　宁	Liaoning	30	147	20	117	3617	6918	8.7
吉　林	Jilin	60	423	18	89	4615	72666	41.2
黑龙江	Heilongjiang	73	356	21	176	2844	47956	19.4
上　海	Shanghai	20	221	25	50	1312	2227	6.4
江　苏	Jiangsu	130	856	38	206	7253	17272	43.7
浙　江	Zhejiang	129	795	70	309	10041	22399	64.8
安　徽	Anhui	64	329	22	157	6975	5193	17.1
福　建	Fujian	130	426	32	126	8659	22702	32.8
江　西	Jiangxi	78	382	26	102	4602	2469	5.8
山　东	Shandong	107	1084	66	407	14535	14421	30.7
河　南	Henan	195	1332	22	174	4381	77335	87.4
湖　北	Hubei	124	766	49	122	3032	2886	17.0
湖　南	Hunan	140	910	28	120	6093	5164	17.8
广　东	Guangdong	165	1203	46	221	7158	4133	27.6
广　西	Guangxi	103	476	23	124	3068	63459	105.8
海　南	Hainan	11	92	11	26	1844	518	2.6
重　庆	Chongqing	40	258	19	110	5351	19243	72.0
四　川	Sichuan	135	757	51	242	6160	9989	25.8
贵　州	Guizhou	86	458	43	99	3841	2055	7.9
云　南	Yunnan	107	427	49	165	6618	1666	8.2
西　藏	Tibet	3	6	1	9	93		
陕　西	Shaanxi	94	699	27	170	8287	5040	13.4
甘　肃	Gansu	62	440	27	135	5682	72987	54.6
青　海	Qinghai	25	199	10	77	1802	675	2.4
宁　夏	Ningxia	8	100	10	43	2139	1302	4.1
新　疆	Xinjiang	71	361	25	202333	2728	5332	5.8
新疆兵团	Xinjiang Production and Construction Corps	6	18	2	15	502	462	1.1

4-10-4　乡(镇、街道)残联
Disabled Persons'Federations at Township Level

地　区	Region	乡(镇、街道)已建残联 Disabled Persons' Federations Established in Townships (Towns, Sub-districts)	残联机关 Disabled Persons' Federation			
			实有人员 Total Staff	专职残联理事长 Full-time Presidents	兼职残联理事长 Part-time Presidents	专职委员 Full-time Commissioners on Disability Issues
		个 unit	人 person	人 person	人 person	人 person
全　国	**Nationwide**	**37184**	**43221**	**8907**	**10008**	**59019**
北　京	Beijing	336	394	182	58	1724
天　津	Tianjin	243	367	160	19	288
河　北	Hebei	2291	2372	453	658	2459
山　西	Shanxi	1314	1356	113	569	1672
内蒙古	Inner Mongolia	1075	1239	92	314	1335
辽　宁	Liaoning	1364	1418	282	879	1989
吉　林	Jilin	893	974	126	273	977
黑龙江	Heilongjiang	1306	1312	122	395	1079
上　海	Shanghai	221	443	57	139	721
江　苏	Jiangsu	1263	1577	590	260	2102
浙　江	Zhejiang	1361	1676	994	126	1586
安　徽	Anhui	1539	1827	495	410	2449
福　建	Fujian	1102	1125	285	391	1701
江　西	Jiangxi	1650	2268	308	535	2782
山　东	Shandong	1822	2114	546	389	3401
河　南	Henan	2431	2878	911	685	4728
湖　北	Hubei	1217	1390	264	304	2115
湖　南	Hunan	1915	2047	531	456	3857
广　东	Guangdong	1625	2143	438	336	1919
广　西	Guangxi	1256	1366	235	559	1872
海　南	Hainan	224	213	11	88	334
重　庆	Chongqing	1031	1347	275	222	1489
四　川	Sichuan	2618	3695	182	813	4726
贵　州	Guizhou	1509	1637	309	198	4743
云　南	Yunnan	1425	1527	482	459	1696
西　藏	Tibet					
陕　西	Shaanxi	1254	1372	129	99	2310
甘　肃	Gansu	1362	1567	236	167	1541
青　海	Qinghai	409	404	10	44	354
宁　夏	Ningxia	247	248	12	26	392
新　疆	Xinjiang	861	874	77	131	557
新疆兵团	Xinjiang Production and Construction Corps	20	51		6	121

4-10-4 续表 Continued

地 区	Region	干部队伍综合培训情况 Training of Staff		志愿者助残情况 Volunteers	
		乡镇级举办综合培训班 Township-level General Trainings	参加乡镇级培训人次 Trainees on Township-level Trainings	志愿者登记在册 Registered Volunteers	受助残疾人 PWDs Helped by Volunteers
		期 session	人次 person-time	人 persons	万人次 10,000 person-times
全 国	**Nationwide**	**25697**	**354460**	**666485**	**955.3**
北 京	Beijing	328	5422	6442	144.9
天 津	Tianjin	155	2796	8366	6.8
河 北	Hebei	1400	18366	108069	83.8
山 西	Shanxi	636	8503	1353	3.4
内蒙古	Inner Mongolia	499	6106	1276	1.2
辽 宁	Liaoning	473	3629	12276	10.5
吉 林	Jilin	708	10260	53582	27.7
黑龙江	Heilongjiang	501	5623	57712	36.7
上 海	Shanghai	375	3939	2101	49.4
江 苏	Jiangsu	1152	17828	31594	67.6
浙 江	Zhejiang	1196	24435	14115	41.0
安 徽	Anhui	1119	15468	5252	10.0
福 建	Fujian	647	7040	16969	18.1
江 西	Jiangxi	772	13762	2756	3.7
山 东	Shandong	1899	37680	13818	27.5
河 南	Henan	1913	15639	148538	171.1
湖 北	Hubei	508	5567	3433	8.0
湖 南	Hunan	923	16230	8911	15.2
广 东	Guangdong	1004	15653	4410	15.5
广 西	Guangxi	623	6955	20979	18.9
海 南	Hainan	292	798	257	0.7
重 庆	Chongqing	1361	11521	21185	35.1
四 川	Sichuan	1691	24723	12478	40.7
贵 州	Guizhou	870	14968	6849	6.8
云 南	Yunnan	959	11359	3003	7.0
西 藏	Tibet				
陕 西	Shaanxi	1260	12508	3863	3.4
甘 肃	Gansu	1357	22253	92745	87.3
青 海	Qinghai	307	2700	304	1.3
宁 夏	Ningxia	200	5066	1203	4.3
新 疆	Xinjiang	543	7493	1950	4.3
新疆兵团	Xinjiang Production and Construction Corps	26	170	696	3.2

4-10-5 村(社区)残疾人组织
Disabled Persons' Federations at Village /Community Level

地 区	Region	已建残协 Associations of PWDs		残协情况 Associations		
		村 In Villages	社区 In Communities	已建残疾人活动室 Recreational Rooms for PWDs	村 In Villages	社区 In Communities
		个 unit	个 unit	个 unit	个 unit	个 unit
全 国	**Nationwide**	**508107**	**81054**	**213980**	**178588**	**35392**
北 京	Beijing	3756	2552	3544	2206	1338
天 津	Tianjin	3209	1393	3867	2914	953
河 北	Hebei	48892	3726	32627	30008	2619
山 西	Shanxi	19454	2374	5718	4759	959
内蒙古	Inner Mongolia	11553	2169	2236	1718	518
辽 宁	Liaoning	11816	4145	10208	7159	3049
吉 林	Jilin	9034	1665	2911	2318	593
黑龙江	Heilongjiang	9487	2761	3184	2037	1147
上 海	Shanghai	1629	3971	2918	844	2074
江 苏	Jiangsu	15297	4993	12786	9534	3252
浙 江	Zhejiang	21226	3505	15917	13499	2418
安 徽	Anhui	15092	2414	7766	6552	1214
福 建	Fujian	14164	2157	4719	4195	524
江 西	Jiangxi	17565	2779	7750	6673	1077
山 东	Shandong	55374	5467	8043	6689	1354
河 南	Henan	47154	4307	26190	23979	2211
湖 北	Hubei	21808	3293	5285	4558	727
湖 南	Hunan	25554	3440	10108	8842	1266
广 东	Guangdong	18661	5158	6132	4327	1805
广 西	Guangxi	14832	1670	3499	3086	413
海 南	Hainan	2839	359	174	144	30
重 庆	Chongqing	9139	2033	4268	3195	1073
四 川	Sichuan	28900	3964	10792	9234	1558
贵 州	Guizhou	16054	1888	2268	1872	396
云 南	Yunnan	12879	1923	4788	4104	684
西 藏	Tibet	4246	65	172	86	86
陕 西	Shaanxi	17737	2296	4803	4138	665
甘 肃	Gansu	16009	1221	8425	7781	644
青 海	Qinghai	4187	420	602	426	176
宁 夏	Ningxia	2249	601	652	378	274
新 疆	Xinjiang	7869	1994	1628	1333	295
新疆兵团	Xinjiang Production and Construction Corps	442	351			

4-10-5 续表 Continued

地 区	Region	残协专职委员选聘情况 Full-time Commissioners on Disability Issues			志愿者助残情况 Volunteers	
		残协专职委员 Full-time Commissioners on Disability Issues	村 In Villages	社区 In Communties	志愿者登记在册 Registered Volunteers	受助残疾人 PWDs Assisted by Volunteers
		人 person	人 person	人 person	人 persons	万人次 10,000 person-times
全 国	**Nationwide**	**497743**	**432674**	**65069**	**724456**	**837.7**
北 京	Beijing	4382	3154	1228	6798	38.1
天 津	Tianjin	4029	2978	1051	10956	7.5
河 北	Hebei	50320	46627	3693	98315	62.6
山 西	Shanxi	21440	18815	2625	2421	4.8
内蒙古	Inner Mongolia	12749	10839	1910	3195	3.9
辽 宁	Liaoning	13757	10141	3616	22141	46.0
吉 林	Jilin	9407	7998	1409	74033	39.2
黑龙江	Heilongjiang	3901	2071	1830	40448	28.7
上 海	Shanghai	2189	789	1400	960	21.0
江 苏	Jiangsu	16654	12610	4044	41297	57.1
浙 江	Zhejiang	22723	18625	4098	8538	20.9
安 徽	Anhui	13352	11351	2001	5413	9.6
福 建	Fujian	15012	12742	2270	8746	19.2
江 西	Jiangxi	11481	9479	2002	4558	2.8
山 东	Shandong	65696	59324	6372	17208	22.5
河 南	Henan	44730	40663	4067	178004	212.8
湖 北	Hubei	22017	19101	2916	8494	15.8
湖 南	Hunan	21898	19078	2820	8096	13.1
广 东	Guangdong	16600	14072	2528	6370	14.0
广 西	Guangxi	14773	13175	1598	21132	7.8
海 南	Hainan	2322	1977	345	699	1.9
重 庆	Chongqing	9446	7491	1955	21985	52.0
四 川	Sichuan	35551	34207	1344	18280	37.2
贵 州	Guizhou	8387	6902	1485	7505	8.8
云 南	Yunnan	12564	11045	1519	3313	12.3
西 藏	Tibet	71	71		10	
陕 西	Shaanxi	20312	17907	2405	5567	7.7
甘 肃	Gansu	15586	14520	1066	87047	58.7
青 海	Qinghai	1533	1342	191	551	1.0
宁 夏	Ningxia	2591	2012	579	2385	4.9
新 疆	Xinjiang	2215	1561	654	9728	5.6
新疆兵团	Xinjiang Production and Construction Corps	55	7	48	263	0.4

十一、残疾人服务设施建设
Service Facilities for Persons with Disabilities

4-11-1　残疾人综合服务设施
Comprehensive Service Facilities for Persons with Disabilities

地　区	Region	已竣工 Completed Projects		
		本年度新竣工 Projects Completed in 2022		
		项目数 Projects	建设面积 Construction Area	总投资 Total Investment
		个 unit	平方米 square meter	万元 10,000 yuan
全　国	**Nationwide**	**25**	**121637**	**87487.2**
北　京	Beijing			
天　津	Tianjin			
河　北	Hebei			
山　西	Shanxi			
内蒙古	Inner Mongolia	1	2000	750.0
辽　宁	Liaoning			
吉　林	Jilin			
黑龙江	Heilongjiang	2	404	9.8
上　海	Shanghai			
江　苏	Jiangsu			
浙　江	Zhejiang	5	29514	34535.9
安　徽	Anhui	2	5475	1453.0
福　建	Fujian			
江　西	Jiangxi			
山　东	Shandong	2	6100	1955.0
河　南	Henan	2	6870	1830.0
湖　北	Hubei			
湖　南	Hunan			
广　东	Guangdong	6	46181	34623.4
广　西	Guangxi			
海　南	Hainan			
重　庆	Chongqing			
四　川	Sichuan			
贵　州	Guizhou			
云　南	Yunnan	1	1817	182.7
西　藏	Tibet	2	1525	660.0
陕　西	Shaanxi	1	2471	1106.0
甘　肃	Gansu	1	19280	10381.5
青　海	Qinghai			
宁　夏	Ningxia			
新　疆	Xinjiang			
新疆兵团	Xinjiang Production and Construction Corps			

4-11-1 续表 1 Continued 1

地 区	Region	已竣工 Completed Projects		
		累计已竣工 Completed Projects in Total		
		项目数 Projects	建设面积 Construction Area	总投资 Total Investment
		个 unit	平方米 square meter	万元 10,000 yuan
全 国	**Nationwide**	**2263**	**6111136**	**2038353.3**
北 京	Beijing	8	95721	63880.2
天 津	Tianjin	24	113959	63859.9
河 北	Hebei	133	136841	28557.7
山 西	Shanxi	43	123286	35756.7
内蒙古	Inner Mongolia	57	114259	36909.6
辽 宁	Liaoning	109	284905	104337.6
吉 林	Jilin	47	96741	31853.9
黑龙江	Heilongjiang	98	94922	27538.8
上 海	Shanghai	16	23123	11613.5
江 苏	Jiangsu	77	469726	199477.2
浙 江	Zhejiang	87	648397	320340.4
安 徽	Anhui	86	231873	56107.2
福 建	Fujian	82	276586	93456.0
江 西	Jiangxi	68	89376	20415.4
山 东	Shandong	117	340373	90119.7
河 南	Henan	108	287212	71747.2
湖 北	Hubei	88	207639	49156.0
湖 南	Hunan	91	119106	25765.2
广 东	Guangdong	108	654904	249742.8
广 西	Guangxi	100	175107	33109.0
海 南	Hainan	9	11576	3690.0
重 庆	Chongqing	29	101259	34747.1
四 川	Sichuan	165	450398	136682.2
贵 州	Guizhou	54	62809	13333.6
云 南	Yunnan	118	155982	29127.4
西 藏	Tibet	52	64230	21425.0
陕 西	Shaanxi	80	175619	48175.7
甘 肃	Gansu	93	123176	41418.3
青 海	Qinghai	21	73860	21960.0
宁 夏	Ningxia	13	26647	6556.3
新 疆	Xinjiang	80	280323	67282.7
新疆兵团	Xinjiang Production and Construction Corps	2	1200	211.0

4-11-1　续表 2　Continued 2

地　区	Region	在建项目 Projects under Construction		
		项目数 Projects	建设面积 Construction Area	总投资 Total Investment
		个 unit	平方米 square meter	万元 10,000 yuan
全　国	**Nationwide**	**46**	**640551**	**389398.0**
北　京	Beijing			
天　津	Tianjin			
河　北	Hebei			
山　西	Shanxi	1	5986	4249.5
内蒙古	Inner Mongolia	2	22309	8128.6
辽　宁	Liaoning	2	8000	2630.0
吉　林	Jilin			
黑龙江	Heilongjiang	1	1500	200.0
上　海	Shanghai			
江　苏	Jiangsu	4	61651	70920.0
浙　江	Zhejiang			
安　徽	Anhui	1	7441	2400.0
福　建	Fujian	1	10120	4000.0
江　西	Jiangxi	1	960	531.3
山　东	Shandong	2	131200	50800.0
河　南	Henan	3	16943	5304.0
湖　北	Hubei	3	32769	5800.0
湖　南	Hunan	3	18324	8834.0
广　东	Guangdong	7	246921	206343.3
广　西	Guangxi	1	430	43.0
海　南	Hainan	1	4000	1981.0
重　庆	Chongqing	1	900	406.0
四　川	Sichuan	4	12187	4770.0
贵　州	Guizhou	2	9700	2308.0
云　南	Yunnan	1	5560	772.0
西　藏	Tibet			
陕　西	Shaanxi	2	24467	4120.0
甘　肃	Gansu	1	4800	1046.0
青　海	Qinghai	1	1480	712.0
宁　夏	Ningxia			
新　疆	Xinjiang	1	12903	3099.2
新疆兵团	Xinjiang Production and Construction Corps			

4-11-1 续表 3 Continued 3

地 区	Region	筹建项目 Projects under Discussion and Preparation		
		项目数 Projects	建设面积 Construction Area	总投资 Total Investment
		个 unit	平方米 square meter	万元 10,000 yuan
全 国	**Nationwide**	**9**	**67283**	**52743.0**
北 京	Beijing			
天 津	Tianjin			
河 北	Hebei			
山 西	Shanxi			
内蒙古	Inner Mongolia	1	30000	27160.0
辽 宁	Liaoning	2	11068	2584.0
吉 林	Jilin			
黑龙江	Heilongjiang			
上 海	Shanghai			
江 苏	Jiangsu	1	3000	1500.0
浙 江	Zhejiang	1	6000	11400.0
安 徽	Anhui			
福 建	Fujian	1	6100	2998.0
江 西	Jiangxi			
山 东	Shandong			
河 南	Henan			
湖 北	Hubei			
湖 南	Hunan	1	1200	420.0
广 东	Guangdong	1	8915	6281.0
广 西	Guangxi			
海 南	Hainan			
重 庆	Chongqing			
四 川	Sichuan			
贵 州	Guizhou			
云 南	Yunnan			
西 藏	Tibet	1	1000	400.0
陕 西	Shaanxi			
甘 肃	Gansu			
青 海	Qinghai			
宁 夏	Ningxia			
新 疆	Xinjiang			
新疆兵团	Xinjiang Production and Construction Corps			

4-11-2　残疾人康复设施
Rehabilitation Service Facilities for Persons with Disabilities

地　区	Region	已竣工 Completed Projects		
		本年度新竣工 Projects Completed in 2022		
		项目数 Projects	建设面积 Construction Area	总投资 Total Investment
		个 unit	平方米 square meter	万元 10,000 yuan
全　国	**Nationwide**	**50**	**372352**	**136001.6**
北　京	Beijing			
天　津	Tianjin			
河　北	Hebei	1	6333	1175.0
山　西	Shanxi	2	6737	2100.0
内蒙古	Inner Mongolia	5	33936	12279.0
辽　宁	Liaoning			
吉　林	Jilin			
黑龙江	Heilongjiang			
上　海	Shanghai			
江　苏	Jiangsu			
浙　江	Zhejiang	1	4843	2676.0
安　徽	Anhui	1	800	100.0
福　建	Fujian			
江　西	Jiangxi	5	35513	6347.3
山　东	Shandong			
河　南	Henan	6	46900	11529.4
湖　北	Hubei	3	19062	6174.0
湖　南	Hunan	4	40817	12130.3
广　东	Guangdong	2	8065	2159.5
广　西	Guangxi	3	25770	8519.0
海　南	Hainan	1	3941	963.8
重　庆	Chongqing	2	14000	5390.0
四　川	Sichuan	3	11800	3410.0
贵　州	Guizhou	3	61188	22565.4
云　南	Yunnan	3	23294	7180.8
西　藏	Tibet			
陕　西	Shaanxi	2	14334	27472.0
甘　肃	Gansu			
青　海	Qinghai			
宁　夏	Ningxia	1	4784	1700.0
新　疆	Xinjiang	2	10235	2130.0
新疆兵团	Xinjiang Production and Construction Corps			

4-11-2 续表 1 Continued 1

地 区	Region	已竣工 Completed Projects		
		累计已竣工 Completed Projects in Total		
		项目数 Projects	建设面积 Construction Area	总投资 Total Investment
		个 unit	平方米 square meter	万元 10,000 yuan
全 国	**Nationwide**	**1200**	**6069005**	**1978469.5**
北 京	Beijing	3	13221	8273.7
天 津	Tianjin	10	18793	12573.0
河 北	Hebei	17	97253	29026.1
山 西	Shanxi	56	214626	65271.5
内蒙古	Inner Mongolia	41	204896	66490.8
辽 宁	Liaoning	19	97027	24665.6
吉 林	Jilin	15	89762	47263.9
黑龙江	Heilongjiang	9	61546	14567.0
上 海	Shanghai	5	100462	45136.9
江 苏	Jiangsu	68	279280	125505.3
浙 江	Zhejiang	46	354887	155373.0
安 徽	Anhui	29	198341	65513.2
福 建	Fujian	176	81485	22476.6
江 西	Jiangxi	45	311477	66699.4
山 东	Shandong	114	726973	212622.9
河 南	Henan	41	312888	81478.9
湖 北	Hubei	35	230262	79472.3
湖 南	Hunan	59	292717	77954.5
广 东	Guangdong	56	255639	86250.7
广 西	Guangxi	30	184695	51803.2
海 南	Hainan	6	26230	8711.3
重 庆	Chongqing	21	201981	79522.9
四 川	Sichuan	55	284925	110610.9
贵 州	Guizhou	36	326415	91031.1
云 南	Yunnan	20	150750	47995.8
西 藏	Tibet	16	40673	14651.0
陕 西	Shaanxi	49	181133	73245.8
甘 肃	Gansu	40	222765	57516.5
青 海	Qinghai	8	60373	24250.0
宁 夏	Ningxia	23	160185	56278.7
新 疆	Xinjiang	41	202882	47468.9
新疆兵团	Xinjiang Production and Construction Corps	11	84462	28768.2

4-11-2　续表 2　Continued 2

地　区	Region	在建项目 Projects under Construction		
		项目数 Projects	建设面积 Construction Area	总投资 Total Investment
		个 unit	平方米 square meter	万元 10,000 yuan
全　国	**Nationwide**	**190**	**1575012**	**554256.3**
北　京	Beijing			
天　津	Tianjin			
河　北	Hebei	3	84449	46130.0
山　西	Shanxi	7	42366	16250.3
内蒙古	Inner Mongolia	2	11300	3944.0
辽　宁	Liaoning	2	17047	4025.0
吉　林	Jilin	2	14913	4685.0
黑龙江	Heilongjiang	2	15065	4643.0
上　海	Shanghai			
江　苏	Jiangsu	1	44108	39748.0
浙　江	Zhejiang	5	58834	36380.3
安　徽	Anhui	5	39540	9595.0
福　建	Fujian	3	26843	10489.5
江　西	Jiangxi	9	98273	38113.6
山　东	Shandong	3	22212	12400.0
河　南	Henan	16	108758	35643.0
湖　北	Hubei	14	116868	28592.6
湖　南	Hunan	12	89771	24249.0
广　东	Guangdong	1	3000	400.0
广　西	Guangxi	17	186244	74796.1
海　南	Hainan	2	8420	3926.8
重　庆	Chongqing	6	44688	15523.0
四　川	Sichuan	3	22122	8661.2
贵　州	Guizhou	34	232800	53775.5
云　南	Yunnan	8	67794	19754.2
西　藏	Tibet	2	10723	4653.0
陕　西	Shaanxi	8	64395	22250.7
甘　肃	Gansu	12	80634	19193.8
青　海	Qinghai	1	5740	1641.0
宁　夏	Ningxia	1	4945	2432.7
新　疆	Xinjiang	9	53162	12360.0
新疆兵团	Xinjiang Production and Construction Corps			

4-11-2 续表 3 Continued 3

地区	Region	筹建项目 Projects under Discussion and Preparation		
		项目数 Projects	建设面积 Construction Area	总投资 Total Investment
		个 unit	平方米 square meter	万元 10,000 yuan
全国	**Nationwide**	**10**	**124151**	**67251.2**
北京	Beijing			
天津	Tianjin			
河北	Hebei			
山西	Shanxi			
内蒙古	Inner Mongolia	2	47000	42968.2
辽宁	Liaoning			
吉林	Jilin			
黑龙江	Heilongjiang			
上海	Shanghai			
江苏	Jiangsu	1	3000	300.0
浙江	Zhejiang	1	13312	12511.0
安徽	Anhui	1	5800	1700.0
福建	Fujian			
江西	Jiangxi	2	10339	2200.0
山东	Shandong	1	24000	2772.0
河南	Henan			
湖北	Hubei	1	11700	3450.0
湖南	Hunan			
广东	Guangdong			
广西	Guangxi			
海南	Hainan			
重庆	Chongqing			
四川	Sichuan			
贵州	Guizhou	1	9000	1350.0
云南	Yunnan			
西藏	Tibet			
陕西	Shaanxi			
甘肃	Gansu			
青海	Qinghai			
宁夏	Ningxia			
新疆	Xinjiang			
新疆兵团	Xinjiang Production and Construction Corps			

4-11-3　残疾人托养设施
Institutional Care Service Facilities for Persons with Disabilities

地　区	Region	已竣工 Completed Projects		
		本年度新竣工 Projects Completed in 2022		
		项目数 Projects	建设面积 Construction Area	总投资 Total Investment
		个 unit	平方米 square meter	万元 10,000 yuan
全　国	**Nationwide**	**40**	**114575**	**34563.0**
北　京	Beijing			
天　津	Tianjin			
河　北	Hebei			
山　西	Shanxi	1	2300	730.0
内蒙古	Inner Mongolia	1	2800	730.0
辽　宁	Liaoning	1	8900	1888.0
吉　林	Jilin			
黑龙江	Heilongjiang	1	600	1.0
上　海	Shanghai			
江　苏	Jiangsu			
浙　江	Zhejiang	5	25926	10826.0
安　徽	Anhui	1	7500	2250.0
福　建	Fujian	1	2500	200.0
江　西	Jiangxi	2	5578	1200.0
山　东	Shandong			
河　南	Henan			
湖　北	Hubei	2	7898	1918.1
湖　南	Hunan	3	7931	1588.0
广　东	Guangdong			
广　西	Guangxi			
海　南	Hainan			
重　庆	Chongqing			
四　川	Sichuan	1	2800	760.0
贵　州	Guizhou	1	7560	3320.0
云　南	Yunnan	6	19197	5249.9
西　藏	Tibet	1	4506	1700.0
陕　西	Shaanxi	3	4888	818.0
甘　肃	Gansu			
青　海	Qinghai			
宁　夏	Ningxia	1	2110	994.9
新　疆	Xinjiang	8	590	59.0
新疆兵团	Xinjiang Production and Construction Corps	1	992	330.0

4-11-3 续表 1 Continued 1

地 区	Region	已竣工 Completed Projects		
		累计已竣工 Completed Projects in Total		
		项目数 Projects	建设面积 Construction Area	总投资 Total Investment
		个 unit	平方米 square meter	万元 10,000 yuan
全 国	**Nationwide**	**1076**	**3179672**	**877759.1**
北 京	Beijing			
天 津	Tianjin	10	7803	3572.4
河 北	Hebei	27	93011	19371.4
山 西	Shanxi	21	55848	15056.7
内蒙古	Inner Mongolia	38	93836	32158.4
辽 宁	Liaoning	25	97301	39221.7
吉 林	Jilin	11	35833	11217.0
黑龙江	Heilongjiang	30	68802	16813.3
上 海	Shanghai	12	7260	1593.0
江 苏	Jiangsu	109	333492	98915.4
浙 江	Zhejiang	57	396392	163938.9
安 徽	Anhui	18	65575	18027.3
福 建	Fujian	49	77251	16270.7
江 西	Jiangxi	38	99860	21760.7
山 东	Shandong	37	123156	31763.9
河 南	Henan	38	123135	23867.0
湖 北	Hubei	36	85886	16822.5
湖 南	Hunan	57	123050	29429.9
广 东	Guangdong	14	73211	15779.1
广 西	Guangxi	29	71559	15819.1
海 南	Hainan	5	14211	4879.3
重 庆	Chongqing	13	64226	19347.3
四 川	Sichuan	42	115162	32005.8
贵 州	Guizhou	70	261393	69577.2
云 南	Yunnan	51	130358	38088.4
西 藏	Tibet	5	19800	6749.8
陕 西	Shaanxi	55	138654	22262.0
甘 肃	Gansu	41	115670	29372.4
青 海	Qinghai	30	59670	18104.2
宁 夏	Ningxia	15	36744	12433.0
新 疆	Xinjiang	57	110397	19199.8
新疆兵团	Xinjiang Production and Construction Corps	36	81128	14341.7

4-11-3　续表 2　Continued 2

地　区	Region	在建项目 Projects under Construction		
		项目数 Projects	建设面积 Construction Area	总投资 Total Investment
		个 unit	平方米 square meter	万元 10,000 yuan
全　国	**Nationwide**	**105**	**506851**	**213492.6**
北　京	Beijing			
天　津	Tianjin			
河　北	Hebei	1	6000	1000.0
山　西	Shanxi	4	8149	2384.3
内蒙古	Inner Mongolia	1	1962	730.0
辽　宁	Liaoning	1	2000	520.0
吉　林	Jilin	2	4084	1320.0
黑龙江	Heilongjiang	1	2120	424.0
上　海	Shanghai			
江　苏	Jiangsu			
浙　江	Zhejiang	9	80638	42686.7
安　徽	Anhui	1	1382	446.0
福　建	Fujian	2	6026	1990.0
江　西	Jiangxi	1	2000	365.0
山　东	Shandong	3	13149	2810.0
河　南	Henan	5	28739	7662.5
湖　北	Hubei	6	40186	17771.1
湖　南	Hunan	7	34733	13762.9
广　东	Guangdong	2	73565	63725.4
广　西	Guangxi	9	38546	11466.9
海　南	Hainan	1	1983	1899.0
重　庆	Chongqing	1	4606	1381.0
四　川	Sichuan	2	5700	1530.0
贵　州	Guizhou	17	51304	10353.0
云　南	Yunnan	11	36772	10507.8
西　藏	Tibet	1	5748	2095.0
陕　西	Shaanxi	1	1300	730.0
甘　肃	Gansu	8	35132	10602.1
青　海	Qinghai	1	2430	730.0
宁　夏	Ningxia	1	2040	740.0
新　疆	Xinjiang	3	10459	2280.0
新疆兵团	Xinjiang Production and Construction Corps	3	6097	1580.0

4-11-3 续表 3 Continued 3

地区	Region	筹建项目 Projects under Discussion and Preparation		
		项目数 Projects	建设面积 Construction Area	总投资 Total Investment
		个 unit	平方米 square meter	万元 10,000 yuan
全国	**Nationwide**	**11**	**39419**	**20543.2**
北京	Beijing			
天津	Tianjin			
河北	Hebei			
山西	Shanxi			
内蒙古	Inner Mongolia	2	16000	11290.0
辽宁	Liaoning	2	3200	1100.0
吉林	Jilin			
黑龙江	Heilongjiang			
上海	Shanghai			
江苏	Jiangsu			
浙江	Zhejiang	2	7800	4348.0
安徽	Anhui			
福建	Fujian			
江西	Jiangxi			
山东	Shandong			
河南	Henan			
湖北	Hubei	1	2000	410.0
湖南	Hunan	1	870	265.0
广东	Guangdong			
广西	Guangxi	1	2549	930.2
海南	Hainan			
重庆	Chongqing			
四川	Sichuan	1	5000	1500.0
贵州	Guizhou			
云南	Yunnan			
西藏	Tibet			
陕西	Shaanxi	1	2000	700.0
甘肃	Gansu			
青海	Qinghai			
宁夏	Ningxia			
新疆	Xinjiang			
新疆兵团	Xinjiang Production and Construction Corps			

十二、信息化建设
Application of IT

4-12-1　残疾人事业信息化建设
Application of IT in the Work for Persons with Disabilities

地　区	Region	门户网站 Websites	省级 At Provincial Level	地级 At Municipal Level	县级 At County Level
		个 unit	个 unit	个 unit	个 unit
全　国	**Nationwide**	**1032**	**31**	**233**	**768**
北　京	Beijing	8	1		7
天　津	Tianjin	3	1		2
河　北	Hebei	56	1	9	46
山　西	Shanxi	20	1	5	14
内蒙古	Inner Mongolia	37	1	8	28
辽　宁	Liaoning	22	1	11	10
吉　林	Jilin	20	1	5	14
黑龙江	Heilongjiang	18	1	3	14
上　海	Shanghai	11	1		10
江　苏	Jiangsu	60	1	13	46
浙　江	Zhejiang	47	1	10	36
安　徽	Anhui	89	1	16	72
福　建	Fujian	102	1	10	91
江　西	Jiangxi	62	1	8	53
山　东	Shandong	42	1	15	26
河　南	Henan	55	1	18	36
湖　北	Hubei	42	1	12	29
湖　南	Hunan	42	1	14	27
广　东	Guangdong	51	1	18	32
广　西	Guangxi	38	1	9	28
海　南	Hainan	4	1	1	2
重　庆	Chongqing	5	1		4
四　川	Sichuan	66	1	16	49
贵　州	Guizhou	15	1	3	11
云　南	Yunnan	20	1	6	13
西　藏	Tibet	1	1		
陕　西	Shaanxi	32	1	9	22
甘　肃	Gansu	31	1	7	23
青　海	Qinghai	13	1	2	10
宁　夏	Ningxia	8	1	3	4
新　疆	Xinjiang	9	1	1	7
新疆兵团	Xinjiang Production and Construction Corps	3		1	2

分省统计报告

Provincial Statistical Reports

2022 年北京市残疾人事业发展统计公报

2022 年是首都残疾人事业发展历程中极为重要的一年。习近平总书记出席北京冬残奥会开闭幕式，在党的二十大和北京冬奥会、冬残奥会总结表彰大会上，都对“完善残疾人社会保障制度和关爱服务体系，促进残疾人事业全面发展”提出明确要求，为残疾人工作指明了方向、提供了根本遵循。市委、市政府坚持以人民为中心的发展思想，以北京冬残奥会为契机大力推动残疾人事业全面发展。

一、康复

坚持首善标准制定《北京市残疾预防行动计划（2022—2025 年）》，西城区成为全国残疾预防 15 个重点联系地区之一。加大政策落实力度，15.6 万名残疾人享受专项康复政策服务。会同民政部门规范残疾儿童康复定点机构认定，协调消防、食品卫生等部门加强行业管理，组织第三方开展全覆盖监督。组织对 1692 名康复从业人员开展专业培训，推进持证上岗。实施辅助器具进校园工程，设立残疾人“心理健康热线”。全年为 16.4 万名残疾人提供个性化康复服务，康复服务覆盖率超过 98%。

180021 名残疾人得到基本康复服务，其中 92028 名残疾人得到基本辅助器具适配服务。得到康复服务的持证残疾人中，有视力残疾人 7646 名、听力残疾人 20116 名、言语残疾人 172 名、肢体残疾人 74609 名、智力残疾人 7731 名、精神残疾人 53181 名、多重残疾人 14432 名。

截至 2022 年底，有残疾人康复机构 173 个。康复机构在岗人员达 3617 人，其中，管理人员 413 人，业务人员 2776 人，其他人员 428 人。

二、教育

贯彻落实《“十四五”特殊教育发展提升行动计划》，全市共有特殊教育学校 20 所，特殊教育在校生 7722 人。建设市级特殊教育中心 1 个，市级视障儿童教育资源中心 1 个，市级听障儿童教育资源中心 1 个，市级自闭症及情绪行为障碍儿童教育训练基地（简称自闭症基地）14 个，区级特殊教育中心 16 个，学区级融合教育资源中心 76 个，资源教室 499 个。

三、就业

持续实施残疾人就业状况动态监测，截至 2022 年底，全市劳动年龄内持证残疾人 15.63 万人，城乡残疾人就业率 67.1%，就业局势保持总体稳定。

21 个市相关部门启动实施促进残疾人就业三年行动（2022-2024 年），深入开展 2022 残疾人就业宣传年活动。党政机关常态化定向招录残疾人公务员 12 人。抓实落细残疾人就业促进政策，9800 余家用人单位享受招用残疾人岗位补贴和社会保险补贴，2.7 万名城乡残疾人享受自主创业、灵活就业社保补贴。3.1 万劳动年龄内农村残疾人就业参保。

427 家职业康复站为 8800 余名智力、稳定期精神和重度肢体残疾人提供职业康复服务。菜单式免费培训惠及 4123 人次。圆满举办第十届残疾人职业技能竞赛，共设 16 个竞赛项目，1321 名残疾人报名参加，112 名选手获得奖项。开展农村困难残疾人实用技术培训，为 1590 人次残疾人赋能。为残疾人高校毕业生提供“一对一”精准就业服务纳入 2022 年度重要民生实事项目，240 名残疾人高校毕业生就业帮扶全覆盖。培训盲人医疗按摩人员 162 人。现有保健按摩机构 316 个，医疗按摩机构 3 个。15 人获得盲人医疗按摩人员初级职务任职资格，3 人获得中级职务任职资格。

四、社会保障

配合健全残疾人“两项补贴”主动发现服务机制，提供政策宣传、协助办理等便利化服务。截至 2022 年底，困难残疾人生活补贴 11.59 万人，重度残疾人护理补贴 9.39 万人。

协助完善困难人员代缴基本养老保险保费工作流程。截至 2022 年底，参加城乡居民基本养老保险的残疾人 136435 人。91666 名残疾人领取养老金。60 岁以下参保的残疾人中，27681 名重度残疾人和 17088 名非重度残疾人享受代缴保费政策。

督促城乡居民医保残疾人参保和状态核查，实现“应保尽保”。截至 2022 年底，参加城乡居民基本医疗保险的残疾人 216000 人，其中 216000 名残疾人获得参保缴费资助。

开展残疾人托养服务的各级各类机构达 732 个，其中寄宿制服务机构 305 个，日间照料机构 427 个。10383 名残疾人通过寄宿制和日间照料服务机构接受了托养服务，34869 名残疾人接受居家服务。

五、宣传文化

配合市委宣传部提供十余万字对外宣传材料，冬残奥会和残疾人事业发展宣传报道 3.6 万篇。深入贯彻冬奥遗产战略，20 项成果入选《北京 2022 年冬奥会和冬残奥会遗产报告集（2022）》。

截至 2022 年底，共有市级电视手语栏目 1 个，区级电视手语栏目 3 个。

各级公共图书馆设立盲文及盲文有声读物阅览室 8 个，开展残疾人文化周活动 392 场次。

六、体育

冬残奥会参赛取得历史性成绩，市残联被党中央、国务院表彰为“北京冬奥会、冬残奥会突出贡献集体”，8 个集体、15 名个人受到市委、市政府、北京冬奥组委和中国残联表彰。

12 名北京运动员入选中国冬残奥代表团，助力轮椅冰壶成功卫冕，雪上项目夺取冬残奥会首金，实现北京在冬残奥会参赛史上人数最多、项目最全、成绩最好的历史性突破。连续开展冰雪嘉年华等系列活动，累计近 10 万人次乐享冰雪。

七、维权

全面完成无障碍环境建设 2019-2021 年专项行动，截至冬残奥会闭幕，全市累计整改整治点位 36.6 万个，首都城市功能核心区和冬奥赛事服务保障相关区域基本实现无障碍化，城市无障碍环境规范性、适用性、系统性水平显著提升。

8 个竞赛场馆、2 个冬奥村（冬残奥村）实现全流线无障碍，25 家冬奥定点医院、60 家冬奥会签约饭店、7 家冬残奥会签约饭店全部完成无障碍改造，涉奥场所周边 1 公里范围内 9905 个点位完成改造提升，为 3225 人次有需求观众提供全流程无障碍观赛服务，获国际残奥委会和各国运动员广泛赞誉。

持续推进全市无障碍环境建设和人性化服务水平，协调抓好《北京市无障碍环境建设条例》贯彻落实，逐步建立无障碍公交导乘系统，创建“一刻钟无障碍便民服务圈”，完善 110、119、120、122 等紧急热线和 12345 市民服务热线的文字信息传送、语音呼叫功能，方便残疾人咨询求助。累计完成居家环境无障碍改造 8876 户。

制定或修改关于残疾人的专门法规和规章：市级 1 个；制定或修改保障残疾人权益的规范性文件：市级 1 个。区级以上人大开展《中华人民共和国残疾人保障法》执法检查和专题调研 1 次；政协开展视察和专题调研 1 次。开展市级普法宣传教育活动 50 次，3500 人次参加；举办市级法律培训班 1 个，80 人次参加。各地残联办理建议、提案 22 件。

共出台了 37 个市、区级无障碍环境建设与管理法规、政府令和规范性文件；开展无障碍环境建设检查 1693 次，无障碍培训 7560 人次。

八、组织建设

截至 2022 年底，区、乡镇（街道）共有残联 353 个，其中区级（含燕山）残联 17 个，乡镇（街道）残联 336 个。村（社区）已建残协 6329 个，并全部完成换届。

市、区、乡镇（街道）残联工作人员 1305 人。乡镇（街道）残联、村（社区）残协专职委员 6599 人。各区残联通过采取专（兼）职的方式，全部配备了残疾人领导干部。

建立温馨家园星级评估机制，新建温馨家园 34 个，全市总量达到 684 个，服务残疾人 358.7 万人次。

市区残疾人专门协会 90 个，市区残联业务主管的助残社会组织 261 个。

九、服务设施

截至 2022 年底，已竣工的各级残疾人综合服务设施 8 个，总建设规模 95721.1 平方米，总投资 63880.2 万元；已竣工的各级残疾人康复设施 3 个，总建设规模 13221.4 平方米，总投资 8273.7 万元。

2022 年天津市残疾人事业发展统计公报

2022 年，天津市残联坚持以习近平新时代中国特色社会主义思想为指导，全面贯彻党的二十大和市第十二次党代会精神，以推动残疾人事业高质量发展为主题，以促进残疾人全面发展和共同富裕为主线，深入实施《天津市“十四五”残疾人保障和发展规划》，完善残疾人社会保障制度和关爱服务体系，努力开创残疾人事业发展新局面。

一、康复

出台《天津市残疾预防行动计划（2022-2025 年）》，对残疾预防工作作出全面部署。广泛开展残疾预防知识宣传，提升全社会预防残疾意识，推动“十四五”残疾预防和残疾人康复工作高质量发展。2022 年共有 51541 名残疾儿童和持证残疾人得到了基本康复服务。各类康复对象人数及占比如下：

1．视力残疾人共 3995 人，约占 7.8%。其中接受康复医疗服务的 190 人，接受康复训练服务的 362 人，接受辅助器具服务的 1378 人，接受支持性服务的 2416 人。

2．听力、言语残疾人共 3146 人，约占 6.1%。其中接受康复医疗服务的 294 人，接受康复训练服务的 192 人，接受辅助器具服务的 958 人，接受支持性服务的 2013 人。

3．肢体残疾人共 28271 人，约占 54.9%。其中接受康复医疗服务的 2412 人，接受康复训练服务的 453 人，接受辅助器具服务的 12140 人，接受支持性服务的 15299 人。

4．智力残疾人共 3747 人，约占 7.3%。其中接受康复医疗服务的 192 人，接受康复训练服务的 572 人，接受支持性服务的 3409 人，其他 35 人。

5．精神残疾人共 7419 人，约占 14.4%。其中接受康复医疗服务的 5334 人，接受康复训练服务的 2748 人，接受支持性服务的 2530 人，其他 10 人。

6．多重残疾人共 1661 人，约占 3.2%。

7. 0-17 岁未持证残疾儿童共 3302 人，约占 6.4%。

加强残疾人康复机构与人才队伍建设，深化社区康复工作。截至 2022 年底，全市共有社区康复协调员 4420 人，康复服务设施 445 个。全市建立残疾人康复服务机构 99 个，其中残联系统所属康复机构 17 个。按机构属性划分，民办机构最多，共计 29 个；按康复类别划分，精神康复机构最多，共计 54 个。康复机构在岗人员为 2853 人，其中，管理人员 290 人，业务人员 1926 人，其他人员 637 人。

二、教育

实施第二期国家通用手语和通用盲文推广行动，认真落实残疾人教育扶残助学金政策，为 11417 个残疾人家庭发放助学金。成立市文博系统手语推广研究中心，开发文博手语讲解词汇 200 个、制作导览视频 100 套。广泛开展校园手语推广活动，天津理工大学聋人工学院入选国家通用语言文字推广普及典型案例，在第 25 届全国推普周开幕式上，向全国展示我市手语研究成果。开展首次残疾学生创新创业竞赛，成为助力大学生就业亮点。全面落实残疾考生参加普通高考工作，为残疾考生提供便利。有 55 名残疾人被普通高等院校录取，135 名残疾人进入高等特殊教育学院学习。开办特殊教育普通高中 2 所，在校生 114 人。其中聋生 87 人，盲生 27 人。

三、就业

2022 年新增残疾人就业 5607 人，其中城镇新增就业 3638 人、农村新增就业 1969 人。制定《天津市残疾人职业技能培训补贴实施办法》，出台《天津市促进残疾人就业三年行动实施方案（2022-2024 年）》、《天津市机关、事业单位、国有企业带头安置残疾人若干举措》。充分发挥农村助残就业帮扶基地作用，安置 121 名残疾人就业，辐射带动 58 户残疾人家庭增收。建设“圆梦家园”驿站，落实“创翼计划”，开展“残疾人就业宣传年”活动，全市举办“暖心活动”等各类专场招聘会 210 余场，发放新招用残疾人就业补贴、超比例安排残疾人就业奖励、残疾人个体工商户社会保险缴费补贴、残疾人自主创业补贴等，让疫情下的残疾人就业更加稳定多元。

城乡持证残疾人就业人数为 63486 人。就业形式主要集中在按比例就业、个体就业和农业种养加，其中：按比例就业为 43924 人，个体就业为 4301 人，农业种养加为 11814 人。

全市培训盲人保健按摩人员 30 人次，培养盲人医疗按摩人员 111 人次；保健按摩机构 143 个，医疗按摩机构 2 个，9 人获得盲人医疗按摩人员初级职务任职资格。

四、社会保障

截至 2022 年底，全市参加城乡居民基本养老保险的残疾居民为 80715 人，较 2021 年增加了 1723 人。其中领取待遇的有 53370 人[①]，较 2021 年增加了 1444 人。60 周岁以下参保残疾居民 27345 人。23293 名 60 岁以下参保重度残疾人与 4052 名非重度残疾人全部享受了参保个人缴费资助政策。

残疾人托养服务工作稳步推进。残疾人托养服务机构 29 个，其中寄宿制托养服务机构 7 个，日间照料机构 21 个，综合性服务机构 1 个。托养残疾人总数 59742 人，其中享受居家托养服务残疾人 59544 人，占残疾人托养总数的 99.67%。

五、维权

2022 年，制定或修改保障残疾人权益的规范性文件 3 个。开展“信访联连看”专项调研、普法宣传教育活动，举办市级法律培训班，对残疾人保障法的贯彻实施起到了推动作用。

积极推动残疾人、残疾人亲属和残疾人工作者参选人大代表、政协委员工作，各级残联担任人大代表、政协委员共 44 名，办理人大、政协建议、提案 12 件。

建立无障碍环境建设领导协调组织 17 个，开展无障碍环境建设督导 75 次；提升改造“融畅”手机无障碍导向标识系统，为 6287 户残疾人家庭进行无障碍改造。开展无障碍环境建设公益诉讼专项监督行动，妥善办理残疾人来访来信 436 件、来电 7316 通，接待来访 1925 人次，有效保障残疾人合法权益。

六、宣传文化体育

举办“同声颂党恩、喜迎二十大”天津市第十四届残疾人歌唱大赛、第十二届“牵手残疾人、走进图书馆”活动、“绘中国画卷、赞时代征程”天津市残疾人艺术作品展、残疾人文化周活动，积极参加京津冀三地残疾人文化交流活动。组织残疾人文化宣讲“七进”100 场，成为残疾人文艺宣传“三贴近”的新亮点。在滨海新区和市内六区建设 10 个残疾人“文化进社区”站点，在全市实施 1000 户文化进残疾人家庭“五个一”文化助残项目。举办残疾人文化周活动 114 场，残疾人参加文化活动 19142 人次，全市设立公共图书馆盲文及盲人有声读物图书室 7 个，丰富残疾人文化生活。

开展第十二届残疾人健身周、全国特奥日、残疾人冰雪运动季等残疾人群众体育健身活动 93 次，36395 人次残疾人群众参加，促进残疾人身心健康。选拔残疾人运动员开展运动试训，积极探索暑期夏令营、射箭、乒乓球等项目。实施残疾人康复健身体育进家庭项目，将健身器材、健身方法和健身服务送到 200 户重度残疾人家庭，满足重度残疾人居家锻炼需求。

七、组织建设

截至 2022 年底，全市共建立区及以下残联 259 个，其中：区残联 16 个，乡镇（街道）残联 243 个；建立村（社区）残协 4602 个，建立残疾人活动室 3867 个。全市共建立各类残疾人专门协会 85 个，助残社会组织 6 个。各级残联组织全面开展干部职工和专职委员培训工作，基层组织队伍建设得到进一步加强。

[①] 注：领取待遇人员为“实际参保的残疾居民”中，已年满 60 周岁、未享受城镇职工基本养老保险待遇、直接按月领取城乡居民社会养老保险基础养老金的残疾居民。

2022 年河北省残疾人事业发展统计公报

2022 年，河北省各级残联在省委、省政府的坚强领导和中国残联的有力指导下，坚持以习近平新时代中国特色社会主义思想为指导，全面贯彻党的二十大精神，认真落实习近平总书记关于残疾人工作的重要指示批示精神，深入实施“十四五”残疾人保障和发展规划，全面推进残疾人事业高质量发展取得新成效。

一、康复

贯彻落实《河北省残疾预防行动计划（2022-2025 年）》《河北省“十四五”残疾人康复服务实施方案》，推动“十四五”残疾预防和残疾人康复工作高质量发展。深入贯彻实施《河北省残疾儿童康复救助实施方案》，加强和改进残疾儿童康复救助服务，优化救助流程，提升经办服务效能，10512 名残疾儿童得到康复救助。以农村低收入残疾人为重点，持续开展残疾人精准康复服务行动，299368 名残疾人得到基本康复服务，85262 名残疾人得到基本辅助器具适配服务。获得康复服务的持证残疾人中，视力残疾人 16837 名、听力残疾人 15360 名、言语残疾人 1920 名、肢体残疾人 185789 名、智力残疾人 13765 名、精神残疾人 44630 名、多重残疾人 14221 名。

加强残疾人康复机构和康复人才队伍建设，深化社区康复工作，制定《河北省残联系统康复机构业务规范建设评估细则（试行）》，落实《河北省残疾儿童定点康复机构评估办法（试行）》《河北省残疾人康复专业技术人员规范化培训实施方案》，组织开展康复机构业务规范化建设评估和全省残联系统康复专业技术人员规范化培训。截至 2022 年底，全省有残疾人康复机构 572 个，康复机构在岗人员达 15398 人，其中管理人员 1846 人、业务人员 10746 人、其他人员 2806 人。全年完成省级康复专业技术人员规范化培训 300 人。

二、教育

落实“十四五”特殊教育发展提升行动计划，实施辅助器具进校园工程，加强残疾人中等职业学校基础能力建设和规范化管理，特殊教育得到有力保障。2022 年共为 249 名高考残疾考生提供了不同形式的合理便利，对全省 1223 名新入学困难残疾大学生和困难残疾人家庭子女大学生进行资助，其中残疾研究生 12 名、残疾本科生 58 名、残疾人家庭子女研究生 123 名、残疾人家庭子女本科生 1030 名。

全省共有特殊教育普通高中（部、班）10 个，在校生 846 人，其中聋生 646 人、盲生 101 人、其他 99 人。残疾人中等职业学校（班）4 个，在校生 327 人，毕业生 214 人，毕业生中 148 人获得职业资格证书。高等教育阶段，有 540 名残疾人被普通高等院校录取。

三、就业

城乡持证残疾人就业人数为 419612 人，其中按比例就业 19693 人、集中就业 3976 人、个体就业 12602 人、公益性岗位就业 2575 人、辅助性就业 1981 人、灵活就业（含社区、居家就业）70482 人、从事农业种养加 308303 人。

为 6963 人次农村困难残疾人提供实用技术培训，切实提高增收能力。全省 129 个残疾人就业帮扶基地共安置 1995 名残疾人就业，带动 2045 户残疾人家庭增收。

全省共培训盲人保健按摩人员 349 人次、盲人医疗按摩人员 510 人次。现有保健按摩机构 546 个，医疗按摩机构 47 个。989 人获得盲人医疗按摩人员初级职务任职资格，172 人获得中级职务任职资格。

四、社会保障

截至 2022 年底，参加城乡居民基本养老保险的残疾人数达 1547656 名。620209 名残疾人领取养老金。60 岁以下参保的残疾人中，359703 名重度残疾人和 132131 名非重度残疾人得到参保缴费资助。

开展残疾人托养服务的各级各类机构达 313 个，其中寄宿制服务机构 60 个、日间照料机构 5 个、综合性服务机构 73 个，居家服务机构 175 个。3151 名残疾人通过寄宿制和日间照料服务机构接受托养服务，19217 名残疾人接受居家服务。

五、宣传文化

2022 年紧密结合北京冬残奥会成功举办和党的二十大胜利召开，组织开展“喜迎二十大奋进新征程”主题宣传教育，精心打造具有残联特色、图文并茂的机关党建与业务融合文化墙；举办河北省残疾人事业十年回顾成就展，推出“十年温暖答卷”新闻报道网上阅读点击量超 140 万。举办“建功新时代，一起向未来——河北冬残奥运动员先进事迹情景报告会”，引发强烈社会反响，全网信息曝光量超 450 万条（次）。组织“我和我的残疾人朋友”主题宣传活动，共收到来自全省各地 522 篇应征稿件，精选改编成声波和视频故事，进行了多媒体传播。建成、完善“河北省残联发布”新媒体矩阵，创建微信、快手、抖音等多个新媒体传播平台。与河北广播电视台签署了战略合作协议，打造残疾人事业宣传的新范式。截至 2022 年底，全省共有省市级残疾人专题广播节目 8 个、电视手语栏目 11 个。

开展残疾人文化进家庭、进社区，为 2500 户残疾人提供文化进家庭“五个一”服务，组织开展京津冀摄影诗歌手工艺品文化交流、残疾人书法绘画作品展览等线上线下活动，开展残疾人文化周活动 1171 场次，残疾人精神文化生活更加丰富。完善残疾人文化服务基础设施，各级公共图书馆设立盲文及盲文有声读物阅览室 33 个，市级残疾人艺术团 7 个。

六、体育

残疾人竞技体育位居全国前列。冬季项目方面，2022 年北京冬残奥会取得历史性辉煌战绩，河北省 34 名运动员参加了全部 6 个大项 61 个小项的比赛，夺得 10 金 15 银 12 铜，金牌数、奖牌数占到中国体育代表团的 55%、60%，为祖国、为河北赢得了巨大荣誉。省残联和 5 名运动员被党中央、国务院分别授予“突出贡献集体”和“突出贡献个人”称号，受到习近平总书记的亲切接见。残联系统 47 个单位和个人受到省委、省政府和中国残联表彰。在 2022 年世界残奥单板滑雪国家锦标赛上，河北运动员共夺得 4 金 4 银 4 铜。

夏季项目方面，我省 4 名运动员赴韩国参加举重亚锦赛，夺得了 8 金 7 银 1 铜。2 名运动员赴法国沙托鲁参加 2022 年世界残奥射击世界杯赛，夺得 3 金 2 铜。

群体项目方面，组织参加第五届全国残疾人排舞公开赛，获得二等奖。为 4000 户生活困难的残疾人提供康复健身“三进”服务，组织开展残疾人健身周、“全国特奥日”、冰雪运动季等线上线下活动，更多的残疾人通过康复健身体育融入社会生活。

七、维权

制定或修改保障残疾人权益的规范性文件 13 个，其中市级 1 个、县级 12 个。县级以上人大开展《中华人民共和国残疾人保障法》执法检查和专题调研 15 次；政协开展视察和专题调研 16 次。开展省级普法宣传教育活动 2 次，200 人次参加。举办省级法律培训班 1 个，100 人次参加。各地残联办理建议、提案 37 件，全部按时办结。

全省共出台 50 个省、市、县级无障碍环境建设与管理法规、政府令和规范性文件；开展无障碍环境建设检查 200 次，无障碍培训 744 人次。为有需求的 12894 户困难重度残疾人家庭实施无障碍改造；为 4787 名残疾人发放了机动轮椅车燃油补贴。

2022 年，12385 热线通过电话、短信、微信、网站四大平台共为 38570 名残疾人提供服务，涉及事项 73069 件。其中，坐席即办 72939 件，向各地市交办转办函 130 件，限时办理 129 件，办理中 1 件，无逾期办理事项。对涉及事项进行综合分析，共划分出 7 类残疾人重点关注和集中反映的问题。其中，残疾人证问题 22373 件，较上年度增长 3.06%；社会保障类问题 13910 件，较上年度增长 9.54%；教育类问题 6613 件，较上年度增长 17.8%；残保金类问题 5842 件，较上年度增长 31.7%；家庭无障碍改造类 3280 件，较上年度增长 9.1%；残疾儿童康复救助类问题 1967 件，较上年度下降 3.4%；疫情类问题 80 件。

八、组织建设

市、县、乡共有残联 2476 个，其中设区市已建残联 11 个、县（市、区）残联 174 个、乡镇（街道）残联 2291 个、社区（村）已建残协 52618 个。

省、市、县、乡残联工作人员 5384 人，乡镇（街道）残联、村（社区）残协专职委员总计 52778 人。7 个市级残联配备了残疾人领导干部，101 个县级残联配备了残疾人干部。

残疾人专门协会 901 个，助残社会组织 25 个。

九、服务设施

截至 2022 年底，已竣工的各级残疾人综合服务设施 133 个，总建设规模 136841.4 平方米，总投资 28557.7 万元；已竣工的各级残疾人康复设施 17 个，总建设规模 97252.9 平方米，总投资 29026.1 万元；已竣工的各级残疾人托养服务设施 27 个，总建设规模 93011.4 平方米，总投资 19371.4 万元。

2022 年山西省残疾人事业发展统计公报

2022 年，山西省残疾人事业坚持以习近平新时代中国特色社会主义思想为指导，全面贯彻落实党的二十大精神、习近平总书记考察调研山西重要讲话重要指示精神和关于残疾人事业的重要论述，深入实施《山西省“十四五”残疾人保障和发展规划》，全面推进全省残疾人事业高质量发展。

一、康复

贯彻落实《山西省“十四五”残疾人康复服务实施方案》《山西省残疾预防行动计划（2022—2025年）》《山西省残疾儿童康复救助制度》，扎实推进残疾人精准康复服务行动，不断提高残疾儿童康复救助水平，努力实现残疾人“人人享有康复服务”的目标。

9.2 万名残疾人得到基本康复服务，4.2 万名残疾人得到基本辅助器具适配服务。得到康复服务的持证残疾人中，有视力残疾人 4857 名、听力残疾人 5556 名、言语残疾人 117 名、肢体残疾人 5.3 万名、智力残疾人 6233 名、精神残疾人 1.3 万名、多重残疾人 4935 名。

截至 2022 年底，有残疾人康复机构 286 个。康复机构在岗人员达 9748 人，其中，管理人员 1046 人，业务人员 6681 人，其他人员 2021 人。

二、教育

贯彻落实《山西省“十四五”特殊教育发展提升行动实施方案》，为全省残疾人教育创造更好的条件和环境。会同省教育厅转发《辅助器具进校园工程实施方案》，为义务教育阶段有需要的残疾学生提供适配服务；实施《山西省“十四五”国家手语和盲文规范化行动计划实施方案的通知》，大力推广国家手语和国家盲文。

2022 年，共有特殊教育普通高中（部、班）9 个，在校生 695 人，其中聋人学生 374 名，盲人学生 44 名，其他 277 名。残疾人中等职业学校（班）2 个，在校生 449 名，毕业生 70 名，毕业生中 17 名获得职业资格证书。

三、就业

城乡持证残疾人就业人数为 25.2 万人，其中按比例就业 6970 人，集中就业 5977 人，个体就业 1.3 万人，公益性岗位就业 1165 人，辅助性就业 1047 人，灵活就业（含社区、居家就业）5.8 万人，从事农业种养加 16.5 万人。

开展农村困难残疾人实用技术培训，为 1803 人次残疾人赋能。21 个残疾人就业帮扶基地共安置 584 名残疾人就业，带动 546 户残疾人家庭增收。

共培训盲人保健按摩人员 386 人次、盲人医疗按摩人员 775 人次。现有保健按摩机构 617 个，医疗按摩机构 30 个。8 人获得盲人医疗按摩人员初级职务任职资格，7 人获得中级职务任职资格。

四、社会保障

截至 2022 年底，参加城乡居民基本养老保险的残疾人数达 87.1 万名。36.8 万名残疾人领取养老金。60 岁以下参保的残疾人中，20.5 万名重度残疾人和 7.5 万名非重度残疾人得到参保缴费资助。

开展残疾人托养服务的各级各类机构达 95 个，其中寄宿制服务机构 5 个，日间照料机构 1 个，综合性服务机构 24 个。339 名残疾人通过寄宿制和日间照料服务机构接受了托养服务，4037 名残疾人接受居家服务。

五、宣传文化

截至 2022 年底，共有省级残疾人专题广播节目 1 个、电视手语栏目 1 个，市级残疾人专题广播节目 6 个、电视手语栏目 6 个。

各级公共图书馆设立盲文及盲文有声读物阅览室 21 个，开展残疾人文化周活动 97 场次，省市两级残联艺术团 7 个。

六、维权

2022 年，修改县级保障残疾人权益的规范性文件 1 个。县级以上人大开展《中华人民共和国残疾人保障法》执法检查和专题调研 10 次；政协开展视察和专题调研 5 次。开展省级普法宣传教育活动 2 次，630 余人次参加；举办省级法律培训班 1 个，85 人次参加。各地残联办理建议、提案 45 件。

省市县共出台了 19 个无障碍环境建设与管理法规、政府令和规范性文件；开展无障碍环境建设检查 33 次，无障碍环境建设培训 290 人次。

七、组织建设

2022 年，市县乡共有残联 1443 个，各市已建残联 11 个，县（市、区）已建残联 118 个，乡镇（街道）已建残联 1314 个，社区（村）已建残协 2.2 万个。

省市县乡残联工作人员 4242 人，乡镇（街道）残联、村（社区）残协专职委员总计 2.3 万人。配备残疾人领导干部的市级残联 4 个，配备残疾人干部的县级残联 72 个。残疾人专门协会 648 个，助残社会组织 17 个。

八、服务设施

截至 2022 年底，已竣工的各级残疾人综合服务设施 43 个，总建设规模 12.3 万平方米，总投资 35756.7 万元；已竣工的各级残疾人康复设施 56 个，总建设规模 21.5 万平方米，总投资 65271.4 万元；已竣工的各级残疾人托养服务设施 21 个，总建设规模 5.6 万平方米，总投资 15056.7 万元。

2022年内蒙古自治区残疾人事业发展统计公报

2022年，自治区残联在自治区党委和政府的正确领导下，在中国残联的精心指导下，坚持以习近平新时代中国特色社会主义思想为指导，全面贯彻党的二十大精神和习近平总书记关于残疾人工作的重要指示批示精神，深入贯彻实施《内蒙古自治区“十四五”残疾人事业发展规划》，推进残疾人事业高质量发展，认真履行“代表、服务、管理”职能，克服疫情影响，较好地完成了年度任务。

一、康复

全区各级残联认真贯彻落实《内蒙古自治区残疾预防行动计划（2022-2025年）》《内蒙古自治区“十四五”残疾人康复服务实施方案》，全区6.46万名残疾人得到基本康复服务，31701名残疾人得到基本辅助器具适配服务。得到康复服务的残疾人中，有视力残疾人4499名、听力残疾人5567名、言语残疾人222名、肢体残疾人33859名、智力残疾人2218名、精神残疾人11706名、多重残疾人3403名，未持证的残疾儿童3162人。

加强残疾人康复服务机构与人才队伍建设，开展残疾预防日宣传教育活动，深化康复工作，提升康复服务质量，推进“大爱北疆•助康圆梦”各项公益行动。印发《内蒙古自治区残疾儿童康复救助定点服务机构协议管理实施细则（试行）》和《残疾人定点康复服务机构评估指导方案》。截至2022年底，全区共有残疾人康复机构293个。康复机构在岗人员7187人，其中管理人员682人、业务人员5074人、其他人员1431人。

二、教育

制定印发《内蒙古自治区“十四五”特殊教育发展提升计划实施方案》。实施“学前残疾儿童助学项目”，对全区3000名学前儿童给予补贴。加强内蒙古特殊职业技术学校建设，印发《内蒙古特殊职业技术学校“十四五”发展规划》。落实《第二期国家手语和盲文规范化行动计划（2021-2025年）》。

全区共有特殊教育普通高中（部、班）4个，在校生492人，其中聋生112人，其他380人。残疾人中等职业学校（班）4个，在校生235人，毕业生39人，毕业生中1人获得职业资格证书。

三、就业

印发《内蒙古自治区促进残疾人就业三年行动实施方案（2022-2024年）》《内蒙古自治区促进残疾人职业技能提升实施方案》，组织城乡残疾人职业技能和实用技术培训1.1万人。启动“大爱北疆助业自强”助残公益行动。出台《内蒙古自治区残疾人就业创业示范（孵化）基地管理办法》。全年城乡残疾人新增就业9741人。

截至2022年底，全区城乡持证残疾人就业人数为19.15万人，其中按比例就业1.1万人，集中就业4683人，个体就业1.7万人，公益性岗位就业1886人，辅助性就业1054人，灵活就业（含社区、居家就业）54771人，从事农业种养殖10.1万人。

开展农村困难残疾人实用技术培训，为9033人次残疾人赋能。105个残疾人就业帮扶基地共安置660名残疾人就业，带动648户残疾人家庭增收。

全区共培训盲人保健按摩人员45人次、盲人医疗按摩人员470人次。现有保健按摩机构410个，医疗按摩机构146个。5人获得盲人医疗按摩人员初级职务任职资格，1人获得中级职务任职资格。

四、社会保障

截至2022年底，全区参加城乡居民基本养老保险的残疾人数达53.71万名，26.04万名残疾人领取养老金。在60岁以下参保的残疾人中，12.51万名重度残疾人和5.4万名非重度残疾人得到参保缴费资助。

开展残疾人托养服务的各级各类机构达145个，其中寄宿制服务机构58个，日间照料机构4个，综合性服务机构35个。972名残疾人通过寄宿制和日间照料服务机构接受了托养服务，4417 名残疾人接受居家服务。

审定“两项补贴”申请人数 62.6 万人次，为全区 41.3 万 0-59 周岁残疾人购买意外伤害保险。

五、宣传文化

截至 2022 年底，自治区本级开设电视手语栏目 2 个，盟市开设残疾人专题广播节目 3 个、电视手语栏目 6 个。

全区各级公共图书馆设立盲文及盲文有声读物阅览室 58 个，开展残疾人文化周活动 214 场次。为 2843 名盲人发放文化无障碍产品。扶持建设 16 个基层残疾人文体示范点和 7 个残疾人文创基地。开展残疾人文艺公益巡演 2 场。

六、体育

全区举办运动会或单项选拔赛 47 场次，开展残疾人群众体育健身活动 229 次。选派运动员赴韩国参加残疾人举重亚洲大洋洲锦标赛，夺得 4 枚金牌。

七、维权

制定修改保障残疾人权益的规范性文件盟市级 2 个、旗县（市、区）4 个。旗县（市、区）以上人大开展《中华人民共和国残疾人保障法》执法检查和专题调研 8 次，政协开展视察和专题调研 2 次。开展自治区级普法宣传教育活动 6 次，1700 人次参加。举办自治区级法律培训班 2 个，89 人次参加。各级残联办理建议、提案 29 件。

截至 2022 年底，全区共出台了 21 个无障碍环境建设与管理法规、政府令和规范性文件；开展无障碍环境建设检查 71 次，无障碍培训 133 人次。

共接待来访残疾人 57 人次，处理中国残联网上信访件 25 件，自治区信访局网上信访件 3 件，共接听 12385 残疾人服务热线来电 1096 通，办理 12345 政务服务热线平台诉求 34 件。

八、组织建设

截至 2022 年底，全区（不含自治区本级）共有残联 1190 个，其中：盟市级残联 12 个，旗县（市、区）残联 103 个，乡镇（街道）残联 1075 个；社区（村）已建残协 13722 个。

全区各级残联工作人员 3044 人，乡镇（街道）残联、村（社区）残协专职委员总计 14085 人。已有 10 个盟市残联配备了残疾人领导干部，52 个旗县（市、区）残联配备了残疾人干部。残疾人专门协会 567 个，助残社会组织 37 个。

九、服务设施

截至 2022 年底，全区已竣工各级残疾人综合服务设施 57 个，总建设规模 11.43 万平方米，总投资 3.69 亿元；已竣工的各级残疾人康复设施 41 个，总建设规模 20.49 万平方米，总投资 6.65 亿元；已竣工的各级残疾人托养服务设施 38 个，总建设规模 9.38 万平方米，总投资 3.22 亿元。

2022 年辽宁省残疾人事业发展统计公报

2022 年，辽宁省残联以迎接党的二十大和学习宣传贯彻党的二十大精神为主线，深刻领悟“两个确立”的决定性意义，增强“四个意识”、坚定“四个自信”、做到“两个维护”，深入学习贯彻习近平总书记关于东北、辽宁振兴发展的重要讲话和指示批示精神，主动服务和融入全省振兴发展大局，按照省委、省政府工作要求，全力保民生、抓服务，强机制、促效能，深入开展“两个找到”“2+4”“五个一”专项行动，扎实推进“兜底线、抓两头、促两业”重点任务，残联改革和建设迈出新步伐，全省残疾人工作呈现稳中有进、稳中提质、稳中向好新局面，残疾人事业步入全面高质量发展新阶段。

一、康复

2022 年，192284 名残疾人得到基本康复服务，40755 名残疾人得到基本辅助器具适配服务。得到康复服务的持证残疾人中，有视力残疾人 17398 名、听力残疾人 11809 名、言语残疾人 796 名、肢体残疾人 97062 名、智力残疾人 14135 名、精神残疾人 33059 名、多重残疾人 12579 名。

截至 2022 年底，有残疾人康复机构 462 个。康复机构在岗人员达 9943 人，其中，管理人员 1151 人，业务人员 7160 人，其他人员 1632 人。

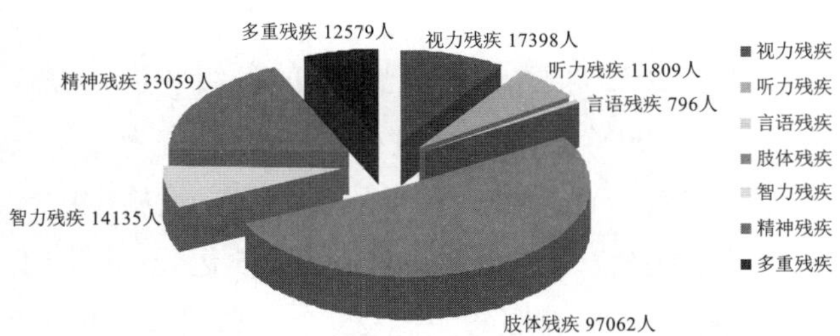

图 1　2022 年持证残疾人接受康复服务情况（单位：人）

二、教育

2022 年，全省共有特殊教育普通高中（部、班）5 个，在校生 291 人，其中聋生 117 人，盲生 4 人，其他 170 人。残疾人中等职业学校（班）15 个，在校生 1002 人，毕业生 222 人。全省有 241 名残疾人被普通高等院校录取，49 名残疾人进入高等特殊教育学院学习。

三、就业

2022 年全省城乡持证残疾人就业人数为 241716 人，其中按比例就业 34273 人，集中就业 11330 人，个体就业 18271 人，公益性岗位就业 5973 人，辅助性就业 5208 人，灵活就业（含社区、居家就业）41484 人，从事农业种养加 125177 人。

培训盲人保健按摩人员 93 人次、盲人医疗按摩人员 124 人次；现有保健按摩机构 655 个、医疗按摩机构 30 个；1 人获得盲人医疗按摩人员初级职务任职资格，1 人获得中级职务任职资格。

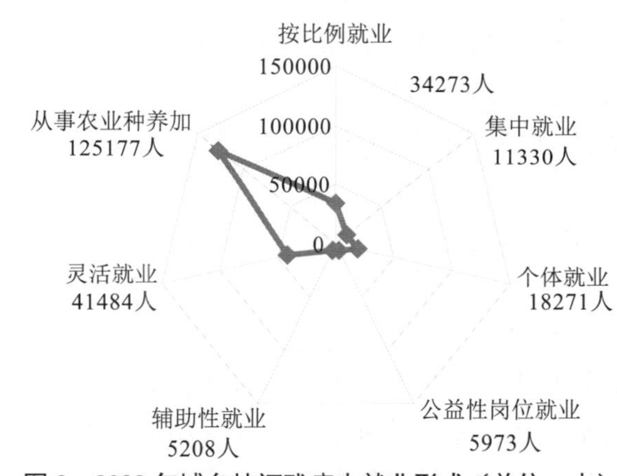

图 2　2022 年城乡持证残疾人就业形式（单位：人）

四、社会保障

截至 2022 年底，残疾居民参加城乡社会养老保险人数达到 518793 名，232091 名残疾人领取养老金。130880 名 60 岁以下参保重度残疾人中，127874 名享受了参保个人缴费资助政策，占比 97.7%。同时，37188 名非重度残疾人参保也得到了个人缴费资助。

全省共有残疾人托养服务机构 155 个，其中寄宿制托养服务机构 67 个，日间照料机构 25 个，综合性托养服务机构 27 个。3763 名残疾人通过寄宿制和日间照料服务机构接受了托养服务。15423 名残疾人接受居家服务。

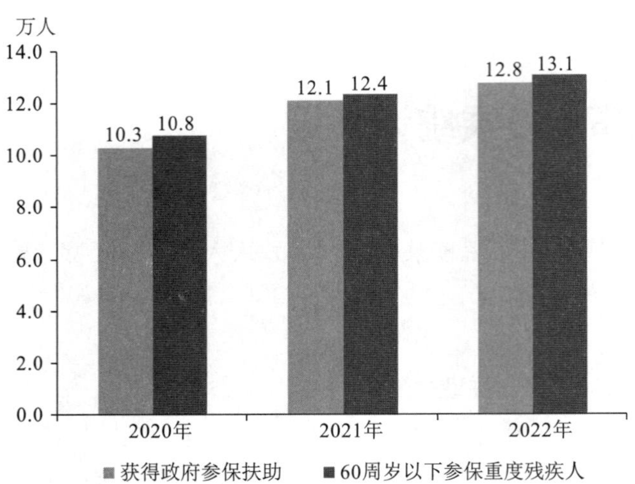

图 3　2020-2022 年 60 周岁以下参保重度残疾人获得政府参保扶助情况（单位：万人）

五、宣传文化

截至 2022 年底，全省共有省级残疾人专题广播节目 1 个、电视手语栏目 1 个；市级残疾人专题广播节目 6 个、电视手语栏目 11 个。

截至 2022 年底，省市县三级公共图书馆共设立盲文及盲文有声读物阅览室 57 个，共开展残疾人文化周活动 178 场次；省地两级残联艺术团 15 个。

六、体育

2022 年，在做好疫情防控的前提下，全省积极推进残疾人竞技体育、群众体育和特奥体育均衡协同发展，承接中国残联残奥、冬残奥训练项目，夯实残奥、群体、特奥发展基础，充分发挥残运会大型体育融入全民健身，促进特奥体育融合活动。

在北京 2022 年冬残奥会上，辽宁籍残疾人运动员发挥稳定，在冬残奥会参赛历史上取得金牌、奖牌零的突破，共获得 2 枚金牌、3 枚银牌、5 枚铜牌共 10 枚奖牌。辽宁省残联通过承接国家高山滑雪、单板滑雪、越野滑雪、冬季两项、冰球等服务保障任务，锻炼了队伍，提高了全省残疾人体育冬季项目的竞技水平。通过本届冬残奥会，残疾人事业得到社会的广泛关注，残疾人冰雪运动普及率也显著提升，极大地提高了残疾人群体的幸福感和满意度。

七、维权

2022 年，制定或修改县级保障残疾人权益的规范性文件 1 个；县级以上人大开展《中华人民共和国残疾人保障法》执法检查和专题调研 1 次。开展省级普法宣传教育活动 7 次，900 人参加；举办省级法律培训班 2 个，300 人参加。

残疾人参政议政工作稳步开展，各地办理议案、建议、提案 40 件。

无障碍建设法规、标准进一步完善。共出台 6 个省、市级无障碍环境建设与管理法规、政府令和规范性文件；8 个市、县系统开展无障碍环境建设；全省开展无障碍环境建设检查 103 次，无障碍培训 1975 人次。

八、组织建设

2022 年，全省市县乡共有残联 1483 个，其中各市残联 14 个，县（市、区）残联 105 个，乡镇（街道）残联 1364 个；社区（村）残协 15961 个。

省市县乡残联工作人员 3048 人，乡镇（街道）残联、村（社区）残协专职委员总计 15746 名。11 个市级残联、41 个县级残联配备了残疾人领导干部。

全省共建立各类残疾人专门协会 600 个，其中省级专门协会 5 个，市级专门协会 70 个，县级专门协会 525 个。全省助残社会组织共有 54 个。

九、服务设施

截至 2022 年底，全省已竣工的各级残疾人综合服务设施 109 个，总建设规模 28.5 万平方米，总投资 10.4 亿元；已竣工的各级残疾人康复设施 19 个，总建设规模 9.7 万平方米，总投资 2.5 亿元；已竣工的各级残疾人托养服务设施 25 个，总建设规模 9.7 万平方米，总投资 3.9 亿元。

2022 年吉林省残疾人事业发展统计公报

2022 年，吉林省残联深入学习宣传贯彻党的二十大精神和省委第十二次党代会精神，全面贯彻习近平新时代中国特色社会主义思想和习近平总书记关于残疾人事业的重要论述和重要指示批示精神，认真落实省委、省政府和中国残联工作要求，克服疫情不利影响，较为顺利地完成了年度各项工作任务。

一、康复

为 133541 名持证残疾人和残疾儿童提供基本康复服务，其中：49891 名残疾人得到基本辅助器具适配服务、3443 名 0-6 岁残疾儿童得到康复救助，有视力残疾人 11900 名、听力残疾人 9452 名、言语残疾人 532 名、肢体残疾人 80481 名、智力残疾人 7921 名、精神残疾人 14948 名、多重残疾人 5887 名。

截至 2022 年底，为全省 1258 个村配置基本型康复器材。现有残疾人康复机构 243 个。康复机构在岗人员达 8042 人，其中，管理人员 1109 人，业务人员 5813 人，其他人员 1120 人。

二、教育

共有特殊教育普通高中（部、班）5 个，在校生 210 人，其中聋生 84 人，其他 126 人。残疾人中等职业学校（班）2 个，在校生 371 人，毕业生 71 人。

三、就业

城乡持证残疾人就业人数为 181033 人，其中按比例就业 8688 人，集中就业 4181 人，个体就业 15670 人，公益性岗位就业 2855 人，辅助性就业 1078 人，灵活就业（含社区、居家就业）45852 人，从事农业种养加 102709 人。

开展农村困难残疾人实用技术培训，为 6751 人次残疾人赋能。161 个残疾人就业帮扶基地共安置 966 名残疾人就业，带动 1818 户残疾人家庭增收。

共培训盲人保健按摩人员 158 人次、盲人医疗按摩人员 225 人次。现有保健按摩机构 351 个，医疗按摩机构 38 个。

四、社会保障

截至 2022 年底，参加城乡居民基本养老保险的残疾人数达 557315 名。225880 名残疾人领取养老金。60 岁以下参保的残疾人中，166404 名重度残疾人和 57089 名非重度残疾人得到参保缴费资助。

开展残疾人托养服务的各级各类机构达 165 个，其中寄宿制服务机构 89 个，日间照料机构 6 个，综合性服务机构 37 个。1891 名残疾人通过寄宿制和日间照料服务机构接受了托养服务，6920 名残疾人接受居家服务。

五、宣传文化

截至 2022 年底，共有省级残疾人专题广播节目 1 个、电视手语栏目 1 个，地级电视手语栏目 5 个。各级公共图书馆设立盲文及盲文有声读物阅览室 51 个，开展残疾人文化周活动 188 场次，省地两级残联艺术团 12 个。

六、体育

以推动残疾人康复、健身体育、竞技体育协调发展为重点，组织开展了内容丰富的特奥日、健身周活动，进一步扩大了群众性体育的普惠和受众面，调动了残疾人的参与热情。举办了残疾人旱地冰壶城市挑战赛、“喜迎冬残奥一起向未来”等形式多样的残疾人冰雪运动季活动，助力北京冬残奥会成功举办。为全省 2000 个村级残疾人服务场所配备文体活动器材，在 12 个社区（村）建设“新时代残疾人文体活动示范点”，进一步满足残疾人的文体活动需求。举办了全省残疾人体育健身指导员培训班，为开展基层残疾人群众性体育健身活动提供了保障。

七、维权

制定或修改保障残疾人权益的规范性文件：省级 1 个、县级 1 个。县级以上人大开展《中华人民共和国残疾人保障法》执法检查和专题调研 2 次；政协开展视察和专题调研 2 次。开展省级普法宣传教育活动 1 次，269 人次参加；举办省级法律培训班 3 个，120 人次参加。各地残联办理建议、提案 20 件。

共出台了 17 个省、地、县级无障碍环境建设与管理法规、政府令和规范性文件；开展无障碍环境建设检查 13 次，无障碍培训 468 人次。

八、组织建设

2022 年，市县乡共有残联 974 个，各地市已建残联 10 个，县（市、区）已建残联 71 个，乡镇（街道）已建残联 893 个，社区（村）已建残协 10699 个。

省市县乡残联工作人员 2713 人，地级配备了残疾人领导干部的残联 4 个，县级配备了残疾人干部的残联 25 个。

残疾人专门协会 369 个，助残社会组织 56 个。

九、服务设施

截至 2022 年底，已竣工的各级残疾人综合服务设施 47 个，总建设规模 96741.2 平方米，总投资 31853.9 万元；已竣工的各级残疾人康复设施 15 个，总建设规模 89761.7 平方米，总投资 47263.9 万元；已竣工的各级残疾人托养服务设施 11 个，总建设规模 35832.8 平方米，总投资 11217.0 万元。

十、信息化

2022 年，全国残疾人按比例就业业务申办系统落地并应用；省残联无障碍门户网站改版升级全新上线，首批通过工信部适老化网站达标测评；支撑吉林政务服务网“吉事办 app”残疾人服务“弱有所扶”和“跨省通办”服务专区建设；“信息助残”项目稳定推进，“智慧残联”服务保障残疾人事业能力持续增强。

通过与相关职能部门开展信息数据共享，有力的推动各领域各部门残疾人工作开展，利用大数据资源，有效提升了残疾人事业保障和发展能力。

省残联门户网站等新媒体累计发布信息 2226 条，快手政务号粉丝近 320 万。相关工作有力保障残联重点工作、重大政策的开展落实，为残疾人事业发展提供良好舆论氛围。

2022 年黑龙江省残疾人事业发展统计公报

2022 年，黑龙江省残联以习近平新时代中国特色社会主义思想为指导，全面贯彻党的二十大精神，认真贯彻落实习近平总书记重要指示批示精神和习近平总书记关于残疾人事业重要论述，深入实施《“十四五”残疾人保障和发展规划》，全面推进残疾人事业高质量发展。

一、康复

73081 名残疾人得到基本康复服务，31056 名残疾人得到基本辅助器具适配服务。得到康复服务的持证残疾人中，有视力残疾人 6046 名、听力残疾人 4406 名、言语残疾人 48 名、肢体残疾人 46021 名、智力残疾人 4034 名、精神残疾人 7457 名、多重残疾人 2263 名。

截至 2022 年底，有残疾人康复机构 271 个。康复机构在岗人员达 5240 人，其中，管理人员 582 人，业务人员 3701 人，其他人员 957 人。

二、教育

共有残疾人中等职业学校（班）5 个，在校生 359 人，毕业生 73 人。

三、就业

城乡持证残疾人就业人数为 21433 人，其中按比例就业 15102 人，集中就业 4040 人，个体就业 23146 人，公益性岗位就业 5402 人，辅助性就业 1227 人，灵活就业（含社区、居家就业）74355 人，从事农业种养加 91060 人。

开展农村困难残疾人实用技术培训，为 3815 人次残疾人赋能。50 个残疾人就业帮扶基地共安置 751 名残疾人就业，带动 527 户残疾人家庭增收。

共培训盲人保健按摩人员 480 人次、盲人医疗按摩人员 140 人次。现有保健按摩机构 219 个，医疗按摩机构 36 个。130 人获得盲人医疗按摩人员初级职务任职资格，25 人获得中级职务任职资格。

四、社会保障

截至 2022 年底，参加城乡居民基本养老保险的残疾人数达 477863 名。193958 名残疾人领取养老金。60 岁以下参保的残疾人中，97372 名重度残疾人和 44498 名非重度残疾人得到参保缴费资助。

开展残疾人托养服务的各级各类机构达 70 个，其中寄宿制服务机构 3 个，日间照料机构 2 个，综合性服务机构 7 个。152 名残疾人通过寄宿制和日间照料服务机构接受了托养服务，4593 名残疾人接受居家服务。

五、宣传文化

截至 2022 年底，共有省级残疾人专题广播节目 1 个、电视手语栏目 2 个，地级残疾人专题广播节目 5 个、电视手语栏目 5 个。

各级公共图书馆设立盲文及盲文有声读物阅览室 50 个，开展残疾人文化周活动 211 场次，省地两级残联艺术团 12 个。

六、体育

在举国关注、举世瞩目的北京 2022 年冬残奥会上，黑龙江残疾人运动员、教练员充分展现了自强不息的精神风貌、奋勇争先的拼搏力量、点亮梦想的生命绽放，书写了“残奥之美重在精神之美”的感人篇章。以王海涛为队长的中国轮椅冰壶队夺得本届冬残奥会我国唯一一枚冰上项目金牌；首次参赛的中国残奥冰球队运动员吕志取得了铜牌的历史性突破；15 名黑龙江籍教练员入选本届中国体育代表团，占教练员总数的 50%，其中，岳清爽在开幕式上代表全体教练员及官员宣誓，向世界展现了中国形象、龙江形象；朱德文作为国家残疾人越野滑雪和冬季两项教练，带队获得了 8 金 4 银 7 铜的好成绩。4 月 8 日，在北京冬奥会、冬残奥会总结表彰大会上，黑龙江省残联被党中央、国务院授予突出贡献集体荣誉称号。

七、维权

制定或修改保障残疾人权益的规范性文件地级2个、县级1个。县级以上人大开展《中华人民共和国残疾人保障法》执法检查和专题调研3次；政协开展视察和专题调研6次。开展省级普法宣传教育活动5次，40000人次参加。各地残联办理建议、提案21件。

共出台了1个省、地、县级无障碍环境建设与管理法规、政府令和规范性文件；开展无障碍环境建设检查9次，无障碍培训665人次。

八、组织建设

2022年，市县乡共有残联1445个，各地市已建残联13个，县（市、区）已建残联126个，乡镇（街道）已建残联1306个，社区（村）已建残协12248个。

省市县乡残联工作人员2626人，乡镇（街道）残联、村（社区）残协专职委员总计4979人。地级配备了残疾人领导干部的残联7个，县级配备了残疾人干部的残联33个。

残疾人专门协会690个，助残社会组织15个。

九、服务设施

截至2022年底，已竣工的各级残疾人综合服务设施98个，总建设规模94921.9平方米，总投资27538.8万元；已竣工的各级残疾人康复设施9个，总建设规模61545.8平方米，总投资14567.0万元；已竣工的各级残疾人托养服务设施30个，总建设规模68802.4平方米，总投资16813.3万元。

2022 年上海市残疾人事业发展统计公报

2022 年，上海市残联以习近平新时代中国特色社会主义思想为指导，以习近平总书记关于残疾人事业的重要指示批示精神为遵循，全面学习贯彻党的二十大精神和市第十二次党代会精神，围绕全市工作大局，坚持“防疫情、稳经济、保安全”，统筹推进疫情防控和残疾人事业发展，努力推动残疾人事业高质量发展、残疾人高品质生活。

一、康复

全市有 13.1 万残疾儿童及持证残疾人得到基本康复服务，其中 0-17 岁儿童 0.4 万人。得到康复服务的持证残疾人中，有视力残疾人 2 万人、听力残疾人 1.5 万人、言语残疾人 0.1 万人、肢体残疾人 7 万人、智力残疾人 1 万人、精神残疾人 1 万人、多重残疾人 0.4 万人，得到康复服务的未持证残疾人 0.2 万人。全年共为 5.4 万名残疾人提供各类辅助器具适配服务。

截至 2022 年底，全市提供残疾康复服务的机构有 956 个，其中，68 个机构提供视力残疾康复服务，30 个机构提供听力言语残疾康复服务，254 个机构提供肢体残疾康复服务，267 个机构提供智力残疾康复服务，309 个机构提供精神残疾康复服务，262 个机构提供辅助器具服务（部分机构提供多种形式的康复服务）。残疾康复在岗人员达 7569 人，其中，管理人员 1187 人，业务人员 4035 人，其他人员 2347 人。

二、教育

进一步完善特殊教育体系，加快特殊职业教育发展。全市设立了 18 个特殊职业教育办学点，其中 1 个特殊教育普通高中（班）；在校盲人学生 122 人。残疾人中职教育（班）17 个，在校生 1061 人，已毕业 169 人，其中有 19 人获得职业资格证书。共有 68 名残疾人考生被普通高校录取，另有 6 名残疾人考生被高等特殊教育机构录取。

三、就业与扶贫

2022 年，全市持证残疾人就业年龄段内（男：16 岁-59 岁，女：16 岁-54 岁）的就业人数为 6.7 万人，其中分散按比例就业 4.6 万人，集中就业 0.8 万人，务农 0.1 万人，辅助性就业、公益性岗位就业 0.6 万人，灵活就业、自主创业等 0.6 万人。共培训盲人保健按摩人员 1800 人次、盲人医疗按摩事人员 100 人次；现有保健按摩机构 310 个，医疗按摩机构 2 个。强化东西部帮扶协作，2022 年上海市区两级残联共有帮扶项目 19 个，帮扶资金 577.9 万元，惠及云南省残疾人 2570 人。

四、社会保障

截至 2022 年底，9.7 万名残疾人参加城乡居民基本养老保险，4.7 万名残疾人领取养老金。60 岁以下参保的残疾人中，4.1 万名重度残疾人和 0.2 万名非重度残疾人得到参保缴费资助。开展残疾人托养服务的各级各类机构 816 个，其中寄宿制服务机构 381 个，日间照料机构 435 个。8903 名残疾人通过寄宿制和日间照料服务机构接受托养服务，2.7 万名残疾人接受居家养护服务。持续开展精准帮扶，帮扶资金 955.29 万元，帮扶惠及 10819 名困难残疾人。

五、宣传文化

举办第三十二次“全国助残日”和第二十三次“上海助残周”活动。截至 2022 年底，共有电视手语栏目 1 个，地级残疾人专题广播节目 3 个、电视手语栏目 12 个。

继续推进公共图书馆盲人阅览室建设、无障碍电影放映和残疾人文化活动。截至 2022 年底，全市共设立 38 个盲文及盲人有声读物图书馆；制作社区无障碍电影剧本 40 部。市、区两级开展残疾人文化周活动 508 场次，全年有 12.3 万人次残疾人参加各级各类文化活动。

六、体育

全年通过线上线下深度融合模式，开展了围棋、五子棋、电竞、残疾人足球训练营等项目，通过丰富多彩的各类活动，满足了不同类别残疾人的健身需求。累计开展市级各类残疾人群众体育健身活动 3 次，举办市级残疾人体育比赛 3 次，区级各类残疾人群众体育健身活动 1873 次。全市残疾人群众体育健身活动参与人数约 6.9 万人次，参加市级赛事残疾人运动员 586 人次，聘任教练员 36 名，全市设有 4 个残疾人体育训练基地。

七、维权

全市制定或修改保障残疾人权益的规范性文件 5 个。区级人大开展《中华人民共和国残疾人保障法》执法检查和专题调研 4 次，区级政协开展视察和专题调研 2 次；开展市级普法宣传教育活动 3 次，线上线下累计 5.27 万人次参加；举办市级法律培训班 1 个，75 人参加。

全市设有残疾人法律救助工作协调机构 18 个，设有残疾人法律救助工作站 17 个。全年受理残疾人群众来信 835 件，来电 9196 次，来访 2334 人次。

截至 2022 年底，本市残联系统有人大代表 38 人，其中市级 3 人，区、街道（乡镇）代表 36 人，其中 1 人同时兼任市、区级人大代表；本市残联系统有政协委员 15 人，其中市级 2 人，区级 13 人。全市残联系统办理建议、提案 53 件。

截至 2022 年底，全市累计出台 5 个区级无障碍环境建设与管理规范性文件；全市开展无障碍环境建设检查 932 次，无障碍工作培训 665 人次。

八、组织建设

全市市、区、街道（乡镇）有残联组织 238 个，其中市级 1 个、区级 16 个、街道（乡镇）级 221 个。全市已建居（村）残疾人协会 5560 个，已建比例为 99.48%，其中：有固定办公场所 5361 个，占 96.42%；有办公经费 3989 个，占 71.74%；配备办公设备 5273 个，占 94.83%。

全市残联系统实有人员 1094 名，其中：市残联 48 名、区残联 139 名、街道（乡镇）907 名。市、区残联领导班子已配备 24 名兼职副理事长，其中：市残联 2 名、区残联 22 名。街道（乡镇）残联领导班子已配备 221 名理事长，486 名理事。居（村）残疾人工作专职委员 5935 名。

全市共建立市级及以下各类残疾人专门协会 85 个，其中：市级 5 个、区级 80 个，有办公场所 85 个，占 100%。全市有助残社会组织 170 个。

九、服务设施建设

截至 2022 年底，本市累计投入使用的各级残疾人综合服务设施 16 个，总建设规模为 2.3 万平方米，总投资额 1.2 亿元。累计已投入使用的各级残疾人托养设施 12 个，总建设规模为 7260 平方米，总投资额为 1593 万元。累计已投入使用的各级残疾人康复设施 5 个，总建设规模为 10.05 万平方米，总投资额 4.5 亿元。

十、其他

截至 2022 年底，全市残疾人人口基础数据库持证残疾人 60.3 万人，比上年减少 0.2 万人。

2022 年，实现“上海市残疾人交通补贴申请”事项免申即享，符合业务办理条件的残疾人无需申请即可享受本市残疾人交通补贴。

实现多个市残联“一网通办”业务事项信息通过市办件库标准化流转。

2022 年江苏省残疾人事业发展统计公报

2022 年，全省残联系统以习近平新时代中国特色社会主义思想为指导，深入学习贯彻党的二十大和习近平总书记关于残疾人事业重要论述、重要指示批示精神，深入实施《江苏省“十四五”残疾人事业发展规划》，认真落实省委、省政府决策部署，推动残疾人工作高质量发展走在前列，促进残疾人事业全面发展，圆满完成各项目标任务。

一、康复

依据省“十四五”残疾人康复服务实施方案，细化落实各项康复工作，推进残疾人康复事业高质量发展。积极组织实施省政府民生实事项目“实现全省孤独症儿童基本康复服务全覆盖”。印发《江苏省残疾预防行动计划（2021-2025 年）》，开展全生命周期残疾预防活动。印发《江苏省残联系统康复机构业务规范建设评估实施方案》，规范残疾儿童康复救助服务，完善康复机构定点流程措施。出台《关于进一步做好江苏省听力残疾儿童人工耳蜗康复救助项目工作的通知》，优化听障儿童人工耳蜗救助政策。

2022 年，全省共计 23.3 万持证残疾人及残疾儿童得到基本康复服务，其中 0-6 岁残疾儿童 2.8 万人，7-17 岁残疾儿童 0.8 万人；得到康复服务的持证残疾人中，视力残疾人 1.6 万名、听力残疾人 0.8 万名、言语残疾人 0.02 万名、肢体残疾人 9.02 万名、智力残疾人 1.8 万名、精神残疾人 6.9 万名、多重残疾人 0.9 万名；全年共为 5.9 万名残疾人提供各类辅助器具适配服务；全年共为 40 名听障儿童实施人工耳蜗手术和康复训练。

截至 2022 年底，全省共有残疾人康复机构 530 个，其中，残联系统康复机构 96 个；康复机构在岗人员达 1.53 万人，其中，管理人员 0.18 万人，业务人员 1.09 万人，其他人员 0.26 万人；全年完成康复管理人员培训 0.5 万人次，康复专业技术人员培训 2.5 万人次。

二、教育

联合省教育厅等部门出台《江苏省“十四五”特殊教育发展提升行动计划》，继续推进学前融合教育试点。印发《关于进一步健全精准资助部门协调工作机制的通知》，进一步提升困难学生资助精准水平的广度和深度。

2022 年，全省共有特殊教育普通高中 4 个，在校生 573 人，其中聋生 454 人，盲生 27 人，其他 92 人；残疾人中等职业学校（班）11 个，在校生 1368 人，毕业生 399 人，毕业生中 79 人获得职业资格证书；全省有 799 名残疾人被普通高等院校录取，137 名残疾人通过单考单招途径进入省内外高等特殊教育学院学习。

三、就业

贯彻落实国务院办公厅《促进残疾人就业三年行动方案（2022-2024 年）》，以省政府办公厅名义印发《江苏省促进残疾人就业三年行动方案（2022-2024 年）》，联合省委组织部等七部门转发《机关、事业单位、国有企业带头安排残疾人就业办法》，发挥机关事业单位、国有企业按比例安排残疾人就业示范作用。联合省乡村振兴局制定印发《关于落实巩固拓展残疾人脱贫攻坚成果有关工作的通知》，将残疾人相关工作纳入强村富民帮促行动统筹推进。强化残疾人职业技能培训，通过按比例就业、集中就业、辅助性就业、灵活就业、自主创业等多种形式，持续扩大就业创业规模。将残疾人就业产品纳入乡村振兴消费帮促范畴，促进残疾人就业增收。

2022 年，全省城乡持证残疾人就业人数为 37.3 万人，其中按比例就业 9.1 万人，集中就业 4.2 万人，个体就业 2.6 万人，公益性岗位就业 3.9 万人，辅助性就业 1.8 万人，灵活就业（含社区、居家就业）7.0 万人，从事农业种养加 8.7 万人；与 2021 年比净增残疾人就业 40173 人。开展农村困难残疾人实用技术培训，为 8283 名残疾人赋能；108 个残疾人就业帮扶基地共安置 1210 名残疾人就业，带动 1266 户残疾人家庭增收。全省共有保健按摩机构 1048 个，盲人医疗按摩机构 70 个。

四、社会保障

紧紧围绕“完善残疾人社会保障制度和关爱服务体系，促进残疾人事业全面发展”总要求，扎实开展各项工作。完成省政府“新增 16-59 周岁无业智力、精神和重度肢体残疾人托养 1.3 万名”民生实事项目，全年新增残疾人托养 16132 人。开展“残疾人之家”规范化建设，联合人社部门在全省“残疾人之家”开发公益性岗位。出台《江苏省“残疾人之家”提升三年行动方案》，提高“残疾人之家”建设运营水平。

截至 2022 年底，126.2 万名残疾人参加城乡居民基本养老保险；57.7 万名残疾人领取养老金；60 岁以下参保的 31.3 万名重度残疾人中，31.0 万人享受参保个人缴费资助政策，占比 99%，20.2 万名非重度残疾人享受参保个人缴费资助政策。

2022 年，全省共计 6.5 万名残疾人接受托养服务，其中接受寄宿制托养服务 0.5 万人，接受日间照料托养服务 2.5 万人，接受居家服务 3.5 万人。

五、宣传文化

通过微信公众号、视频号、抖音和喜马拉雅号开展常态化新媒体宣传。持续发挥交汇点《同追求 共奋斗—残疾人立体声》专题和中国江苏网《残疾人之窗》专栏的阵地作用。推进“书香残疾人之家”项目实施，推选 100 个“书香残疾人之家”。

截至 2022 年底，共有省级残疾人专题广播节目 1 个、电视手语栏目 1 个，地级残疾人专题广播节目 12 个、电视手语栏目 16 个。各级公共图书馆设立盲文及盲文有声读物阅览室 85 个，开展残疾人文化周活动 1143 场次，省地两级残联艺术团 9 个。

六、体育

全省开展残疾人群众体育健身活动 1130 次，参加人员 69897 人次。

举办省第十一届残疾人运动会，首次实现省残运会与省运会在同城同期举办，首次实现省残运会和省特奥会同时举办。

创新项目设置，首次在省残运会竞技比赛中设置青年组，首次将掼蛋、魔方、盲人板铃球群众性体育纳入省残运会比赛项目。13 个设区市共 1005 名运动员在竞体、群体、特奥 18 个项目上决出 528 枚金牌、247 枚银牌、154 枚铜牌。

七、维权

推进党建与法治工作融合，促进科学民主决策和依法行政，落实国家和省法治政府建设各项任务。修订《江苏省按比例安排残疾人就业办法》。印发《贯彻落实<江苏省无障碍环境建设实施办法>加快推进无障碍环境建设的通知》《江苏省无障碍环境建设“十四五”实施方案》《江苏省残疾人家庭无障碍改造服务管理暂行办法》。制定实施《全省残疾人信访突出问题攻坚化解行动实施方案》。

2022 年，制定或修改关于残疾人的专门法规和规章：地级 1 个；制定或修改保障残疾人权益的规范性文件：省级 1 个、地级 4 个、县级 2 个；县级以上人大开展《中华人民共和国残疾人保障法》执法检查和专题调研 35 次；政协开展视察和专题调研 22 次；开展省级普法宣传教育活动 6 次，2600 人次参加；举办省级法律培训班 1 个，80 人次参加；各地残联办理建议、提案 122 件。

2022 年 3 月 1 日《江苏省无障碍环境建设实施办法》施行，各地开展无障碍环境建设检查 336 次，无障碍培训 4112 人次，完成残疾人家庭无障碍改造 7541 户。按国家标准，为 1.1 万残疾人发放残疾人机动轮椅车燃油补贴。

八、组织建设

开展市县乡三级残联换届工作，加强各级残联主席团、执行理事会、各专门协会领导班子建设。积极推动残疾人证管理动态更新工作。打造“茉莉芬芳”社会助残服务品牌，深化志愿助残服务活动。

2022 年，市县乡共有残联 1381 个，其中，地级市、县（市、区）、乡镇（街道）全部成立残联；乡镇（街道）残联共 1263 个；村（社区）全部建立残协，共计 20290 个。

截至 2022 年底，省市县乡残联实有工作人员

4711人，乡镇（街道）残联、村（社区）残协专职委员总计18756人。地市级残联配备20名残疾人干部，县级残联配备61名残疾人干部。

截至2022年底，全省共建立各类残疾人专门协会556个，其中省级5个、市级65个、县级486个；全省共有助残社会组织543个。

九、服务设施

全省残联系统持续开展残疾人服务设施建设工作。

截至2022年底，已建成各级残疾人综合服务设施77个，总建设规模47.0万平方米，总投资199477.2万元；已建成各级残疾人康复设施68个，总建设规模28.0万平方米，总投资125505.3万元；已建成各级残疾人托养服务设施109个，总建设规模33.3万平方米，总投资98915.4万元。

十、信息化建设

完成“智慧残联”上线工作，推进全省“互联网+助残服务”平台和全省残联一体化工作平台试运行。

截至2022年底，全省残联系统独立建立网站25个，其中省级1个、地级7个、县级17个；搭载上级残联、同级政府网站35个，其中地级6个、县级29个。

2022 年浙江省残疾人事业发展统计公报

2022 年，全省残疾人工作在省委省政府坚强领导和中国残联精心指导下，以习近平新时代中国特色社会主义思想为指导，紧紧围绕“两个先行”目标，扎实推进残疾人事业高质量发展，促进残疾人共同富裕。

一、康复

推动残疾预防和残疾人康复工作高质量发展。印发《浙江省贯彻〈国家残疾预防行动计划（2021—2025 年）〉实施方案》，推进“全国残疾预防重点联系地区”建设。加强和改进残疾儿童康复救助服务工作，有 1.2 万残疾儿童得到康复救助。以农村低收入残疾人为重点，持续开展残疾人精准康复服务行动，有 67.1 万残疾人得到基本康复服务，4.4 万残疾人得到基本辅助器具适配服务。得到康复服务的持证残疾人中，视力残疾人 6 万、听力残疾人 8.9 万、言语残疾人 0.9 万、肢体残疾人 22.5 万、智力残疾人 9.3 万、精神残疾人 14.9 万、多重残疾人 4.1 万。

2022 年，全省提升建设规范化残疾儿童康复机构 71 家。截至年底，全省共有残疾人康复机构 314 个。康复机构在岗人员 12646 人，其中，管理人员 1219 人、业务人员 9551 人、其他人员 1876 人。

二、教育

2022 年，全省各级残联共资助残疾学生和残疾人家庭子女 2.9 万人。全省共有特殊教育普通高中（部、班）6 个，在校生 709 人，其中，聋生 227 人、盲生 305 人、其他 177 人。残疾人中等职业学校（班）30 个，在校生 1977 人，毕业生 542 人，毕业生中 145 人获得职业资格证书。全省有 291 名残疾人被普通高等院校录取，浙江特殊教育职业学院录取残疾考生 454 名。

三、就业

2022 年，全省新增残疾人就业 2.3 万人，组织残疾人职业技能培训 2.6 万人次。截至年底，全省持证残疾人就业人数 32.9 万人，其中，按比例就业 9.4 万人、集中就业 3.4 万人、个体就业 3.3 万人、公益性岗位就业 0.5 万人、辅助性就业 1.8 万人、灵活就业（含社区、居家就业）9.8 万人、从事农业种养殖 4.7 万人。

开展农村困难残疾人实用技术培训，为 3559 人次残疾人赋能。全省 220 个残疾人就业帮扶基地共安置 938 名残疾人就业，带动 2366 户残疾人家庭增收。

全省共培训盲人保健按摩人员 518 人次、盲人医疗按摩人员 165 人次。全省共有保健按摩机构 1105 个、医疗按摩机构 83 个。获得盲人医疗按摩初级专业技术职务任职资格 69 人、中级专业技术职务任职资格 3 人。

四、社会保障

2022 年，全省享受困难残疾人生活补贴 29.4 万人、重度残疾人护理补贴 67.1 万人，累计发放资金 28.9 亿元。全省纳入低保残疾人 24.74 万人，占低保总数 44.12%。截至年底，残疾人参加城乡居民基本养老保险人数 81.7 万名。60 周岁以下参保的残疾人中，14.3 万名重度残疾人和 20.8 万名非重度残疾人得到参保缴费资助，44.7 万名残疾人领取养老金。

残疾人托养服务工作稳步推进，全省开展残疾人托养服务的各级各类机构共有 1494 个，其中，寄宿制服务机构 215 个、日间照料机构 1127 个、综合性服务机构 152 个。3 万名残疾人通过寄宿制和日间照料服务机构接受托养服务。

五、宣传文化

2022 年，在全国助残日、全国残疾预防日、国际残疾人日等重要节点，协调中央、省级媒体积极报道我省残疾人事业。扎实开展就业宣传年活动，分别在浙江日报和省残联微信公众号推出系列报道。推动实现省、市两会开幕会直播加配手语翻译全覆盖，首次在省党代会开幕会直播加配手语翻译。在浙江日报发布残疾人就业企业百强榜和五星级残疾人之家光荣榜。拍摄制作《一个人的升旗仪式》，点击量超10万。组织开展浙江省第二届“最美浙江人•最美残疾人工作者”评选发布宣传活动。举办残疾人就业工作媒体通气会。推出“二十大精神学思汇”“心相约•梦闪耀”等专栏，微信传播指数位居全国各省（区、市）前列。省残疾人艺术团49名演职人员精彩亮相冬残奥会开闭幕式。扎实开展“喜迎杭州亚残运会•浙江省千场残疾人文体活动进社区”活动，各地组织开展文体活动2797场，9.8万人次参与。

全省共有省级残疾人专题广播节目1个、电视手语栏目3个，市级残疾人专题广播节目12个、电视手语栏目12个。省市县三级公共图书馆共设立盲文及盲文有声读物阅览室88个，开展残疾人文化周活动824场次。省市两级残联共有残疾人艺术团17个。

六、体育

残疾人竞技体育进一步提升。在北京冬残奥会上，取得2枚铜牌，实现奖牌“零”的突破。以浙江籍运动员为主力的中国盲人门球男队在2022年葡萄牙盲人门球世锦赛获得亚军，顺利取得巴黎残奥会入场券。我省运动员谭玉娇在残奥举重亚锦赛上夺得4枚金牌。扎实组织开展省第十一届残运会15个提前项目比赛，各地积极承办赛事。

残疾人体育基础进一步夯实。继续开展“冰雪季”、健身周、“特奥日”等全国品牌活动，扎实组织开展康复体育“三进”家庭工作。继续推广残疾人旱地冰壶比赛，带动各类残疾人康复健身。举办全国“第12届残疾人健身周”浙江主场活动，开展“线上迎亚残运”轮椅舞蹈、盲人跳绳比赛，线上浏览量达128万次，网络投票达22万。积极推进残疾人体育后备人才队伍建设，对全省11957名8－25岁残疾人进行筛选，确定112人参加冬季集训。

七、维权

制定或修改关于残疾人的专门法规、规章：市级2个；制定或修改保障残疾人权益的规范性文件：省级8个、市级7个、县级15个。全省已出台67个无障碍环境建设与管理法规、政府令和规范性文件。县级以上人大开展《中华人民共和国残疾人保障法》执法检查和专题调研52次，县级以上政协开展视察和专题调研49次。各地残联办理建议、提案246件。

省级开展普法宣传教育活动4次，1.8万人次参加。省级举办法律培训班3个，4200人次参加。全省成立残疾人法律救助工作协调机构102个，建立残疾人法律救助工作站102个。

大力推进无障碍环境建设，全省开展无障碍环境建设检查746次，无障碍培训9984人次。创建省级无障碍社区108个，完成重要公共服务场所无障碍改造1056个，实施残疾人家庭无障碍改造7994户，发放残疾人机动轮椅车燃油补贴13589人。

八、组织建设

全省市县乡共有残联1465个，其中，设区市残联11个、县（市、区）残联93个、乡镇（街道）残联1361个。村（社区）已建残协24731个。

省市县乡残联共有工作人员5405人，乡镇（街道）、村（社区）残协专职委员总计24308人。9个设区市残联配备残疾人领导干部，64个县级残联配备残疾人干部。

全省共建立六大专门协会597个，其中，省级6个、设区市66个、县级525个。全省共有助残社会组织373个。

九、服务设施

截至2022年底，全省已竣工的各级残疾人综合服务设施87个，总建设规模64.8万平方米，总投资32亿元；已竣工的各级残疾人康复设施46个，总建设规模35.5万平方米，总投资15.5亿元；已竣工的各级残疾人托养服务设施57个，总建设规模39.6万平方米，总投资16.4亿元。

2022 年安徽省残疾人事业发展统计公报

2022 年，全省各级残联坚持以习近平新时代中国特色社会主义思想为指导，深入学习宣传贯彻党的二十大精神，认真贯彻落实习近平总书记关于残疾人工作的重要指示批示精神，深入实施《安徽省“十四五”残疾人保障和发展规划》，全力推进全省残疾人事业高质量发展。

一、康复

贯彻落实《安徽省“十四五”残疾人保障和发展规划》《安徽省残疾预防行动计划(2022-2025 年)》和《安徽省“十四五”残疾人康复服务实施方案》，推动“十四五”残疾预防和残疾人康复工作高质量发展。深入实施残疾儿童康复救助制度，加强和改进残疾儿童康复救助服务，提升残疾儿童家庭获得感，35535 名残疾儿童得到康复救助。持续开展精准康复服务行动，361032 名残疾人得到基本康复服务，50649 名残疾人得到基本辅助器具适配服务。得到康复服务的持证残疾人中，有视力残疾人 19785 人、听力残疾人 15471 人、言语残疾人 1416 人、肢体残疾人 102734 人、智力残疾人 21297 人、精神残疾人 164686 人、多重残疾人 25382 人。

加强康复机构规范化和康复人才队伍建设，截至 2022 年底，全省有残疾人康复机构 309 个，康复机构在岗人员达 10877 人，其中，管理人员 916 人，业务人员 8651 人，其他人员 1310 人。完成培训康复管理人员 1999 人次，培训康复业务人员 13389 人次。

二、教育

落实《安徽省“十四五”特殊教育发展提升行动计划》，做好适龄残疾儿童少年入学安置工作，实施彩票公益助学项目，与省教育厅等联合印发《安徽省中等职业教育残疾学生资助暂行办法》，实施辅助器具进校园工程，为残疾人教育创造更好的条件和环境。

全省共有特殊教育普通高中（部、班）2 个，在校生 503 人，其中聋生 350 人、盲生 152 人、其他 1 人。残疾人中等职业学校（班）7 个，在校生 1049 人，毕业生 304 人，毕业生中 288 人获得职业资格证书。高等教育阶段，招收 674 名残疾学生，其中专科（高职）330 人，本科 305 人，研究生 39 人。

三、就业

大力促进残疾人就业创业，出台《安徽省促进残疾人就业三年行动实施方案（2022-2024 年）》，开展残疾人就业宣传年系列活动。

2022 年，全省城镇新增残疾人就业 0.6 万人，农村新增残疾人就业 2.2 万人；培训残疾人 2.12 万人次。

全省城乡持证残疾人就业人数为 51.3 万人，其中按比例就业 1.3 万人，集中就业 0.7 万人，个体就业 4.3 万人，公益性岗位就业 0.3 万人，辅助性就业 0.5 万人，灵活就业 16.2 万人，从事农业种养加 28.0 万人。

开展农村困难残疾人实用技术培训，为 1.3 万人次残疾人赋能。全省 110 个残疾人就业帮扶基地共安置 1470 名残疾人就业，带动 956 户残疾人家庭增收。

全省共培训盲人保健按摩人员 247 人次、盲人医疗按摩人员 202 人次。现有保健按摩机构 277 个，医疗按摩机构 95 个。390 人获得育人医疗按摩人员初级职务任职资格，67 人获得中级职务任职资格。

四、社会保障

截至 2022 年底，参加城乡居民基本养老保险的残疾人数达 162.5 万。65.7 万残疾人领取养老金。60 岁以下参保的残疾人中，47.4 万重度残疾人和 7 万非重度残疾人得到参保缴费资助。

残疾人托养服务工作稳步推进，开展残疾人托养服务的各级各类机构达 332 个，其中寄宿制服务机构 153 个，日间照料机构 33 个，综合性服务机构 86 个。0.4 万残疾人通过寄宿制和日间照料服务机构接受托养服务，1.9 万残疾人接受居家服务。

五、宣传文化

积极开展第三十二次“全国助残日”活动，会同省文明办等 12 部门联合印发《安徽省新时代扶残助残文明实践活动行动方案》，会同省文旅厅联合开展年度“残疾人文化周”活动。实施困难残疾人家庭“五个一”文化助残项目。会同省委宣传部等共同举办以“贯彻二十大奋进新征程”为主题的安徽省第八届残疾人读书达人演讲大赛，共有 20 多万人次参与网上互动，进一步扩大了残疾人文化品牌的影响力，丰富了残疾人精神文化生活。

全省共有省级残疾人专题广播节目 1 个、电视手语栏目 1 个，地级残疾人专题广播节目 16 个、电视手语栏目 15 个。全省各级公共图书馆设立盲文及盲文有声读物阅览室 62 个，开展残疾人文化周活动 301 场次，省市两级残联艺术团 9 个。

六、体育

在滁州市成功举办安徽省第八届残疾人运动会。全省 16 个市 500 余名残疾人运动员参加比赛，共产生 240 枚金牌、159 枚银牌、104 枚铜牌，16 个代表团获得“体育道德风尚奖”，实现了“安全、简约、精彩、有序”目标。

七、维权

制定或修改保障残疾人权益的规范性文件：地级 4 个、县级 7 个。全省县级以上人大开展《中华人民共和国残疾人保障法》执法检查和专题调研 4 次；政协开展视察和专题调研 5 次。全省开展省级普法宣传教育活动 1 次，60 人次参加；举办省级法律培训班 1 个，50 人次参加。各地残联办理建议、提案 73 件。

全省共出台了 10 个省、地、县级无限碍环境建设与管理法规、政府令和规范性文件；全省开展无障碍环境建设检查 115 次，无障碍培训 261 人次。截至 2022 年底，共为 21717 困难重度残疾人家庭实施无障碍改造，为 7840 残疾人发放残疾人机动轮椅车燃油补贴。

八、组织建设

全省共有市县乡残联组织 1672 个，其中市级残联 16 个，县（市、区）残联 117 个，乡镇（街道）残联 1539 个。现有社区（村）残协 17506 个。

省市县乡残联工作人员 3674 人，乡镇（街道）残联、村（社区）残协专职委员总计 15810 人。残疾人专门协会 590 个，助残社会组织 46 个。

九、服务设施

截至 2022 年底，全省已竣工的各级残疾人综合服务设施 86 个，总建设规模 23.2 万平方米，总投资 5.6 亿元；已竣工各级残疾人康复设施 29 个，总建设规模 19.8 万平方米，总投资 6.6 亿元；已竣工的各级残疾人托养服务设施 18 个，总建设规模 6.6 万平方米，总投资 1.8 亿元。

2022年福建省残疾人事业发展统计公报

2022年，福建省残联以习近平新时代中国特色社会主义思想为指导，认真学习贯彻党的二十大精神及习近平总书记关于残疾人事业的重要论述，深入实施《福建省“十四五”残疾人保障和发展规划》，全面推进残疾人事业高质量发展。

一、康复

2022年，全省32.3万名残疾人得到基本康复服务，3.8万名残疾人得到基本辅助器具适配服务。得到康复服务的持证残疾人中，分别有：视力障碍残疾人1.9万名、听力障碍残疾人4.0万名、言语障碍残疾人1455名、肢体障碍残疾人13.3万名、智力障碍残疾人3.9万名、精神障碍残疾人6.2万名、多重障碍残疾人1.8万名。

截至2022年底，全省共有残疾人康复机构394个。康复机构从业人员达1.2万人，其中，管理人员1449人，业务人员8434人，其他人员2399人。

二、教育

2022年，共有特殊教育普通高中（部、班）5个，在校生827人，其中，听力障碍残疾学生232人，视力障碍残疾学生58人，其他537人。残疾人中等职业学校（班）16个，在校生523人，毕业生155人，毕业生中60人获得职业资格证书。

三、就业

2022年，城乡持证残疾人就业人数为22.1万人，其中，按比例就业1.4万人，集中就业3934人，个体就业1.8万人，公益性岗位就业2409人，辅助性就业2532人，灵活就业（含社区、居家就业）7.9万人，从事农业种养加10.1万人。

开展农村困难残疾人实用技术培训，为8727人次残疾人赋能。全省38个残疾人就业帮扶基地共安置511名残疾人就业，带动414户残疾人家庭增收。

四、社会保障

截至2022年底，参加城乡居民基本养老保险的残疾人数达72.9万名。35.5万名残疾人领取养老金。60岁以下参保的残疾人中，20.5万名重度残疾人和15.7万名非重度残疾人得到参保缴费资助。

残疾人托养服务工作稳步推进，开展残疾人托养服务的各级各类机构达99个，其中，寄宿制服务机构47个，日间照料机构39个，综合性服务机构9个。1870名残疾人通过寄宿制和日间照料服务机构接受了托养服务，1.8万名残疾人接受居家服务。

五、宣传

残疾人宣传文化工作持续推进。截至2022年底，全省共有省级残疾人电视手语栏目2个，地级残疾人专题广播节目4个、电视手语栏目9个。各级公共图书馆设立盲文及盲文有声读物阅览室49个。以“心向党花开红艳艳”为主题，开展2022年全省残疾人文化周，省领导、省残工委成员单位、宁夏残疾人艺术团以及助残志愿者、演职人员等470余人参加活动，是历年来规格最高的一届。文化周开幕式文艺演出线上展播点击量达14.7万人次。

六、体育

残疾人竞技体育水平不断提高。做好杭州亚残运会筹备工作，推荐25人参加中国残联年度训练营。为助力北京冬残奥会，积极开展我省“第六届中国残疾人冰雪运动季”活动，约有380名残疾人体验冰壶、冰球、滑雪等旱地冰雪运动。残疾人群众体育活动日益活跃，全省残疾人社区文体活动参与率达43.1%，高于全国平均水平。

七、维权

各级残联维权组织建设进一步加强，残疾人事业法律法规体系更加完善，无障碍环境建设取得新突破，残疾人维权工作全面开展。

2022 年，制定或修改保障残疾人权益的规范性文件省级 2 个、县级 3 个。县级以上人大开展《中华人民共和国残疾人保障法》执法检查和专题调研 6 次；政协开展视察和专题调研 3 次。开展省级普法宣传教育活动 9 次，覆盖对象 2.0 万人。残疾人参政议政工作稳步开展，各地残联办理建议、提案 47 件。

无障碍建设法规、标准进一步完善。共出台了 24 个省、地、县级无障碍环境建设与管理法规、政府令和规范性文件；全省完成家庭无障碍改造 5849 户；开展无障碍环境建设检查 199 次，培训无障碍环境体验督导人员 3094 人次。

八、组织建设

2022 年，市县乡共有残联 1212 个，地市及平潭综合实验区已建残联 10 个，县（市、区）已建残联 89 个（含代管行政职能的开发区 7 个，泉州 1 个、福州 1 个、漳州 5 个），乡镇（街道）已建残联 1109 个，平潭综合实验区 4 个片区成立残联，社区（村）已建残协 1.7 万个。

省市县乡残联工作人员 2758 人，乡镇（街道）残联、村（社区）残协专职委员总计 1.8 万人。地级配备了残疾人领导干部的残联 10 个，县级配备了残疾人干部的残联 44 个。

残疾人专门协会 454 个，助残社会组织 82 个。

九、服务设施

截至 2022 年底，已竣工的各级残疾人综合服务设施 82 个，总建设规模 27.7 万平方米；已竣工的各级残疾人康复设施 176 个，总建设规模 8.1 万平方米；已竣工的各级残疾人托养服务设施 49 个，总建设规模 7.7 万平方米。

2022 年江西省残疾人事业发展统计公报

2022 年，全省残联在党的二十大胜利召开之年，深入贯彻落实习近平总书记关于残疾人事业的重要指示批示和视察江西重要讲话精神，紧扣全面建设“六个江西”主题，大力实施“政治引领、固本强基、制度助残、提质增效”行动，聚焦“作示范、勇争先”目标定位，以实干实绩强攻民生保障，以仁爱之心关爱之情推动全省残疾人事业高质量发展取得新成效。

一、康复

16.2 万名残疾人得到基本康复服务，5.5 万名残疾人得到基本辅助器具适配服务。得到康复服务的持证残疾人中，有视力残疾人 1.3 万名、听力残疾人 1.1 万名、言语残疾人 270 名、肢体残疾人 6.7 万名、智力残疾人 1 万名、精神残疾人 4.6 万名、多重残疾人 1 万名。

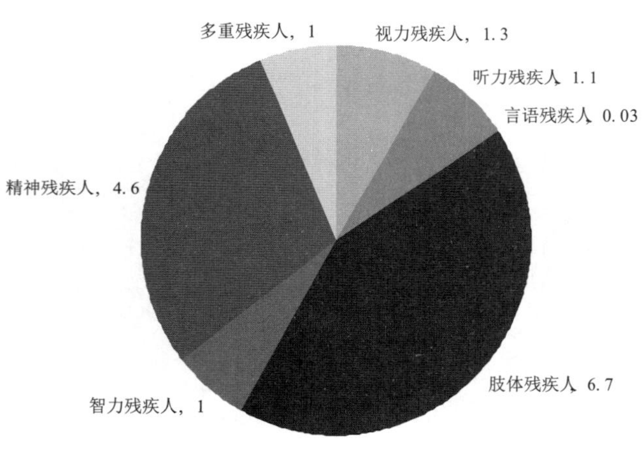

图 1　得到康复服务的持证残疾人情况（单位：万人）

截至 2022 年底，有残疾人康复机构 316 个。康复机构在岗人员达 8221 人，其中，管理人员 949 人，业务人员 5392 人，其他人员 1880 人。

二、教育

共有特殊教育普通高中（部、班）1 个，在校生 32 人，其中聋生 26 人，盲生 6 人。残疾人中等职业学校（班）8 个，在校生 888 人，毕业生 283 人，毕业生中 92 人获得职业资格证书。

三、就业

城乡持证残疾人就业人数为 39.8 万人，其中按比例就业 1.3 万人，集中就业 1.8 万人，个体就业 4 万人，公益性岗位就业 1.1 万人，辅助性就业 0.7 万人，灵活就业（含社区、居家就业）18.7 万人，从事农业种养加 12.1 万人。

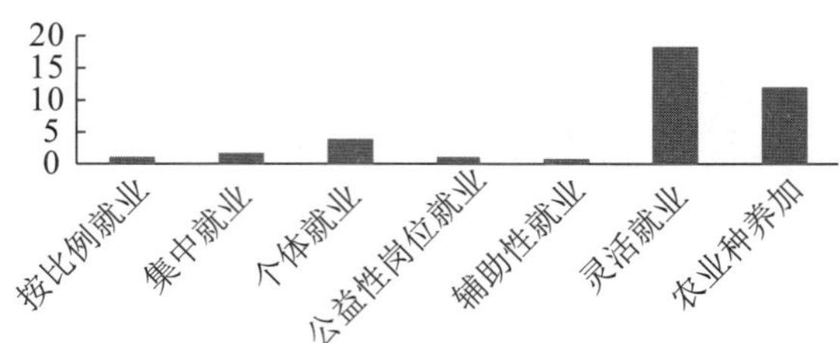

图 2　城乡持证残疾人就业情况（单位：万人）

开展农村困难残疾人实用技术培训，为 5024 人次残疾人赋能。80 个残疾人就业帮扶基地共安置 944 名残疾人就业，带动 790 户残疾人家庭增收。共培训盲人保健按摩人员 528 人次、盲人医疗按摩人员 62 人次。现有保健按摩机构 180 个，医疗按摩机构 9 个。

四、社会保障

截至 2022 年底，参加城乡居民基本养老保险的残疾人数达 98 万名。36.4 万名残疾人领取养老金。60 岁以下参保的残疾人中，25 万名重度残疾人和 16.2 万名非重度残疾人得到参保缴费资助。

开展残疾人托养服务的各级各类机构达 260 个，其中寄宿制服务机构 16 个，日间照料机构 17 个，综合性服务机构 56 个。2680 名残疾人通过寄宿制和日间照料服务机构接受了托养服务，1.4 万名残疾人接受居家服务。

五、宣传文化

截至 2022 年底，共有省级残疾人专题广播节目 2 个、电视手语栏目 2 个，地级残疾人专题广播节目 6 个、电视手语栏目 7 个。

各级公共图书馆设立盲文及盲文有声读物阅览室 34 个，开展残疾人文化周活动 223 场次，省地两级残联艺术团 5 个。

六、维权

制定或修改保障残疾人权益的规范性文件省级 2 个、地级 10 个、县级 32 个。县级以上人大开展《中华人民共和国残疾人保障法》执法检查和专题调研 20 次。政协开展视察和专题调研 21 次。开展省级普法宣传教育活动 32 次，1850 人次参加。举办省级法律培训班 1 个，340 人次参加。各地残联办理建议、提案 61 件。

共出台了 28 个省、地、县级无障碍环境建设与管理法规、政府令和规范性文件；开展无障碍环境建设检查 161 次，无障碍培训 1165 人次。

七、组织建设

2022 年，市县乡共有残联 1773 个，各地市已建残联 11 个，县（市、区）已建残联 112 个，乡镇（街道）已建残联 1650 个，社区（村）已建残协 2 万个。

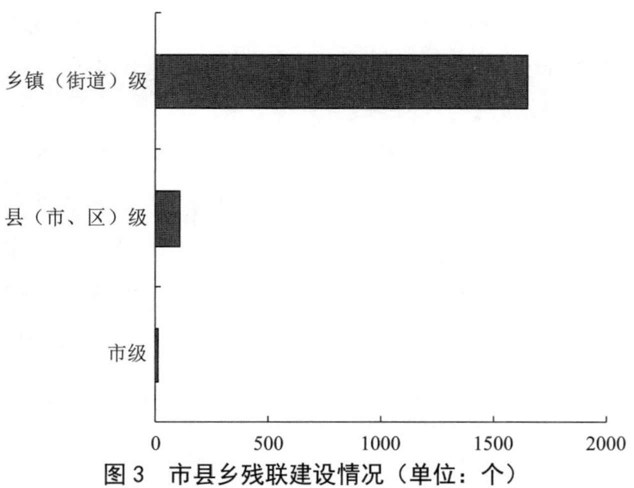

图 3　市县乡残联建设情况（单位：个）

省市县乡残联工作人员 3967 人，乡镇（街道）残联、村（社区）残协专职委员总计 1.4 万人。地级配备了残疾人领导干部的残联 10 个，县级配备了残疾人干部的残联 57 个。残疾人专门协会 497 个，助残社会组织 35 个。

八、服务设施

截至 2022 年底，已竣工的各级残疾人综合服务设施 68 个，总建设规模 8.9 万平方米，总投资 20415.4 万元；已竣工的各级残疾人康复设施 45 个，总建设规模 31.1 万平方米，总投资 66699.4 万元；已竣工的各级残疾人托养服务设施 38 个，总建设规模 10 万平方米，总投资 21760.7 万元。

九、信息化建设

省残联依托“赣服通”“政务服务网”建立完善“异地办理”服务事项，上线运行残疾人高校新生奖励平台，为 1879 人提供残疾人证线上办理服务，为 3279 家用人单位提供残疾人按比例就业情况联网认证“跨省通办”线上服务，安置登记 11367 名残疾人就业，633 名残疾人高校新生获奖励金 238 万元。联合江西联通开展“我为群众办实事，用科技让“‘AI’发声”助残活动，8.4 万名听障人士受益。省气象局在江西卫视天气预报节目上线 AI 气象手语虚拟主播，为听障人士提供无障碍气象服务。

十、民生工程

全省已完成城乡残疾人职业培训 3414 个，为残疾人购买公益性岗位 3896 个，为残疾人购买农家书屋管理员岗位 12062 个，残疾人就业进一步得到保障。

2022 年山东省残疾人事业发展统计公报

2022 年以来，各级残联坚持以习近平新时代中国特色社会主义思想为指导，深入学习贯彻党的二十大精神、省第十二次党代会精神，坚决落实习近平总书记对山东工作的重要指示要求，按照省委工作部署，锚定“走在前、开新局”，坚持守正创新，健全工作机制，加强残疾人权益保障，优化残疾人发展环境，全省残疾人工作取得新的发展。

一、康复

积极推动康复地方立法，出台《山东省残疾预防和残疾人康复条例》，推动健全多元化康复服务体系，完善残疾筛查、康复救助、康教融合、职业教育、庇护性就业等全程服务链条，为康复事业的持续发展提供了法治保障。出台《关于推进山东省残疾人康复事业高质量发展的实施意见》，完善康复目录，推动康复工作纳入经济社会发展大局，进一步保障残疾人康复权益。持续推动扩大康复覆盖面，147 万名残疾人得到基本康复服务，4.5 万名残疾儿童得到康复救助，8.8 万名残疾人得到基本辅助器具适配服务；得到康复服务的持证残疾人中，有视力残疾人 10.4 万名、听力残疾人 11 万名、言语残疾人 1.3 万名、肢体残疾人 86 万名、智力残疾人 12.8 万名、精神残疾人 15.4 万名、多重残疾人 9.3 万名。

推动实施残联系统康复机构运行服务规范提升工程、残疾儿童定点康复机构规范提升工程，推进各级各类机构取得教育、医疗资质，提高设施设备和专业人员配备，为残疾人提供安全有效的康复服务。开展康复专业人员规范化培训，线上线下相结合培训覆盖 1.2 万人次。截至 2022 年底，残疾人康复机构达 1438 个。康复机构在岗人员达 4.3 万人，其中，管理人员 0.3 万人，业务人员 3.5 万人，其他人员 0.5 万人。

二、教育

印发《山东省“十四五”特殊教育发展提升行动计划》，2022 年，共有特殊教育普通高中（部、班）7 个，在校生 915 人，其中聋生 390 人，盲生 247 人，其他 278 人。残疾人中等职业学校（班）10 个，在校生 1006 人，毕业生 421 人，毕业生中 126 人获得职业资格证书。印发《山东省第二期国家手语和盲文规范化行动计划（2021-2025 年）》，培训推广盲文、手语骨干人员 125 名。继续实施山东省残疾人大学生励志助学项目，为全省 1059 名残疾人大学生提供一次性助学保障。

三、就业

省政府办公厅印发《山东省促进残疾人就业三年行动实施方案（2022—2024 年）》。2022 年，城乡持证残疾人就业人数为 558879 人，其中按比例就业 71323 人，集中就业 15833 人，个体就业 30379 人，公益性岗位就业 31134 人，辅助性就业 4374 人，灵活就业（含社区、居家就业）121383 人，从事农业种养加 284453 人。

印发《山东省“十四五”残疾人职业技能提升计划》，全省开展农村困难残疾人实用技术培训，为 19607 人次残疾人赋能。157 个残疾人就业帮扶基地共安置 5058 名残疾人就业，带动 2614 户残疾人家庭增收。

2022 年，共培训盲人保健按摩人员 507 人次、盲人医疗按摩人员 700 人次。现有保健按摩机构 1431 个，医疗按摩机构 109 个。9 人获得盲人医疗按摩人员初级职务任职资格，4 人获得中级职务任职资格。

四、社会保障

截至 2022 年底，参加城乡居民基本养老保险的残疾人数达 1924438 名。964620 名残疾人领取养老金。60 岁以下参保的残疾人中，463588 名重度残疾人和 86229 名非重度残疾人得到参保缴费资助。开展残疾人托养服务的各级各类机构达 682 个，其中寄宿制服务机构 90 个，日间照料机构 392 个，综合性服务机构 132 个。10388 名残疾人通过寄宿制和日间照料服务机构接受了托养服务，12748 名残疾人接受居家服务。全省建成并投入运营“如康家园”残疾人综合服务平台 1447 处。

五、宣传文化

截至 2022 年底，共有省级残疾人专题广播节目 1 个、电视手语栏目 1 个，市级残疾人专题广播节目 12 个、电视手语栏目 8 个。各级公共图书馆设立盲文及盲文有声读物阅览室 77 个，开展残疾人文化周活动 316 场次，省市两级残联艺术团 22 个。

六、体育

组织全省 14 名运动员参加北京第 13 届冬残奥会越野滑雪、冬季两项和残奥冰球三个大项比赛，由中国残联和全省组建的国家残奥冰球队获得铜牌，实现奖牌零的突破，并被党中央、国务院授予北京冬奥会、冬残奥会突出贡献集体。参加越野滑雪和冬季两项比赛的两名运动员分别获得两人次第 8 名、两人次第 9 名的好成绩。在日照市举办省第十一届残运会，全省 17 支代表队共 1500 余名残疾人运动员参加了 17 个大项 700 余个小项的比赛，共决出金牌 786 枚，银牌 539 枚，铜牌 441 枚，实现省残运会与省运会“两个赛事、同样精彩”的目标。开展“残疾人健身周”“残疾人冰雪季”活动等群众性残疾人体育活动。

七、维权

2022 年，制定或修改关于残疾人的专门法规和规章：省级 1 个、地级 0 个；制定或修改保障残疾人权益的规范性文件：省级 0 个、地级 6 个、县级 17 个。县级以上人大开展《中华人民共和国残疾人保障法》执法检查和专题调研 56 次；政协开展视察和专题调研 20 次。出台《山东省残联系统开展法治宣传教育第八个五年规划（2021-2025 年）》，开展省级普法宣传教育活动 4 次，3275 人次参加；举办省级法律培训班 2 个，1067 人次参加。各级残联办理议案、建议、提案 128 件。

截至 2022 年底，全省共出台了 56 个省、市、县级无障碍环境建设与管理法规、政府令和规范性文件。2022 年，印发《山东省无障碍环境建设“十四五”实施方案》《山东省“十四五”困难重度残疾人家庭无障碍改造工作实施方案》，开展无障碍环境建设检查 251 次，无障碍培训 1833 人次，完成困难重度残疾人家庭无障碍改造 34951 户。

八、组织建设

2022 年，全省各级残联共有 1999 个，其中市残联 16 个，县（市、区）残联 161 个，乡镇（街道）残联 1822 个。村（社区）残协 60841 个。

全省各级残联工作人员 6368 人，乡镇（街道）残联、村（社区）残协专职委员总计 69097 人。配备残疾人领导干部的市级残联 10 个，配备残疾人干部的县级残联 87 个。各级残疾人专门协会 770 个，全省助残社会组织 147 个。

九、服务设施

截至 2022 年底，已竣工的各级残疾人综合服务设施 117 个，总建设规模 340373.0 平方米，总投资 90119.6 万元；已竣工的各级残疾人康复设施 114 个，总建设规模 726972.9 平方米，总投资 212622.9 万元；已竣工的各级残疾人托养服务设施 37 个，总建设规模 123155.9 平方米，总投资 31763.9 万元。

2022 年河南省残疾人事业发展统计公报

2022 年，在省委、省政府的正确领导和中国残联的精心指导下，省残联坚持以习近平新时代中国特色社会主义思想为指导，认真落实楼阳生书记“残疾人事业是民生工作的重要组成部分，要切实抓好”的重要批示要求，持续加强党的领导，着力保障和改善残疾人民生，推动全省残疾人事业高质量发展，各项工作取得新成绩。现将 2022 年度残疾人事业统计数据公报如下：

一、康复

2022 年，为 34 万名残疾人提供基本康复服务，其中 0—6 岁残疾儿童 3.2 万名，7—17 岁残疾儿童 1.5 万名，未持证残疾儿童 2.5 万名，残疾人基本康复服务率达到 96.89%。得到康复服务的持证残疾人中，有视力残疾人 2.3 万名、听力残疾人 2.2 万名、言语残疾人 2688 名、肢体残疾人 20 万名、智力残疾人 2.1 万名、精神残疾人 3 万名、多重残疾人 1.6 万名。全年为 10.7 万名残疾人提供基本辅助器具适配服务，残疾人辅助器具适配服务率 98.07%。

截至 2022 年底，全省已建残疾人康复机构 546 个，比上年增加 12 个，其中残联系统已建康复机构 124 个。全省康复机构在岗人员 1.8 万名，其中管理人员 1512 名，业务人员 1.5 万名，其他人员 1524 名。

二、教育

协同教育部门共同稳定解决适龄残疾儿童少年接受义务教育问题，2022 年全省适龄残疾儿童少年入学率 98.26%。

2022 年，全省共有特殊教育普通高中（部、班）8 个，在校生 740 人，其中聋生 457 人，盲生 88 人，其他 195 人。残疾人中等职业学校（班）4 个，在校生 670 人，毕业生 231 人，毕业生中 10 人获得职业资格证书。全年有 1063 名残疾人被普通高等院校录取，317 名残疾人进入高等特殊教育机构学习。

三、就业

2022 年，全省城乡持证残疾人就业人数为 53.6 万人，其中按比例就业 2.4 万人，集中就业 1.1 万人，个体就业 8.1 万人，公益性岗位就业 6873 人，辅助性就业 1.5 万人，灵活就业（含社区、居家就业）13.6 万人，从事农业种养加 26.3 万人。

开展农村困难残疾人实用技术培训，为 2.1 万人次残疾人赋能。全省 64 个残疾人就业帮扶基地共安置 3917 名残疾人就业，带动 4026 户残疾人家庭增收。

全年共培训盲人保健按摩人员 750 人次、盲人医疗按摩人员 600 人次。全省现有保健按摩机构 1401 个，医疗按摩机构 43 个。7 名残疾人获得中级职务任职资格。

四、社会保障

截至 2022 年底，全省参加城乡居民基本养老保险的残疾人数达 269.4 万名。129.8 万名残疾人领取养老金。60 岁以下参保的残疾人中，49.2 万名重度残疾人和 6.7 万名非重度残疾人得到参保缴费资助。

残疾人“两项补贴”标准自 2022 年 12 月 1 日起由每人每月不低于 60 元提高到每人每月不低于 75 元。截至 2022 年底，全省 93.8 万困难残疾人享受生活补贴，119.6 万重度残疾人享受护理补贴。

全省目前开展残疾人托养服务的各级各类机构达 397 个，其中寄宿制服务机构 198 个，日间照料机构 26 个，居家服务机构 51 个，综合性服务机构 122 个。11261 名残疾人通过寄宿制和日间照料服务机构接受了托养服务，5731 名残疾人接受居家服务。

五、宣传文化

组织中央媒体走基层“云看河南”残疾人事业活动，举办河南省第十六届残疾人事业好新闻评选，通过电视、高速公路电子屏、移动通讯开展残疾人事业公益宣传，营造扶残助残浓厚氛围。截至 2022 年底，全省共有省级残疾人专题广播节目 1 个、电视手语栏目 1 个，地级残疾人专题广播节目 11 个、电视手语栏目 8 个。全省各级公共图书馆设立盲文及盲文有声读物阅览室 77 个，开展残疾人文化周活动 247 场次，省地两级残联艺术团 6 个。

六、体育

2022 年，全省组织各级残疾人体育健身活动 201 次，残疾人参加活动 6089 人次，全省有残疾人体育训练基地 6 个，聘任教练员 55 名。

七、维权

2022 年，全省制定或修改保障残疾人权益的地级规范性文件 2 个、县级规划性文件 4 个。县级以上人大开展《中华人民共和国残疾人保障法》执法检查和专题调研 23 次；政协开展视察和专题调研 7 次。开展省级普法宣传教育活动 1 次，72 人次参加；举办省级法律培训班 1 个，72 人次参加。全省各地残联办理建议、提案 23 件。

全省共出台了 102 个省、地、县级无障碍环境建设与管理法规、政府令和规范性文件，比上年增加 2 个；全省开展无障碍环境建设检查 58 次，无障碍培训 660 人次。截至 2022 年底，全省共为 3.14 万户困难重度残疾人家庭实施无障碍改造。

八、组织建设

2022 年，全省已建残联 2623 个，省辖市（含济源示范区）已建残联 18 个，县、市、区（含各类开发区等）已建残联 174 个，乡镇（街道）已建残联 2431 个，社区（村）已建残协 5.2 万个。

2022 年，全省各级残联工作人员 7588 人，乡镇（街道）残联、村（社区）残协专职委员总计 5 万人。6 个地级残联配备了残疾人领导干部，89 个县级残联配备了残疾人干部。

截至 2022 年底，全省已建各级残疾人专门协会 891 个，其中省级 5 个、地级 90 个、县级 796 个。全省共有助残社会组织 41 个。

九、服务设施

2022 年，争取中央预算内投资 4160 万元，支持建设地级残疾人康复中心、托养中心各 1 个，并对 37 个已建服务设施项目给予设备购置补贴。

截至 2022 年底，全省已竣工的各级残疾人综合服务设施 108 个，总建设规模 28.7 万平方米，总投资 7.2 亿元；已竣工的各级残疾人康复设施 41 个，总建设规模 31.3 万平方米，总投资 8.2 亿元；已竣工的各级残疾人托养服务设施 38 个，总建设规模 12.3 万平方米，总投资 2.4 亿元。

十、信息化建设

2022 年，持续深化残疾人一体化政务服务事项，实现豫事办残疾人助残服务事项的更新上线，落实残疾人证办理和按比例就业联网认证共计 2 个内容、7 个事项“跨省通办”；持续深化残疾人数据共享应用，及时同步更新全省 280 多万持证残疾人数据，保障全省 33 家厅局、省辖市单位数据订阅服务；持续优化残疾人大数据平台，整合分析 7 个残联业务系统及 10 家相关厅局单位关联数据，囊括全省 280 多万持证残疾人共计 9800 万条信息，形成 1 个基础库、5 个主题库和 10 个专题库。

2022 年，完成省残联网站新版升级和适老化改造，开设学习贯彻党的二十大精神、就业服务三年行动、平安河南、数字技能提升、国家安全等 5 个专题栏目。

2022 年，省残联门户网站共收到上报新闻 5584 篇，发布信息 5243 篇，同比分别增长 13.4%、13.7%，门户网站访问量达七百万余次。2022 年，省残联微信公众号新增订阅用户 3250 人，累计用户总数增至 1.6 万人，同比增长 18.8%。微信公众号发布文章 778 篇，文章总阅读 12.56 万次，分享转发 6923 次，文章总在看数 501 个，总点赞数 1354 个。

2022 年湖北省残疾人事业发展统计公报

2022 年，全省各级残联坚持以习近平新时代中国特色社会主义思想为指导，全面贯彻党的二十大精神，认真贯彻落实习近平总书记关于残疾人工作的重要指示批示精神，认真贯彻落实省第十二次党代会精神，按照中国残联要求，全面实施《湖北省残疾人事业发展“十四五”规划》，全面推进残疾人事业高质量发展。

一、康复

贯彻落实《湖北省“十四五”残疾人康复服务实施方案》《湖北省残疾预防行动计划（2022-2025 年）》，进一步推动全省残疾人康复事业高质量发展。继续组织实施残疾儿童康复救助，为 22195 名 0-15 岁残疾儿童提供了康复救助，为 14224 名残疾儿童发放了家庭生活补贴。持续开展残疾人精准康复服务行动，458819 名残疾人得到基本康复服务，82811 名残疾人得到基本辅助器具适配服务。得到康复服务的持证残疾人中，有视力残疾人 48932 名、听力残疾人 36969 名、言语残疾人 3413 名、肢体残疾人 193212 名、智力残疾人 36486 名、精神残疾人 99814 名、多重残疾人 26477 名。大力推进残疾人家庭医生签约工作，积极开展精神障碍社区康复服务。

加强残疾人康复机构与人才队伍建设，深化社区康复工作。按照《湖北省残联系统康复专业技术人员规范化培训实施方案（试行）》，确定了 5 家基地承担 2022 年度规范化培训任务。印发了《2022 年湖北省残联系统康复专业技术人员省级规范化培训计划》。全年共举办孤独症、脑瘫、智障、听力言语康复专业技术人员规范化培训班和残疾人辅助技术专业技术人员轮训班 11 期，培训学员 488 人次。截至 2022 年底，全省有残疾人康复机构 273 个。康复机构在岗人员达 8944 人，其中，管理人员 924 人，业务人员 6360 人，其他人员 1660 人。

二、教育

着力建设高质量残疾人教育体系。深入贯彻党的二十大精神，拓展学段服务、推进融合教育、提升支撑能力，实施《湖北省特殊教育发展提升行动计划（2022-2025）》。会同教育厅印发《湖北省辅助器具进校园工程实施方案》，为义务教育阶段有需要的残疾学生提供适配服务；会同团委、教育等八部门印发《湖北省“十四五”国家手语和盲文规范化行动计划》，加快手语盲文规范化、标准化、信息化进程。持续实施湖北省特殊教育学校职业培训扶持项目，200 名特教学校贫困残疾学生获得扶助、10 所特校得到职业教育职业培训补助。对当年考入高校的 580 名残疾人大学生进行资助。

2022 年，全省共有特殊教育普通高中（部、班）7 个，在校生 314 人，其中聋生 236 人，盲生 28 人，其他 50 人。残疾人中等职业学校（班）3 个，在校生 481 人，毕业生 80 人。

三、就业

实施湖北省残疾人就业创业扶持项目，扶持残疾人就业创业示范基地 35 个、自主创业残疾人 400 人，培育残疾人技术能手 1000 人。

全省城乡持证残疾人就业人数为 392645 人，其中按比例就业 31859 人，集中就业 16423 人，个体就业 24921 人，公益性岗位就业 4543 人，辅助性就业 5784 人，灵活就业（含社区、居家就业）126035 人，从事农业种养加 183080 人。

开展农村困难残疾人实用技术培训，为 9139 人次残疾人赋能。96 个残疾人就业帮扶基地共安置 1547 名残疾人就业，带动 2797 户残疾人家庭增收。

全省共培训盲人保健按摩人员 421 人次、盲人医疗按摩人员 139 人次；现有保健按摩机构 1101 个，医疗按摩机构 47 个。

四、社会保障

截至 2022 年底，参加城乡居民基本养老保险的残疾人数达 1234833 名。522262 名残疾人领取养老金。60 岁以下参保重度残疾人中，366004 名重度残疾人和 88684 名非重度残疾人得到参保缴费资助。

全省开展残疾人托养服务的各级各类机构达 232 个，其中寄宿制托养服务机构 39 个，日间照料机构 49 个，综合性托养服务机构 47 个。实施“阳光家园计划”项目，5489 名残疾人通过寄宿制和日间照料服务机构接受了托养服务，13874 名残疾人接受居家服务。

五、宣传文化

聚焦重大主题、重大节日开展残疾人事业宣传，中央电视台《午夜新闻》《新闻直播间》《零点故事》三个栏目连续播发我省独臂村医王文艮的故事。《湖北新闻》全年播发我省残疾人事业新闻达到 22 条，与湖北电视台公共新闻频道合作开设宣传专栏，宣传推介 48 个残疾人工作案例。湖北日报推出 1 个专版、6 个专栏和 32 篇报道。4 名残疾人和 4 名助残先进个人和集体上榜“荆楚楷模”。围绕学习贯彻党的二十大精神主题，开展主题征文、公益文艺演出、残疾人书画展等活动。在全省 13 个市（州）施行残疾人文化进社区项目，举办“共享芬芳共铸美好——2022 年残健融合春节文艺晚会”。编排残疾人文艺节目参加“全国助残日”湖北省系列活动暨“残疾人就业创业关爱行动”启动仪式、“十四五”湖北省残疾人精神文化关爱行动暨“光明阅读文化助残”启动仪式等演出。挖掘培养残疾人特艺人才 23 人，创编新节目 3 个。为 10000 个残疾人家庭提供了文化进残疾人家庭“五个一”服务。为 3000 个重度残疾人家庭提供了康复体育器材和训练服务。命名并扶持了 3 个文化创意产业基地。

截至 2022 年底，共有省级残疾人专题广播节目 1 个、电视手语栏目 1 个；地级残疾人专题广播节目 10 个、电视手语栏目 7 个。各级公共图书馆设立盲文及盲文有声读物阅览室 38 个，开展残疾人文化周活动 326 场次。省地两级残联艺术团 5 个。

六、维权

继续加强残疾人法治宣传，与湖北人民广播电台资讯广播《爱心有约》栏目合作，邀请法学专家、资深律师等学者参与节目，以案释法、普及法律知识。2022 年，县级以上人大开展《中华人民共和国残疾人保障法》执法检查和专题调研 7 次；政协开展视察和专题调研 8 次。开展省级普法宣传教育活 3 次，692000 余人次参加；举办省级法律培训班 1 个，200 人次参加。各地残联办理建议、提案 60 件。共出台了 19 个无障碍环境建设与管理法规、政府令和规范性文件，开展无障碍环境建设检查 84 次，无障碍培训 789 人次。

七、组织建设

2022 年，市县乡共有残联 1338 个，各地市已建残联 13 个，县（市、区）残联已建 108 个，乡镇（街道）残联已建 1217 个；社区（村）已建残协 25101 个。

省市县乡残联工作人员 3622 人，乡镇（街道）残联、村（社区）残协专职委员总计 24132 人。地市级配备了残疾人领导干部的残联有 4 个，县级配备了残疾人干部的残联有 39 个。

残疾人专门协会 558 个，助残社会组织 599 个。

八、服务设施

截至 2022 年底，已竣工的各级残疾人综合服务设施 88 个，总建设规模 207638.5 平方米，总投资 49155.9 万元；已竣工的各级残疾人康复设施 35 个，总建设规模 230262.0 平方米，总投资 79472.3 万元；已竣工的各级残疾人托养服务设施 36 个，总建设规模 85885.9 平方米，总投资 16822.5 万元。

2022 年湖南省残疾人事业发展统计公报

2022 年，湖南省残联坚持以习近平新时代中国特色社会主义思想为指导，全面贯彻党的二十大精神，深入贯彻习近平总书记关于残疾人事业重要论述、重要指示批示精神，认真落实中国残联和省委省政府决策部署，深入实施《湖南省“十四五”残疾人保障和发展规划》，推动全省残疾人工作取得新进展新成效。

一、康复

全省残疾人康复重点工作在中国残联的年度评估中获“优秀”等次，得到省领导的充分肯定。

推进残疾预防工作落实。省政府办公厅印发《湖南省残疾预防行动计划（2022—2025 年）》，实施“五大行动”，促进减少残疾发生。实施省重点民生实事项目。圆满完成 2022 年省重点民生实事“1.1 万名残疾儿童康复救助”项目，救助 17517 人，总体进度 159.2%。实施精准康复服务行动。2022 年，全省共有 315762 名残疾人得到基本康复服务，其中 134560 名残疾人得到基本辅助器具适配服务。得到康复服务的持证残疾人中，有视力残疾人 33291 名、听力残疾人 21232 名、言语残疾人 1386 名、肢体残疾人 149429 名、智力残疾人 17030 名、精神残疾人 65518 名、多重残疾人 14534 名。省残联在中国残联“学习贯彻党的二十大精神深化残疾人精准康复服务”研讨会上汇报交流。推进康复服务改革创新。省残联在 11 个县市区开展第二批残疾人康复服务综合改革试点，在 4 个市州试点建立残疾人基本辅助器具补贴制度，支持建设 50 个社区康复服务站，残疾儿童康复救助开通“不见面”线上申请审核，省残疾人互联网+康复综合管理与服务平台完成验收。狠抓康复专业人才队伍建设。全年组织各类残疾人康复专业技术培训 21 期，共培训 2540 人。继续与长沙民政职业技术学院开设订单班，订单班毕业生就业安置率达到 85.7%。组织开展 1 期全省基层康复机构教师进修培训班，开展 2022 年残疾人康复课题申报评审工作，49 个康复课题立项。为 146 个机构和 17228 名 0—14 岁残疾儿童购买责任险与意外伤害险。截至 2022 年底，有残疾人康复机构 497 个。康复机构在岗人员达 16458 人，其中，管理人员 1918 人，业务人员 11939 人，其他人员 2601 人。

二、教育

与省教育厅开展残疾人教育调研，省政府办公厅印发《湖南省特殊教育发展提升行动计划（2022—2025 年）》。成立湖南省特殊教育研究指导中心、湖南省残疾人职业教育研究指导中心，进一步推动全省特殊教育高质量发展。开展适龄残疾儿童入学情况核查，全省适龄残疾儿童入学率稳定在 97%以上。开展扶残助学，全年对 15522 名高中和大学阶段残疾学生、困难残疾人家庭子女进行资助。继续实施中央彩票公益金中高职助学项目，推动长沙职业技术学院和省特教中专开展实习实训基地建设和师资队伍建设。为 149 名残疾考生提供高考合理便利支持。省直 6 部门制定印发《湖南省第二期国家通用手语和盲文推广工作方案（2022－2025 年）》，进一步提升社会知晓度和扩大无障碍信息社会服务范围。

2022 年，全省共有特殊教育普通高中（部、班）7 个，在校生 462 人，其中聋生 171 人，盲生 42 人，其他 249 人。残疾人中等职业学校（班）3 个，在校生 662 人，毕业生 207 人，毕业生中 14 人获得职业资格证书。高等教育阶段，招收 882 名残疾学生，其中高职（专科）560 人，本科 310 人，研究生 12 人。

三、就业

残疾人就业扶助政策不断完善。省政府办公厅印发《湖南省促进残疾人就业三年行动实施方案（2022—2024 年）》，省直 6 部门印发《关于机关、事业单位、国有企业带头安排残疾人就业工作的实施意见》。

残疾人就业能力持续增强。开展农村困难残疾人实用技术培训，为12323人次残疾人赋能。开展残疾人职业技能培训11689人次。455个残疾人就业帮扶基地共安置6546名残疾人就业，带动9537户残疾人家庭增收。成功举办第七届全省残疾人职业技能竞赛。圆满承办第八届全国残疾人岗位精英职业技能竞赛暨全国残疾人就业服务机构工作人员职业指导竞赛，湖南省获团体总分第一名，岗位精英职业技能竞赛3名选手被人社部授予“全国技术能手”称号，职业指导竞赛3名选手均获“职业指导模范”荣誉称号，湖南省获“就业服务成效奖”，参赛成绩创历史最佳。选送2名选手参加第十届国际残疾人职业技能大赛，勇夺1枚银牌。

残疾人就业服务更加优化。全年对463078名就业年龄段未就业残疾人进行摸底调查，掌握就业需求。组织“就业援助月”“就业宣传年”等活动，融合开展残疾人就业帮扶、就业宣传。一体推进技能培训、资格考试、职称评审、门店扶持，促进盲人按摩行业健康发展。全年共培训盲人保健按摩人员669人次、盲人医疗按摩人员366人次。现有保健按摩机构668个，医疗按摩机构19个。36人获得盲人医疗按摩人员初级职务任职资格，11人获得中级职务任职资格。“一对一”为高校残疾人毕业生提供职业指导、心理疏导和能力测评等就业服务，高校残疾人毕业生就业率达到90.69%。省残疾人就业创业网络服务平台有688家企业注册，动态提供就业职位千余个。目前全省共建有9个残疾人创业孵化基地、68家残疾人辅助性就业机构、1050个残疾人就业示范基地。

2022年，全省城乡持证残疾人就业人数为429492人，其中按比例就业23782人，集中就业12390人，个体就业31133人，公益性岗位就业3042人，辅助性就业6425人，灵活就业（含社区、居家就业）145325人，从事农业种养加207395人。

四、社会保障

社会保障政策全面落实。截至2022年底，参加城乡居民基本养老保险的残疾人数达1595393名。675069名残疾人领取养老金。60岁以下参保的残疾人中，475462名重度残疾人和166888名非重度残疾人得到参保缴费资助。

开展残疾人托养服务的各级各类机构达264个，其中寄宿制服务机构44个，日间照料机构72个，综合性服务机构56个。6503名残疾人通过寄宿制和日间照料机构接受了托养服务，16277名残疾人接受居家服务。

残疾人托养服务工作稳步推进。在全国残疾人社会保障工作研讨会上，介绍了残疾人托养服务等方面的典型工作经验。加强残疾人托养服务规范化、专业化建设，由省市场监督管理局立项，出台首个助残服务类地方标准。残疾人照护工作列入向省委常委会汇报事项，省民政厅会同省残联、省财政厅等有关部门开展专题调研，为下步谋划发展困难重度残疾人集中照护服务工作打下基础。

五、宣传文化

2022年，省残联门户网站全年共编发各类稿件5465篇。依托主流媒体和新兴传播平台，围绕“全国助残日”和“残疾预防日”等重要节点进行专题报道，并在长沙繁华街口、高速路口、机场、高铁站和5条地铁线路的24座地铁站共36个电子大屏及重要室内场所超600块小屏，进行千屏联播海报宣传。整合升级“湖南残联”公众号，全年共推送793篇稿件，粉丝量近2万。联合通信管理局通过三大运营商给全省用户发公益短信宣传助残。

开展为残疾人提供基本、均等公共文化服务工作。截至2022年底，共有省级残疾人专题广播节目1个、电视手语栏目1个，地市级残疾人专题广播节目8个、电视手语栏目5个。全省各级公共图书馆设立盲文及盲文有声读物阅览室31个，开展残疾人文化周活动158场次；地市级残联艺术团28个。

六、体育

残疾人体育全面发展。坚持精心选苗、科学育苗和实战练兵，不断完善省有常训队伍、市州有集训项目、县市区有特训苗子的三级残疾人运动员培育机制。克服疫情影响，成功举办省第十一届残疾人运动会，创造了规模最大、项目最全、参赛人数最多的纪录，增强了残疾人自信自立、积极向上的精神力量。采取“残健融合”“文体结合”方式，举办“2022 年残疾人健身周云竞赛暨文化周活动”，6088 名残疾人参加，关注人次达到 600 万。

七、维权

残疾人工作法治化水平有效提升。配合省人大开展残疾人保障“一法一办法”执法调研，推动“一法一办法”全面实施。加大残疾人法律援助工作力度，全省办理残疾人法律援助案件 1650 件。贯彻落实《信访工作条例》，用心用情处理各类残疾人信访件，全年未发生残疾人重大信访和群访事件，省残联被评为 2022 年度信访工作先进单位。开展全省残疾人服务机构风险隐患排查整治专项行动，共排查整改风险隐患 290 处。全省残疾人保持总体稳定。

2022 年，制定或修改关于残疾人的专门法规和规章：地级 1 个；制定或修改保障残疾人权益的规范性文件：省级 7 个、地级 5 个、县级 6 个。全省县级以上人大开展《中华人民共和国残疾人保障法》执法检查和专题调研 44 次；政协开展视察和专题调研 21 次。开展省级普法宣传教育活动 3 次，120 人次参加；举办省级法律培训班 1 个，80 人次参加。各地残联办理建议、提案 57 件。

无障碍环境建设纵深推进。全面完成《湖南省无障碍环境建设五年行动计划》年度任务。编制发布一批无障碍环境建设标准和规范，扎实推进老旧小区和公共服务场所的无障碍设施改造，完善首届全省旅游发展大会和省第十一届残运会的无障碍设施，制定残疾人通信资费调优政策。承办第三届全国肢残人轮椅马拉松赛，宣传展示湖南无障碍环境建设成绩。在住建部与中国残联联合召开的全国无障碍环境建设工作会议上，先后介绍了无障碍环境建设的典型工作经验。

全省共出台了 34 个省、地市、县级无障碍环境建设与管理法规、政府令和规范性文件；开展无障碍环境建设检查 165 次，无障碍培训 3764 人次。截至 2022 年底，圆满完成 2022 年省重点民生实事“1.2 万户困难残疾人家庭无障碍改造”项目 13337 户，总体进度 111%；发放残疾人机动轮椅车燃油补贴 3 万余人。

八、组织建设

省残联进一步加强组织建设工作。召开省残联七届主席团三次会议。出台实施意见，指导市县残联平稳换届。协调省委组织部、省委编办，健全县级残联党组设置，未设立党组的 29 个县级残联已有 28 个完成设置。举办首届全省残联专职委员知识竞赛有力促进专职委员能力素质的提升。组织对全省 196 万持证残疾人开展基本状况调查，对 744 户残疾人家庭开展收入状况抽样调查，动态掌握残疾人生活状况和服务需求。会同省卫健委成功举办第三届全省评残医生培训班。第五批次调整评残指定医院，全省现有评残医院 223 家。省残联会同省卫健委、省政务局共同制定出台文件，推动残疾人证“一次办”“网上办”，在全国较快推进残疾人证电子证照汇聚制发和应用。全省共换发三代残疾人证 98.7 万本。全国残联组联工作会议等会议上，第三次介绍了残疾人证核发管理方面的典型工作经验。加强志愿助残服务，完善“湘助残”平台运行管理，组织助残志愿者骨干培训，吸引带动青少年等群体积极参与志愿助残服务。

2022 年，市县乡共有残联 2058 个，14 个地市全部成立残联，县（市、区，含经开区）已建残联 129 个，乡镇（街道）已建残联 1915 个；社区（村）已建残协 28994 个。全省各级残联工作人员 4942 人，乡镇（街道）残联、村（社区）残协专职委员总计 25756 人。7 个地市级残联配备了残疾人领导干部，66 个县级残联配备了残疾人干部，全省各级残疾人专门协会 682 个，其中省级专门协会已建 5 个，市级专门协会已建 70 个，县级专门协会已建 607 个。全省助残社会组织 98 个。

九、服务设施

残疾人服务设施建设得到全面发展。截至 2022 年底，全省已竣工的各级残疾人综合服务设施 91 个，总建设规模 119106.4 平方米，总投资 25765.2 万元；已竣工的各级残疾人康复设施 59 个，总建设规模 292717.4 平方米，总投资 77954.5 万元；已竣工的各级残疾人托养服务设施 57 个，总建设规模 123049.8 平方米，总投资 29429.9 万元。

十、信息化建设

截至 2022 年底，14 个地级、27 个县级残联开通网站。省残联继续管好用好全省残疾人基础数据平台，深化与民政、公安、教育、乡村振兴、人社、医保、住建、卫健、市场监督管理等 10 余个部门常态化数据共享，促进惠残政策的精准落实。加快推进“智慧残联”建设。

2022 年广东省残疾人事业发展统计公报

2022 年全省各级残联以习近平新时代中国特色社会主义思想为指导，全面贯彻落实党的二十大精神，认真贯彻落实习近平总书记关于残疾人事业的重要论述和重要指示批示精神，深入实施《“十四五”残疾人保障和发展规划》，全面推进残疾人事业高质量发展。

一、残疾人康复

2022 年，全省得到基本康复服务的儿童及持证残疾人共 29.9 万人。其中 0-6 岁残疾儿童 2.7 万人；7-17 岁残疾儿童 1.6 万人；18-59 岁残疾人 16.9 万人；60 岁以上残疾人 8.7 万人。从服务的残疾类型来看，服务视力残疾 1.1 万人、听力残疾 1.9 万人、言语残疾 0.2 万人、肢体残疾 7.3 万人、智力残疾 2.0 万人、精神残疾 14.1 万人、多重残疾 1.9 万人、0-17 岁未持证残疾儿童 1.4 万人。从接受康复服务的内容来看，接受康复医疗服务 13.6 万人、接受功能训练服务 3.2 万人、接受辅助器具适配服务 5.1 万人、接受支持性服务 9.3 万人。7.1 万名农村低收入残疾人得到康复服务。

截至 2022 年底，全省各级共有残疾人康复机构 1036 个，其中 162 个机构提供视力残疾康复服务、191 个机构提供听力言语残疾康复服务、404 个机构提供肢体残疾康复服务、459 个机构提供智力残疾康复服务、692 个机构提供精神残疾康复及孤独症儿童康复服务、136 个机构提供辅助器具服务。康复机构在岗人员 31455 人，其中管理人员 2829 人，专业技术人员 22322 人，其他人员 6304 人。

二、残疾人教育

截至 2022 年底，全省共有特殊教育普通高中（部、班）7 个，在校生 607 人，其中聋生 372 人，盲生 71 人，其他 164 人。残疾人中等职业学校（班）9 个，在校生 1811 人，毕业生 446 人，毕业生中 69 人获得职业资格证书。有 820 名残疾人被普通高等院校录取，106 名残疾人进入高等特殊教育学院学习。

三、残疾人就业

截至 2022 年底，全省城乡持证残疾人就业年龄段就业人数为 40.9 万人，其中按比例就业 8.3 万人、集中就业 0.7 万人、个体就业 1.7 万人、公益性岗位就业 0.6 万人、辅助性就业 1.4 万人、灵活就业（含社区、居家就业）12.3 万人、从事农村种养加 15.9 万人。2022 年度培训农村残疾人实用技术 9360 人。培训盲人保健按摩人员 368 名、盲人医疗按摩人员 336 名。现有保健按摩机构 1227 个，医疗按摩机构 12 个。

四、残疾人社会保障

截至 2022 年底，城乡残疾居民参加社会养老保险的残疾人数达 110 万名。39.8 万名残疾人领取养老金。60 岁以下参保的残疾人中，46.9 万名重度残疾人和 13.9 万名非重度残疾人得到参保缴费资助。

2022 年全省开展残疾人托养服务的各级各类机构达 1393 个，其中寄宿制托养服务机构 31 个，日间照料托养服务机构 1344 个，居家服务机构 3 个，综合托养服务机构 15 个。托养残疾人总数 25757 名，其中 1649 名残疾人接受寄宿制托养服务，22267 名残疾人接受日间照料托养服务，1841 名残疾人接受居家服务。

五、残疾人宣传文化

截至 2022 年底，共有省级残疾人专题广播节目 1 个、电视手语栏目 1 个、入驻省级政务客户端平台 5 个；地市级残疾人专题广播节目共 20 个、电视手语栏目 20 个。省市县三级公共图书馆共设立盲文及盲文有声读物图书室 68 个。全年共开展残疾人文化周活动 489 场次，参加活动人数达 33541 人次；省地两级残联共有残疾人艺术团 13 个，举办残疾人文化艺术类的比赛及展览39次。

六、残疾人体育

2022年组织残疾人群众体育健身活动1832次，其中省级5次，地市级202次，县区级1625次，参加活动总人次达6.9万人次。省级残疾人体育训练基地8个，聘任教练员50人。

七、残疾人法治建设与维权

2022年，制定或修改保障残疾人权益的地市级规范性文件13个、县级规范性文件7个；县级以上人大开展《中华人民共和国残疾人保障法》执法检查和专题调研21次；政协开展视察和专题调研9次；开展省级普法宣传教育活动4次，参加人数8320人。

残疾人参政议政工作稳步开展，各地残联协助人大代表、政协委员提出议案、建议、提案58件，办理议案、建议、提案85件。

无障碍建设法规、标准进一步完善。共出台了36个省、地市、县级无障碍环境建设与管理法规、政府令和规范性文件；开展无障碍环境建设检查2190次，无障碍培训1141人次。

2022年全省各级残联收到残疾人信访来信3266件；其中涉及就业帮扶类637件占比19.5%、医疗康复类379件占比11.6%、社会保障类374件占比11.5%，教育类166件占比5.1%、权益保障类152件占比4.7%。残疾人来访5757人次；其中医疗康复类1204人次占比21.0%、社会保障类978人次占比17.0%、权益保障类546人次占9.5%、就业帮扶类539人次占比9.4%、教育类413人次占比7.2%。

八、残疾人组织建设

2022年，省市县乡共成立残联1780个，其中各地市已建残联21个、县（市、区）残联已建133个、乡镇（街道）残联已建1625个；已建社区（村）残协23819个。

省市县乡残联工作人员共7714人，乡镇（街道）、村（社区）选聘负责残疾人工作的专职委员总计18519名。15个地市级残联配备了残疾人领导干部，35个县级残联配备了残疾人干部。

全省共建立各类残疾人专门协会697个，其中省级专门协会已建5个、市级专门协会已建105个、县级专门协会已建587个。助残社会组织共有160个，其中省级8个，地市级72个，县区级80个。

九、残疾人服务设施

截至2022年底，已竣工的各级残疾人综合服务设施108个，总建设规模65.5万平方米，总投资24.9亿元；已竣工的各级残疾人康复设施56个，总建设规模25.6万平方米，总投资8.6亿元；已竣工的各级残疾人托养服务设施14个，总建设规模7.3万平方米，总投资1.6亿元。

2022 年度广西壮族自治区残疾人事业发展统计公报

2022 年，在中国残联和自治区党委、政府的正确领导下，全区各级残联坚持以习近平新时代中国特色社会主义思想为指导，深入贯彻落实习近平总书记关于残疾人事业的重要论述，全面贯彻中国残联和自治区党委、政府关于残疾人事业的新部署新要求，加快推进残疾人小康进程，积极推动落实广西残疾人保障和发展“十四五”规划，残疾人事业发展取得良好成效，广大残疾人得到更多福祉。现将我区 2022 年度残疾人事业统计年报数据公报如下：

一、康复

全区共有残疾人康复机构 452 个，其中残联系统康复机构 82 个。全区康复机构在岗人员 10989 人，其中，管理人员 1164 人，业务人员 7735 人，其他人员 2090 人。

166445 名残疾人得到基本康复服务，其中 0-6 岁残疾儿童 18135 人。得到康复服务的持证残疾人中，有视力残疾人 15318 人、听力残疾人 8499 人、言语残疾人 592 人、肢体残疾人 73062 人、智力残疾人 14355 人、精神残疾人 30479 人、多重残疾人 10893 人。全年共为 36027 名残疾人提供各类辅助器具适配服务。

二、教育

全区共有特殊教育普通高中（部、班）4 个，在校生 360 人，其中聋生 262 人，盲生 43 人，其他 55 人。残疾人中等职业学校（班）1 个，在校生 216 人，毕业生 86 人，毕业生中 4 人获得职业资格证书。有 398 名残疾人被普通高等院校录取。

三、就业

全区城乡持证残疾人就业人数为 326932 人，其中按比例就业 18442 人，集中就业 1656 人，个体就业 12162 人，公益性岗位就业 3680 人，辅助性就业 2543 人，灵活性就业（含社区、居家就业）69962 人，从事农业种养加 218487 人。

开展农村困难残疾人实用技术培训，为 22371 人次残疾人赋能。148 个残疾人阳光助残基地（残疾人就业帮扶基地）共安置 636 名残疾人就业，带动 17412 户残疾人家庭增收。

共培训盲人保健按摩人员 489 人、盲人医疗按摩人员 131 人；现有保健按摩机构 414 个，医疗按摩机构 4 个。

四、社会保障

全区参加城乡居民基本养老保险的残疾人达 995996 名，436751 名残疾人领取养老金。60 岁以下参保的残疾人中，309640 名重度残疾人和 111584 名非重度残疾人得到参保缴费资助。

开展残疾人托养服务机构有 170 个，其中寄宿制托养服务机构 16 个，日间照料托养服务机构 2 个，居家服务机构 122 个，综合性托养服务机构 30 个；为 2814 名残疾人提供了寄宿制和日间照料托养服务，37177 名残疾人接受居家服务。

五、宣传文化

全区共有省级残疾人专题广播节目 1 个、电视手语栏目 1 个；地市级残疾人专题广播节目 1 个、电视手语栏目 6 个。

自治区、市、县（市、区）公共图书馆共设立盲文及盲文有声读物阅览室 31 个，共开展残疾人文化周活动 302 场次；自治区、市残联共举办残疾人文化艺术类的比赛演出及展览 7 次，共有各类残疾人艺术团 6 个。

六、体育

各地深入开展残疾人体育工作，全区县级以上残联组织残疾人群众体育健身活动 163 次，8743 人次参加。

七、维权

县级以上人大开展《中华人民共和国残疾人保障法》执法检查和专题调研 3 次；开展省级普法宣传教育活动 3 次，300 人次参加；各地残联办理建议、提案 20 件。

全区共开展无障碍环境建设检查 62 次，无障碍培训 981 人次。

八、组织建设

市县乡三级残联共有 1382 个，其中地级市残联 15 个，县（市、区）残联 111 个，乡镇（街道）残联 1256 个；已建社区（村）残协 16502 个。

自治区、市、县（市、区）、乡镇残联实有人员达 3512 人，乡镇（街道）残联、村（社区）残协选聘残疾人专职委员总计 16645 人。地市级配备了残疾人领导干部的残联有 11 个，县级配备了残疾人干部的残联有 38 个。

全区共有各类残疾人专门协会 628 个，其中省级专门协会 5 个，市级专门协会 70 个，县级专门协会 553 个。助残社会组织共有 16 个。

九、服务设施

全区已竣工的各级残疾人综合服务设施 100 个，总建设规模 175106.9 平方米，总投资 33109 万元；已竣工的各级残疾人康复设施 30 个，总建设规模 184695.5 平方米，总投资 51803.2 万元；已竣工的各级残疾人托养服务设施 29 个，总建设规模 71559.3 平方米，总投资 15819.1 万元。

2022 年海南省残疾人事业发展统计公报

2022 年，在海南省委、省政府正确领导下，在中国残联有力指导下，海南省残联全面贯彻党的二十大精神，认真贯彻落实习近平总书记关于残疾人事业的重要论述和指示批示精神，深入实施《“十四五”残疾人保障和发展规划》，推动残疾人事业和残联各项工作实现了新发展，为实现残疾人小康目标又向前推进了一步。

一、康复

2022 年，2.8 万名残疾人得到基本康复服务，2231 名残疾人得到基本辅助器具适配服务。得到康复服务的持证残疾人中，有视力残疾人 636 名、听力残疾人 487 名、言语残疾人 193 名、肢体残疾人 5124 名、智力残疾人 1424 名、精神残疾人 1.7 万名、多重残疾人 1062 名。

截至 2022 年底，有残疾人康复机构 62 个。康复机构在岗人员达 3498 人，其中，管理人员 381 人，业务人员 1222 人，其他人员 1895 人。

二、教育

2022 年，残疾人中等职业学校（班）1 个，在校生 133 人，毕业生 36 人。

三、就业

城乡持证残疾人就业人数为 4 万人，其中按比例就业 4484 人，集中就业 452 人，个体就业 1077 人，公益性岗位就业 530 人，辅助性就业 194 人，灵活就业（含社区、居家就业）7930 人，从事农业种养加 2.6 万人。

开展农村困难残疾人实用技术培训，为 4345 人次残疾人赋能。14 个残疾人就业帮扶基地共安置 204 名残疾人就业，带动 276 户残疾人家庭增收。

共培训盲人保健按摩人员 131 人次、盲人医疗按摩人员 16 人次，现有保健按摩机构 174 个。

四、社会保障

截至 2022 年底，参加城乡居民基本养老保险的残疾人数达 15.9 万名。6.5 万名残疾人领取养老金。60 岁以下参保的残疾人中，5.4 万名重度残疾人和 1.1 万名非重度残疾人得到参保缴费资助。

开展残疾人托养服务的各级各类机构达 38 个。712 名残疾人通过寄宿制和日间照料服务机构接受了托养服务，2.2 万名残疾人接受居家服务。

五、宣传文化

截至 2022 年底，共有省级电视手语栏目 1 个，地级电视手语栏目 2 个。

各级公共图书馆设立盲文及盲文有声读物阅览室 4 个，开展残疾人文化周活动 26 场次，省地两级残联艺术团 3 个。

六、维权

制定或修改保障残疾人权益的规范性文件：省级 4 个、县级 1 个。开展省级普法宣传教育活动 8 次，654 人次参加；举办省级法律培训班 5 个，608 人次参加。各地残联办理建议、提案 15 件。

共出台了 11 个省、地、县级无障碍环境建设与管理法规、政府令和规范性文件；开展无障碍环境建设检查 262 次，无障碍培训 1449 人次。

七、组织建设

2022 年，市县乡共有残联 246 个，各地市已建残联 3 个，县（市、区）已建残联 19 个，乡镇（街道）已建残联 224 个，社区（村）已建残协 3198 个。

省市县乡残联工作人员 732 人，乡镇（街道）残联、村（社区）残协专职委员总计 2655 人。地级配备了残疾人领导干部的残联 1 个，县级配备了残疾人干部的残联 7 个。

残疾人专门协会 115 个，助残社会组织 8 个。

八、服务设施

截至 2022 年底，已竣工的各级残疾人综合服务设施 9 个，总建设规模 1.2 万平方米，总投资 3690.0 万元；已竣工的各级残疾人康复设施 6 个，总建设规模 2.6 万平方米，总投资 8711.3 万元；已竣工的各级残疾人托养服务设施 5 个，总建设规模 1.4 万平方米，总投资 4879.3 万元。

2022 年重庆市残疾人事业发展统计公报

2022 年以来，重庆市残联坚持以习近平新时代中国特色社会主义思想为指导，深学笃用习近平总书记关于残疾人事业的重要指示批示精神，认真学习贯彻党的二十大和市第六次党代会精神，深入实施《重庆市“十四五”残疾人保障和发展规划》及配套实施方案，持续深化残联组织改革，着力保障和改善残疾人民生，广大残疾人获得感、幸福感、安全感显著增强，全市残疾人事业发展迈上新台阶。

一、康复

残疾人康复服务质效显著提升。制定出台《重庆市残疾预防行动实施方案（2021—2025 年）》，全面实施覆盖全人群全生命周期的残疾预防三级防控策略。大力开展精准康复服务行动，263076 名残疾人得到基本康复服务，44858 名残疾人得到基本辅助器具适配服务。得到康复服务的持证残疾人中，有视力残疾人 27659 名、听力残疾人 14552 名、言语残疾人 2552 名、肢体残疾人 104516 名、智力残疾人 24161 名、精神残疾人 70661 名、多重残疾人 13346 名。

加强服务工作规范，建设康复人才市级规范化培训基地 12 家，开展康复专业技术骨干培训 1700 余人。截至 2022 年底，有残疾人康复机构 300 个。康复机构在岗人员达 9650 人，其中，管理人员 1100 人，业务人员 6729 人，其他人员 1821 人。

二、教育

依法保障残疾人受教育权利。“一人一案”做好适龄残疾儿童少年入学安置，全市适龄残疾儿童少年义务教育入学率达到 97.63%。

2022 年，全市共有特殊教育普通高中 2 个，在校生 190 人，其中聋生 84 人，盲生 106 人。残疾人中等职业学校（班）3 个，在校生 170 人，毕业生 44 人，毕业生中 10 人获得职业资格证书。

三、就业

残疾人就业状况明显改善。开展就业援助月、“成渝双城残疾人创业先锋”大赛、高校残疾人毕业生双选会暨创业成果展等活动 86 场次，成功举办 2022 年“巴渝工匠”杯重庆市第四届残疾人职业技能竞赛暨全国残疾人岗位精英赛重庆选拔赛。

2022 年，全市城乡持证残疾人就业人数为 240755 人，其中按比例就业 19253 人，集中就业 7902 人，个体就业 18886 人，公益性岗位就业 2668 人，辅助性就业 2336 人，灵活就业（含社区、居家就业）79724 人，从事农业种养加 109986 人。

开展农村困难残疾人实用技术培训，为 11936 人次残疾人赋能。全市 112 个残疾人就业帮扶基地共安置 654 名残疾人就业，带动 1153 户残疾人家庭增收。

全市共培训盲人保健按摩人员 6002 人次、盲人医疗按摩人员 215 人次。现有保健按摩机构 500 个，医疗按摩机构 17 个。

四、社会保障

残疾人社会保障力度持续加大。截至 2022 年底，参加城乡居民基本养老保险的残疾人数达 559673 名。243460 名残疾人领取养老金。60 岁以下参保的残疾人中，146852 名重度残疾人和 49262 名非重度残疾人得到参保缴费资助。

残疾人托养服务工作稳步推进，开展残疾人托养服务的各级各类机构 141 个，其中寄宿制服务机构 21 个，日间照料机构 55 个，综合性服务机构 29 个。2189 名残疾人通过寄宿制和日间照料服务机构接受了托养服务，21265 名残疾人接受居家服务。

五、宣传文化

加大残疾人事业宣传力度，在中央、市级媒体刊发残疾人事业宣传报道 660 余条，重庆残联微信公众号传播力稳居“全国省级残联微信公众号传播指数十佳榜”。

残疾人精神文化生活更加丰富。大力发展残疾人文创产业，实施“微笑计划”，建立残疾人文化创意产业项目库。参加2022年冬残奥会延庆颁奖广场演出6场次，开展残疾人特殊艺术巡演5场次、残疾人励志报告巡讲6场次。“书香有爱•阅读无碍”残健融合阅读系列活动被评为“重庆市优秀全民阅读推广活动”。

截至2022年底，共有市级电视手语栏目1个，区县级残疾人专题广播节目9个、电视手语栏目36个。各级公共图书馆设立盲文及盲文有声读物阅览室41个，开展残疾人文化周活动395场次。市级残联艺术团1个。

六、体育

搭建残疾人康复健身交流平台，开展第十六次全国特奥日和第十二届全国残疾人健身周活动，惠及残疾人3.5万人。参加残奥射击世界杯赛获得1枚金牌，承办全国残疾人啦啦操线上邀请赛，成功举办全市2022年残疾人游泳锦标赛。创建国家级残疾人自强健身示范点1个。

七、维权

依法维护残疾人合法权益取得新成效。积极配合市人大常委会开展残疾人保障“一法一条例”执法检查，牵头做好反馈意见整改，持续提升残疾人保障水平。

2022年，制定或修改保障残疾人权益的区县级规范性文件1个。区县级以上人大开展《中华人民共和国残疾人保障法》执法检查和专题调研19次；政协开展视察和专题调研8次。开展市级普法宣传教育活动6次，500人次参加。各级残联办理建议、提案56件。

共出台了12个市级、区县级无障碍环境建设与管理法规、政府令和规范性文件；开展无障碍环境建设检查52次，无障碍培训1880人次。

着力推动惠残助残政策落实落地，为809名下肢残疾人办理绕城高速套餐，为969名外省残疾人办理主城爱心公交卡，为2357名残疾人机动轮椅车发放燃油补贴，制定出台低保残疾人家庭生活用水、用电、用气优惠政策。实施《重庆市无障碍环境建设与管理规定》，开展困难重度残疾人家庭无障碍改造1.3万余户，建设残疾人家庭无障碍改造示范村（社区）44个。

八、组织建设

基层组织和人才队伍建设焕发新活力。强化基层组织和人才队伍建设，召开全市基层残联组织改革工作推进会，举办高质量发展暨新任理事长培训班，招募87名高校应届毕业生和在读研究生“西部助残志愿者”，全市乡镇（街道）残联和村（社区）残协全部如期完成换届工作。出台《村（社区）残疾人协会工作规范》《专职委员工作规范》《关于加强和改进专门协会工作的意见》，市级专门协会围绕“党旗在残疾人中高高飘扬”主题，广泛开展检测义诊、喘息关爱、特需信托等服务；开展村（社区）残协建设成效抽查，建立“访视五看”工作机制，切实畅通联系服务残疾人的“最后一公里”。创新设立“服务精准率”指标，开展“残疾人服务精准供给行动”。扎实开展持证残疾人基本状况调查。持续推进违规持有残疾人证清理工作。

2022年，全市区县、乡镇（街道）共有残联1072个，其中，区、县残联已建41个，乡镇（街道）残联已建1031个；社区（村）已建残协11172个。

市、区县、乡镇（街道）残联工作人员2162人，乡镇（街道）残联、村（社区）残协专职委员总计10939人。县级配备了残疾人干部的残联20个。

各级残疾人专门协会200个，助残社会组织60个。

九、服务设施

残疾人服务设施建设稳步推进。扎实推进市残疾人康复中心（一期）工程建设。

截至2022年底，全市已竣工的各级残疾人综合服务设施29个，总建设规模101259.2平方米，总投资34747.1万元；已竣工的各级残疾人康复设施21个，总建设规模201980.6平方米，总投资79522.9万元；已竣工的各级残疾人托养服务设施13个，总建设规模64225.9平方米，总投资19347.3万元。

2022 年四川省残疾人事业发展统计公报

2022 年，四川省残联坚定以习近平新时代中国特色社会主义思想为指导，全面贯彻党的二十大精神，认真贯彻落实习近平总书记关于残疾人事业重要论述和重要指示批示精神，深入实施《四川省“十四五”残疾人保障和发展规划》，推进四川省残疾人事业高质量发展。

一、康复

贯彻落实《四川省“十四五”残疾人发展和保障规划》《四川省残疾预防行动计划（2022—2025 年）》《四川省<残疾预防和残疾人康复条例>实施办法》和《四川省残疾人康复服务实施方案（2022—2025 年）》，深入贯彻实施《四川省人民政府关于建立残疾儿童康复救助制度的实施意见》，推动“十四五”残疾预防和残疾人康复工作高质量发展。2022 年四川省有 973287 名残疾人得到基本康复服务，127066 名残疾人得到基本辅助器具适配服务。得到康复服务的持证残疾人中，有视力残疾人 134442 名、听力残疾人 70970 名、言语残疾人 6118 名、肢体残疾人 537705 名、智力残疾人 61801 名、精神残疾人 116712 名、多重残疾人 39267 名。

截至 2022 年底，四川省有残疾人康复机构 365 个，在岗人员达 13347 人，其中，管理人员 1244 人，业务人员 10241 人，其他人员 1862 人。

二、教育

会同教育厅印发《四川省辅助器具进校园工程实施方案》，积极推进“辅具进校园工程”试点工作。积极参与《四川省“十四五”特殊教育发展提升实施方案》，将“加快推广国家通用手语盲文”纳入文件重点任务分工。突出抓好“单考单招”和“重点高校招生专项计划”，单考单招高校增加至 14 所。

2022 年，四川省共有特殊教育普通高中（部、班）9 个，在校生 923 人，其中聋生 585 人，盲生 139 人，其他 199 人。残疾人中等职业学校（班）7 个，在校生 370 人，毕业生 35 人。

三、就业

2022 年，四川省城乡持证残疾人就业人数为 854215 人，其中按比例就业 24481 人，集中就业 10438 人，个体就业 50108 人，公益性岗位就业 6696 人，辅助性就业 14686 人，灵活就业（含社区、居家就业）376908 人，从事农业种养加 370898 人。开展农村困难残疾人实用技术培训，为 47586 人次残疾人赋能。161 个残疾人就业帮扶基地共安置 2150 名残疾人就业，带动 3657 户残疾人家庭增收。四川省共培训盲人保健按摩人员 98 人次、盲人医疗按摩人员 7 人次。现有保健按摩机构 967 个，医疗按摩机构 56 个，1 人获得盲人医疗按摩人员初级职务任职资格。

四、社会保障

截至 2022 年底，四川省参加城乡居民基本养老保险的残疾人数达 2320037 名。1027569 名残疾人领取养老金。60 岁以下参保的残疾人中，527796 名重度残疾人和 227635 名非重度残疾人得到参保缴费资助。残疾人托养工作稳步推进，开展残疾人托养服务的各级各类机构达 260 个，其中寄宿制服务机构 42 个，日间照料机构 35 个，综合性服务机构 61 个。5263 名残疾人通过寄宿制和日间照料服务机构接受了托养服务，70362 名残疾人接受居家服务。

五、宣传文化

2022 年，“四川残联”微信公众号发布图文信息 706 篇，阅读量 113.4 万；官方微博全年阅读量过万博文 400 余条，累计阅读量达 8000 万余次；四川残联官方抖音号发布作品 1244 个，粉丝 100.1 万，2022 年浏览量 9586.7 万。

截至 2022 年底，四川省共有省级残疾人专题广播节目 1 个、电视手语栏目 1 个，地级残疾人专题广播节目 8 个、电视手语栏目 13 个。各级公共图书馆设立盲文及盲文有声读物阅览室 105 个，开展残疾人文化周活动 609 场次，省地两级残联艺术团 8 个。

六、体育

2022 年北京冬残奥会上，四川省残疾运动员首次入选国家队参赛，获得 1 个第四名、1 个第五名。承办四川省第十届残运会暨第五届特奥会，赛事共设置大项 25 个，设项数量和参赛人数均为历届最多；对标全国残运会暨特奥会项目设置，新增跆拳道、女子聋人篮球项目；首次设置五人制聋人足球、飞镖等 5 个残疾人大众比赛项目；响应“三亿人上冰雪”号召，首次设立冰壶运动的陆地版本旱地冰壶项目；完成射击、射箭等 6 个残运会提前比赛项目和特奥田径、游泳等 4 个特奥会提前比赛项目赛事，共产生 294 枚奖牌。联合教育厅、省体育局在全省特殊教育学校开展“体育复健进校园”，进一步推动特校体育常态化、规范化开展，推动我省残疾人竞技体育、群众体育和特奥运动健康协调发展。2022 年全省各级残疾人群众性体育活动 778 场次，较 2021 年增长 26.7%。

七、维权

2022 年，四川省制定《四川省〈残疾预防和残疾人康复条例〉实施办法》；制定或修改保障残疾人权益的规范性文件：地级 1 个、县级 26 个。县级以上人大开展《中华人民共和国残疾人保障法》执法检查和专题调研 40 次；政协开展视察和专题调研 23 次。开展省级普法宣传教育活动 2 次，1000 人次参加；举办省级法律培训班 1 个，70 人次参加。各地残联办理建议、提案 100 件。四川省共出台了 38 个省、地、县级无障碍环境建设与管理法规、政府令和规范性文件；开展无障碍环境建设检查 1480 次，无障碍培训 3184 人次。

八、组织建设

2022 年，四川省共有市县乡残联 2829 个，各地市已建残联 21 个，县（市、区）已建残联 190 个，乡镇（街道）已建残联 2618 个，社区（村）已建残协 32864 个。省市县乡残联工作人员 7075 人，乡镇（街道）残联、村（社区）残协专职委员总计 40277 人。地级配备了残疾人领导干部的残联 12 个，县级配备了残疾人干部的残联 93 个，残疾人专门协会 967 个，助残社会组织 164 个。

九、服务设施

截至 2022 年底，四川省已竣工的各级残疾人综合服务设施 165 个，总建设规模 450398.3 平方米，总投资 136682.2 万元；已竣工的各级残疾人康复设施 55 个，总建设规模 284925.1 平方米，总投资 110610.9 万元；已竣工的各级残疾人托养服务设施 42 个，总建设规模 115162.3 平方米，总投资 32005.8 万元。

2022 年贵州省残联人事业发展统计公报

2022 年，贵州省各级残联坚持以习近平新时代中国特色社会主义思想为指导，深入学习贯彻习近平总书记关于残疾人事业的重要论述和指示批示精神，全面贯彻党的二十大精神，深入实施《贵州省“十四五”残疾人保障和发展规划》，按照党中央、国务院及贵州省委、省政府决策部署，积极推进残疾人事业高质量发展。

一、康复

12.2 万名残疾人得到基本康复服务，3.5 万名残疾人得到基本辅助器具适配服务。得到康复服务的持证残疾人中，有视力残疾人 1.3 万名、听力残疾人 7798 名、言语残疾人 1362 名、肢体残疾人 6.1 万名、智力残疾人 8777 名、精神残疾人 1.3 万名、多重残疾人 1.2 万名。

截至 2022 年底，有残疾人康复机构 295 个。康复机构在岗人员达 1.1 万人，其中，管理人员 1225 人，业务人员 7636 人，其他人员 2161 人。

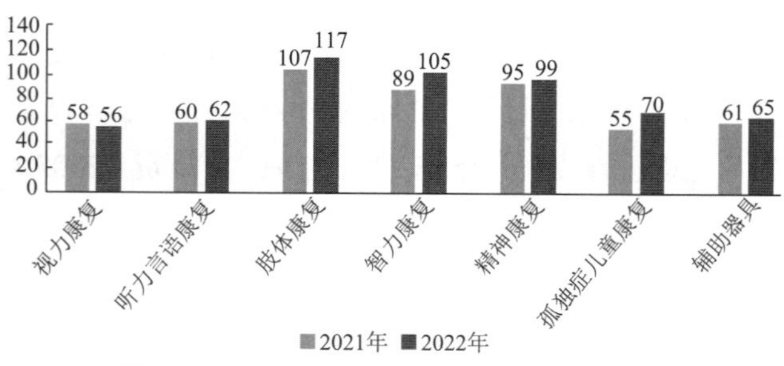

图 1　2021/2022 年度开展康复业务的康复机构数（单位：个）

二、教育

全省共有特殊教育学校 79 所，残疾儿童少年义务教育入学率达到 96.8%。共有特殊教育普通高中（部、班）6 个，在校生 708 人，其中聋生 630 人，盲生 78 人。残疾人中等职业学校 1 所，共有 34 个教学班，在校生 615 人，毕业 4 届学生，毕业生中 15 人获得职业资格证书（盲医资格证）。

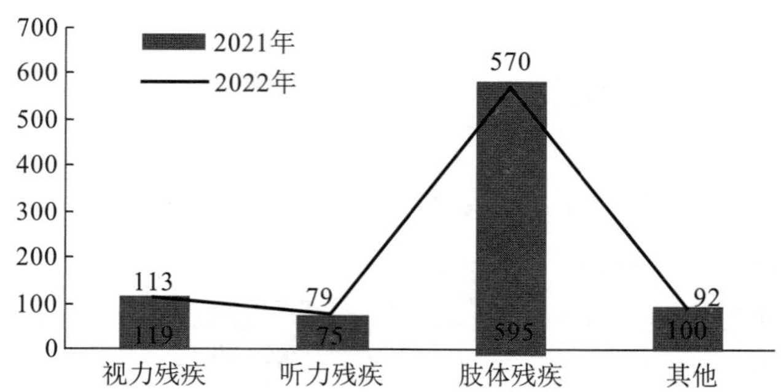

图 2　2021/2022 年普通高等院校当年录取残疾人考生人数对比（单位：人）

三、就业

城乡持证残疾人就业人数为 40 万人，其中按比例就业 1.1 万人，集中就业 6836 人，个体就业 2.3 万人，公益性岗位就业 5231 人，辅助性就业 2887 人，灵活就业（含社区、居家就业）14.3 万人，从事农业种养加 20.8 万人。

开展农村困难残疾人实用技术培训，为 4531 人次残疾人赋能。135 个残疾人就业帮扶基地共安置 1071 名残疾人就业，带动 2075 户残疾人家庭增收。

共培训盲人保健按摩人员 554 人次、盲人医疗按摩人员 199 人次。现有保健按摩机构 352 个，医疗按摩机构 14 个。143 人获得盲人医疗按摩人员初级职务任职资格，34 人获得中级职务任职资格。

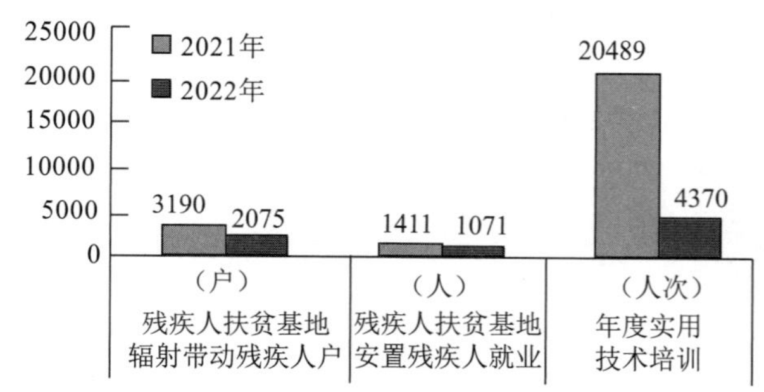

图 3　2021 年与 2022 年扶贫情况比较

四、社会保障

截至 2022 年底，参加城乡居民基本养老保险的残疾人数达 96.6 万名。40.4 万名残疾人领取养老金。60 岁以下参保的残疾人中，21.5 万名重度残疾人和

6.8万名非重度残疾人得到参保缴费资助。

开展残疾人托养服务的各级各类机构达135个，其中寄宿制服务机构9个，综合性服务机构42个。1199名残疾人通过寄宿制和日间照料服务机构接受了托养服务，9581名残疾人接受居家服务。

五、宣传文化

截至2022年底，共有省级残疾人专题广播节目1个、电视手语栏目1个，地级残疾人专题广播节目3个、电视手语栏目7个。

各级公共图书馆设立盲文及盲文有声读物阅览室30个，开展残疾人文化周活动102场次，省地两级残联艺术团5个。

六、体育

截至2022年底，共有省级残疾人群众体育活动示范点32个。积极组织开展“特奥日活动”“残疾人冰雪运动季”“残疾人健身周”等群众性体育活动，共开展残疾人群众体育健身活动107次，3264人次残疾人群众参加活动。

七、维权

制定或修改保障残疾人权益的规范性文件：地级1个、县级3个。县级以上人大开展《中华人民共和国残疾人保障法》执法检查和专题调研3次；政协开展视察和专题调研1次。开展省级普法宣传教育活动2次，300人次参加；举办省级法律培训班1个，200人次参加。各地残联办理建议、提案18件。

共出台了5个省、地、县级无障碍环境建设与管理法规、政府令和规范性文件；开展无障碍环境建设检查254次，无障碍培训385人次。

八、组织建设

2022年，市县乡共有残联1609个，各地市已建残联9个，县（市、区）已建残联91个（含新浦新区、黄果树旅游区社会事务管理局、义龙新区），乡镇（街道）已建残联1509个，社区（村）已建残协1.8万个。

省市县乡残联工作人员3641人，乡镇（街道）残联、村（社区）残协专职委员总计1.3万人。地级配备了残疾人领导干部的残联7个，县级配备了残疾人干部的残联65个。

残疾人专门协会458个，助残社会组织15个。

九、服务设施

截至2022年底，已竣工的各级残疾人综合服务设施54个，总建设规模6.3万平方米，总投资1.3亿元；已竣工的各级残疾人康复设施36个，总建设规模32.6万平方米，总投资9.1亿元；已竣工的各级残疾人托养服务设施70个，总建设规模26.1万平方米，总投资7亿元。

2022 年云南省残疾人事业发展统计公报

2022 年，全省各级残联始终坚持以习近平新时代中国特色社会主义思想为指导，全面贯彻落实党的二十大精神，深入贯彻落实习近平总书记关于残疾人事业的重要论述、重要指示批示和考察云南重要讲话精神，认真贯彻落实省委第十一届三次全会精神，忠诚拥护“两个确立”，切实增强“四个意识”，坚定“四个自信”、做到“两个维护”，紧紧围绕省委“3815”战略目标，深入实施《云南省“十四五”残疾人保障和发展规划》，努力推动残疾人事业全面发展。

一、康复

2022 年，省残联积极推进全省残疾人精准康复服务行动，全面贯彻落实残疾儿童康复救助制度，实施重点残疾人康复救助工程，加快实现残疾人“人人享有康复服务”的目标，残疾人康复水平不断提高。全省共有 24.81 万名残疾儿童和持证残疾人获得基本康复服务，其中，共为 5.03 万名残疾人提供各类辅助器具适配服务，共为 10.4 万名农村低收入残疾人提供服务。

按照年龄结构划分，2022 年全省共有 1.91 万名残疾儿童得到基本康复服务，其中包括 0-6 岁残疾儿童 7088 名，7-17 岁残疾儿童 12044 名；共有 22.9 万名成年残疾人得到康复服务，其中 18-59 岁残疾人 13.85 万名，60 岁以上残疾人 9.05 万名。

按照残疾类别划分，2022 年得到康复服务的持证残疾人中，视力残疾人占 9.72%，为 2.41 万名；听力残疾人占 8.55%，为 2.12 万名；言语残疾人占 0.99%，为 2453 名；肢体残疾人占 45.1%，为 11.22 万名；智力残疾人占 6.2%，为 1.53 万名；精神残疾人占 21.77%，为 5.4 万名；多重残疾人占 6.17%，为 1.53 万名；非持证的残疾儿童占 1.5%，为 3554 名。

按照服务内容划分（包括获得多项服务情况），2022 年获得康复医疗服务 4.37 万名，获得康复训练 1.9 万名，获得辅助器具服务 5.03 万名，获得支持性服务 14.34 万名。

截至 2022 年底，全省 102 个县（市、区）开展了社区康复服务，共建设康复服务设施 1001 个，总共 11771 个社区（村）中配备了 13225 名社区康复协调员；其中 11947 名社区协调员接受过系统培训，接受培训率 90%。

截至 2022 年底，全省共有残疾人康复机构 279 个，其中，50 个机构提供视力残疾康复服务，80 个机构提供听力语言残疾康复服务，115 个机构提供肢体残疾康复服务，107 个机构提供智力残疾康复服务，99 个机构提供精神残疾康复服务，116 个机构提供辅助器具适配服务。在这 279 个康复机构中，属于残联系统的有 102 个，属于卫生系统的有 103 个，属于民政系统的有 5 个，属于教育系统的有 22 个，属于民办机构的有 33 个，其他机构有 14 个。各类康复机构在岗服务人员达 10467 名，其中，管理人员 1108 名，业务人员 7907 名，其他人员 1452 名。各类机构服务人员中，有 774 名提供视力残疾康复服务，有 631 名提供听力语言残疾康复服务，有 2569 名提供肢体残疾康复服务，有 2567 名提供智力残疾康复服务，有 3489 名提供精神残疾康复服务，有 267 名提供辅助器具适配服务，有 170 名提供孤独症康复服务。全年共培训康复管理人员 3496 人次，培训康复业务人员 16231 人次。

二、教育

截至 2022 年底，全省累计共有残疾人中等职业学校（班）5 个，均为教育部门办学，在校生 643 人，其中聋生 365 人、盲生 166 人、肢残 10 人、其他 30 人；本年度毕业生 116 人。

全省共有高等特殊教育机构 1 个，2022 年共招生 101 人，其中聋生 23 人，盲生 9 人，其他 69 人。2022 年，我省残疾人考生达到录取分数线 1191 人，普通高等院校录取残疾考生 1170 人，其中聋生 131 人，盲生 144 人，肢残 761 人，其他 134 人。

共资助家庭经济困难的在校残疾高中生、残疾大学新生和家庭经济困难残疾人子女（在校高中、大学新生）2420名。

三、就业

截至2022年底，全省城乡持证残疾人就业人数为42.63万名，按照就业形式划分，其中按比例就业2.75万名，集中就业6804名，个体就业（含创业）1.74万名，公益性岗位就业3961名，辅助性就业3442名，从事农业种养加27.07万名，灵活就业（包括社区就业、居家就业）10.18万名。

四、社会保障

截至2022年，全省符合参加城乡社会养老保险条件的残疾居民为127.86万人，其中重度残疾人有47.69万名。本年度实际参保残疾居民120.06万名中，领取待遇的有49.19万名，领取待遇的残疾人中有重度残疾人18.33万名，60周岁以下参保残疾人有70.88万名，其中有重度残疾人26.98万名，非重度残疾人43.89万人。参保重度残疾人中有26.39万名获得全额代缴保险费用，0.53万名获得部分代缴保险费用，非重度参保残疾人中有12.05万人获得全额代缴保险费用，12.29万人获得部分代缴保险费用。

全省全年为21882名符合条件的智力、精神和重度肢体残疾人提供托养服务，其中居家托养服务18096人，日间照料1278人，机构托养2508人。

五、宣传文化体育

2022年，全省开展助残日主题宣传活动180多场，残疾人事业得到广泛宣传。涌现出“全国道德模范”“云岭楷模”荣誉称号获得者张顺东、李国秀夫妇等一批自强先进典型。

截至2022年底，省级共有残疾人专题电视手语栏目1个，广播电台残疾人专题节目2个，开通1个省级残疾人联合会官方微信；州（市）残联残疾人广播电台残疾人专题节目5个、电视手语栏目7个。全省各级公共图书馆共设立盲文及盲文有声读物图书室55个，其中省级1个，州市级16个，县区级39个。全年共开展残疾人文化周活动177场次，其中省残联举办1场次，参与300人次，州（市）残联举办12场次，参与3096人次，县（市、区）残联举办164场次，参与10753人次。州（市）级残联共举办残疾人文化艺术类的比赛及展览9次。

2022年云南省向国家输送7名残疾人运动员参加北京冬残奥会，获得了3金2银1铜。

全省各级共组织残疾人群众进行体育健身活动5666场次，参与残疾人4.12万人次。其中省级举办4场次，参与残疾人1262人次；各州（市）举办45场次，参与残疾人3544人次；县区级举办5617场次，参与残疾人3.64万人次。

共有省级残疾人体育训练基地7个，聘任教练员18名。

六、维权与信访

2022年全省各级残联累计接到来信33件，来电10通。来信来电中，残疾人涉法涉诉类12例，占比36%；医疗康复类4例，占比12%；教育类1例，占比3%；就业扶贫类1例，占比3%；社会保障类3例，占比9%；权益保障类3例，占比9%；意见建议类5例，占比15%；控告检举类3例，占比9%；其他类1例，占比4%。

2022年全省各级残联累计接待涉残疾人来访120（114）人次，个人来访120人次，集体来访0批次，0人次。个人来访中涉法涉诉类23人次，占比21%；医疗康复类14人次，占比12%；教育类4人次，占比3%；就业类11人次，占比10%；社会保障类19人次，占比16%；权益保障类10人次，占比9%；意见建议类2人次，占比2%；控告检举类0人次，占比0%；其他类31人次，占比27%。（非残6人次占比5%）

七、组织建设

2022年，云南省残联机关有编制65个，实有人员65名，其中残疾人干部有7名。省残联直属7个事业单位，共有编制206个，实有人员187名。

16个州（市）残联中的12个配备了残疾人领导干部，共有编制208个，实有工作人员214名，其中残疾人领导干部12名，一般残疾人干部30名。州（市）残联共有直属事业单位共28个，共有编制172个，实有人员148名，其中残疾人工作者13名；各州（市）2022年共举办综合培训班7期，参加培训人次达176人次；共举办残疾人干部培训班4期，参加培训人次 246 人次；共有 195 名助残志愿者为 4543 名残疾人提供了志愿助残服务。

全省共有 129 个县（市、区）和 3 个开发区建立了残联，其中 101 个残联机关配备了残疾人领导干部，县（市、区）残联机关共有编制 1073 个，实有人员 1330 名，其中残疾人干部 176 名；县（市、区）残联共有直属事业单位 107 个，共有编制 371 个，实有人员 427 名。各县（市、区）共举办 165 期干部培训班，参加培训人次 6618 人次；共有 1666 名助残志愿者为 82214 万名残疾人提供了志愿助残服务。

全省共有 1425 个乡镇（街道）建立了残联，共有编制 1359 个，实有人员 1527 名，其中专职残联理事长有 482 名，兼职残联理事长有 459 名，乡镇级残疾人专职委员 1694 名。乡镇（街道）残联共举办培训班 959 期，参加培训人次 11359 人次；共有 3003 名助残志愿者为 70238 名残疾人提供了志愿助残服务。

全省已建村（农村社区）残协 12879 个，已建城市社区残协 1923 个；全省共建设残疾人活动室 4788 个，其中村（农村社区）建立 4104 个，城市社区建立 684 个；全省各村、社区共配备残疾人专职委员 12567 名，其中农村（农村社区）配备 11046 名，城市社区配备 1521 名。共有 3313 名助残志愿者为 123023 名残疾人提供了志愿助残服务。

截至 2022 年底，全省共建立省级及以下各类残疾人专门协会 703 个，其中盲人协会省级 1 个、州（市）级 16 个、县（市、区）级 128 个；聋人协会省级 1 个、州（市）级 15 个、县（市、区）级 128 个；肢残人协会省级 1 个、州（市）级 16 个、县（市、区）级 128 个；智力残疾人及亲友协会省级 1 个、州（市）级 15 个、县（市、区）级 118 个；精神残疾人及亲友协会省级 1 个、州（市）级 15 个、县（市、区）级 119 个。

截至 2022 年底，全省各级共有助残社会组织为 17 个，其中，社会团体 7 个，基金会 1 个，社会服务机构 9 个。

八、服务设施

截至 2022 年底，全省累计已竣工的各级残疾人综合服务设施 118 个，总建设规模 15.6 万平方米，总投资 2.9 亿元。2022 年在建项目 1 个，总建设规模 0.56 万平方米，总投资 772 万元。

截至 2022 年底，全省已竣工的各级残疾人托养服务设施 51 个，总建设规模 13.04 万平方米，总投资 3.81 亿元。其中本年度新竣工项目 6 个，总建设规模 1.92 万平方米，总投资 5249.94 万元。2022 年在建项目 11 个，总建设规模 3.68 万平方米，总投资 1.05 亿元。

截至 2022 年底，全省已竣工的各级残疾人康复服务设施 20 个，总建设规模 15.07 万平方米，总投资 4.8 亿元。其中本年度新竣工项目 3 个，总建设规模 2.33 万平方米，总投资 7180.84 万元。2022 年在建项目 8 个，总建设规模 6.78 万平方米，总投资 1.98 亿元。

2022年西藏自治区残疾人事业发展统计公报

2022年，在中国残联的大力指导下，在自治区党委、政府的正确引领下，全区各级残联系统深入学习贯彻习近平新时代中国特色社会主义思想，认真贯彻中国残联、自治区党委、政府的各项决策部署。切实把思想和行动统一到中国残联、自治区党委、政府的安排部署上来，把力量凝聚到聚焦“四件大事”、聚力“四个创建”上来，推动残疾人事业在科学理论指导下全面发展。

一、康复服务取得新成效

着力推进健康西藏建设，制定《西藏自治区残疾人预防行动计划（2022-2025年）》，全面提高全区残疾风险综合防控能力。深入实施《残疾预防和残疾人康复条例》，推进精准康复服务行动和残疾儿童康复救助，2022年，全区共有16502名残疾人得到基本康复服务，13687名残疾人得到基本辅助器具适配服务。其中，视力残疾人2476名、听力残疾人2313名、言语残疾人373名、肢体残疾人9572名、智力残疾人108名、精神残疾人228名、多重残疾人1426名。

截至2022年底，全区共有残疾人康复机构11个。康复机构在岗人员97人，其中，管理人员28人，业务人员40人，其他人员29人，全年共培训康复业务人员110人次。

二、残疾人教育有新提升

教育部门大力推进特殊教育发展，义务教育阶段残疾学生入学率继续保持在97%以上。2022年，全区共有83名残疾考生达到录取分数线，其中72名残疾考生被全国各类高等院校录取。

三、残疾人就业创业状况进一步改善

制定《西藏自治区贯彻落实〈促进残疾人就业三年行动方案(2022-2024年)〉重点任务分工方案》，认真落实《机关、事业单位、国有企业带头安排残疾人就业办法》，统筹落实促进残疾人就业的各项政策措施，发挥就业政策叠加效应，多渠道、多形式、多业态促进残疾人就业。2022年，城乡持证残疾人就业人数为19184人，其中按比例就业1316人，集中就业455人，个体就业747人，公益性岗位就业312人，辅助性就业268人，灵活就业（含社区、居家就业）10353人，从事农业种养加5733人。开展农村困难残疾人实用技术培训，为940人次残疾人赋能。

共培训盲人保健按摩人员14人次、盲人医疗按摩人员10人次。现有保健按摩机构33个。

四、残疾人社会保障水平稳步增长

截至2022年底，参加城乡居民基本养老保险的残疾人数达102343名。30046名残疾人领取养老金。60岁以下参保的残疾人中，18632名重度残疾人和8674名非重度残疾人得到参保缴费资助。

残疾人托养服务工作扎实推进，组织专门力量深入七地市27个县区86户残疾人家中，开展残疾人信息核查工作，自治区残疾人托养中心集中托养首批9名残疾人通过寄宿制和日间照料服务机构接受了托养服务，211名残疾人接受居家服务。

五、残疾人宣传、文体工作收获新成果

为参加第十一届残运会暨第八届特奥会的运动员、教练员兑现奖励资金356.3万元，激励更多的残疾人参与体育康复运动，提高身体素质，积极融入社会。第十届全国残疾人艺术汇演线上比赛（西部片区）中，我区选送的6个节目获得3个一等奖、3个二等奖和组织奖。2022年，全区各级公共图书馆设立盲文及盲文有声读物阅览室4个，开展残疾人文化周活动3场次。持续推进“五个一”服务，残疾人精神文化生活不断丰富。

六、残联自身组织建设持续巩固

2022年，全区各级共有残联82个，各地市已

建残联 7 个，县（市、区）已建残联 74 个，社区（村）已建残协 4311 个。全区各级残联实有工作人员 404 人，乡镇（街道）残联、村（社区）残协专职委员总计 71 人。市、地级配备了残疾人领导干部的残联 3 个，县级配备了残疾人干部的残联 9 个。残疾人专门协会 13 个。

七、残疾人服务设施保障得到增强

截至 2022 年底，已竣工的各级残疾人综合服务设施 52 个，总建设规模 64230.1 平方米，总投资 21425.0 万元；已竣工的各级残疾人康复设施 16 个，总建设规模 40673.1 平方米，总投资 14651.0 万元；已竣工的各级残疾人托养服务设施 5 个，总建设规模 19799.7 平方米，总投资 6749.8 万元。

2022年陕西省残疾人事业发展统计公报

2022年，全省残联系统以习近平新时代中国特色社会主义思想为指导，全面贯彻落实党的二十大精神和习近平总书记来陕考察重要讲话重要指示，按照省第十四次党代会部署，坚持稳中求进工作总基调，紧紧围绕实施《陕西省“十四五”残疾人保障和发展规划》，锐意进取、开拓创新，残疾人事业发展取得新成效。

一、康复

贯彻落实中国残联《“十四五”残疾人保障和发展规划》、陕西省《残疾预防行动计划（2021-2025年）》和《“十四五”残疾人康复服务实施方案》，推动“十四五”残疾预防和残疾人康复工作高质量发展。深入贯彻实施《国务院关于建立残疾儿童康复救助制度的意见》，加强和改进残疾儿童康复救助服务，提升残疾儿童家庭获得感，1.4万残疾儿童得到康复救助。持续开展残疾人精准康复服务行动，2022年全省共有55.4万名有康复需求残疾儿童和持证残疾人接受康复服务，6.8万残疾人得到辅助器具适配服务。得到康复服务的残疾人中，有视力残疾人59756名、听力残疾人48713名、言语残疾人330名、肢体残疾人31.1万名、智力残疾人34042名、精神残疾人52471名、多重残疾人39806名、0-17岁非持证残疾儿童8117名。

加强残疾人康复机构与人才队伍建设，深化社区康复工作。制定了《陕西省残联系统康复专业技术人员省级规范化培训基地遴选及管理办法（试行）》，遴选确定一批省级规范化培训基地，开展全省残联系统康复专业技术人员省级规范化培训，提升康复服务规范化水平。截至2022年底，全省有残疾人康复机构346个，康复机构在岗人员10106人。

二、教育

会同省教育厅等7部门印发《陕西省“十四五”特殊教育发展提升行动方案》，会同省委宣传部、省教育厅等7部门印发《陕西省手语和盲文规范化行动计划（2021—2025年）》，成立全省国家通用手语和盲文推广中心和讲师团，培训手语和盲文骨干150人。对1045名残疾大学生和困难残疾人家庭大学生给予一次性资助，有效减轻了家庭负担。指导省城市经济学校完成172名残疾学生招生任务。

全省共有特殊教育普通高中（部、班）1个，在校生29人均为盲生，残疾人中等职业学校（班）6个，在校生1780人。高等教育阶段，招收272名残疾学生，其中，高职（专科）121人，本科151人。

三、就业

全省城乡新增残疾人就业18481人，其中，城镇新增就业2759人，农村新增就业15722人；全省城乡实名培训残疾人20271人。

全省城乡持证残疾人就业人数为26.1万人，其中，按比例就业10637人，集中就业4013人，个体就业16453人，公益性岗位就业5081人，辅助性就业4133人，灵活就业78384人，从事农村种养加14.2万人。

开展农村困难残疾人实用技术培训，为8521人次残疾人赋能。对5128名农村残疾人开展阳光增收扶持，对79个农村助残增收基地进行扶持，辐射带动2584残疾人户增收。

全省共培训盲人保健按摩人员124人次，盲人医疗按摩人员245人次。现有保健按摩机构575个，医疗按摩机构20个。36人获得盲人医疗按摩人员初级职务任职资格。

四、社会保障

截至2022年底，参加城乡居民基本养老保险残疾人104.6万人，42.4万名残疾人领取养老金。60岁以下参保残疾人中，52.2万名重度残疾人和非重度残疾人得到参保缴费资助。全省发放残疾人两项补贴 120.9 万人次，其中生活补贴 74.8 万人，护理补贴 46.1 万人。全省落实残疾人临时救助 2648 人，解决基本生活困难，摆脱临时困境。为全省 5 万名残疾人专职委员、个体就业（自主创业）、公益性岗位就业以及其他困难残疾人购买意外伤害保险，为实现稳定就业和生活提供了有效保障，减轻了家庭负担和后顾之忧。

残疾人托养服务工作稳步推进，开展残疾人托养服务的机构 197 个，其中，寄宿制服务机构 40 个，日间照料机构 19 个，居家服务机构 80 个，综合托养服务机构 58 个。20308 名残疾人享受托养服务，其中 4920 名残疾人通过寄宿制和日间照料服务机构接受托养服务，15388 名残疾人接受居家服务。

五、宣传文化

深入学习宣传贯彻党的二十大精神，安排部署省残联直属单位意识形态工作责任制督导检查工作，省残联官网审核发布稿件 492 篇，微信公众号 627 篇，头条 757 篇，抖音视频 105 条，“陕西省残疾人联合会微信公众号”获得 2022 年陕西省“走好网上群众路线”百个成绩突出账号优秀账号；编辑《共沐阳光》《秦风热线》等广播节目 40 多期。以“促进残疾人就业，保障残疾人权益”为主题，组织开展第三十二次“全国助残日”活动；积极推荐“人民幸福生活是最大的人权主题采访活动”采访线索；开展“强国复兴有我”主题宣传教育活动；举办 2022 年陕西省残联系统宣传干部暨通讯员培训班；联合省记协开展了 2020-2021 年度全省残疾人事业好新闻评选活动，其中 3 件作品在中国残联第十六届残疾人事业好新闻奖评选活动中，分别获得两个二等奖、一个三等奖；联合中国残疾人事业新闻宣传促进会以“就业优先平等共享”为主题，组织开展“云看陕西残疾人事业”宣传活动；与陕西广播电视台新闻综合频道合作，在《第一新闻午间播报》《晚间新闻站》等栏目开设电视手语栏目；与陕西广电网络传媒（集团）股份有限公司联合开展《陕西省“光明影院”公益点播专区运营项目》，在陕西境内有线电视平台统一上线“光明影院”公益点播专区；认真做好舆情监测及处置，按照《陕西省残疾人联合会舆情应对工作机制》每月对涉及我省残疾人的舆情信息进行汇总，统计舆情月报、半年报、全年报共 14 份；与省委宣传部、省委网信办、省委文明办、省文化和旅游厅、省广播电视局联合制定了《陕西省“十四五”提升残疾人文化服务能力实施方案》；联合省文化和旅游厅印发《2022 年度盲人阅览室规范化建设项目实施方案》；开展主题为“奋进新征程喜迎二十大”残疾人文化周活动，制作播出了 16 期广播人物系列专访节目并同步在“学习强国”陕西学习平台发布，在“学习强国”【百灵•炫】中展播残疾人文艺作品 5 条；联合省图书馆开展“关爱听力健康，聆听精彩未来”全国“爱耳日”科普宣传义诊活动、“传承中华美德弘扬传统文化”成语故事分享沙龙线上活动、“奋进新征程喜迎二十大”2022 年残疾人文化周无障碍观影活动、“在线无障碍观影操作指南分享会”直播活动；高质量出版《陕西残疾人》杂志 10 期，合订本一期。全省共有电视手语栏目 3 个，广播电台残疾人专题节目 2 个，公共图书馆盲文及盲人有声读物图书室 68 个，开展残疾人文化周活动 94 场次，全省各级残疾人艺术团 7 个。

六、体育

实施残疾人康复健身体育行动，组织开展第七届中国残疾人冰雪运动季系列活动、第 12 届残疾人健身周及第十六次全国特奥日系列活动、全国残疾人线上跳绳比赛和全国啦啦操、三人制篮球、轮椅舞蹈邀请赛、旱地冰壶城市挑战赛等 10 多次全国性残疾人线上线下比赛活动。在第 13 届冬残奥会上，陕西省运动员刘子旭、王涛获得 1 金 1 铜和 6 个前七名的好成绩，展现了陕西省残疾人运动员自强不息的奋斗精神。

组织 100 多名残疾人运动员开展 2023 年亚残运会和 2024 年残奥会训练工作。为备战 2025 年粤港澳全国残特奥会，在初选的 125 名后备人才基础上，又选拔出 15 名优秀队员，分配到各训练基地参加集训。

在宝鸡市建成 10 个国家级残疾人康复健身示范点，同时完成 40 个省级残疾人康复健身示范点申报工作。

七、维权

2022 年，县级以上人大、政协开展残疾人“一法四条例”执法检查和专题调研 7 次，开展省级普法宣传教育活动 4 次、38 万人次参加。举办省级法律培训班 1 期、70 人次参加。全省现有残疾人法律救助工作协调机构 121 个、残疾人法律救助工作站 120 个。2022 年度为 16071 名困难重度残疾人家庭实施了无障碍改造，为 7334 名残疾人发放了残疾人机动轮椅车燃油补贴。

八、组织建设

全省市县乡共有残联 1377 个，各市、县、乡已全部成立残联，村（社区）均建立残协，共 20033 个。

地方各级残联工作人员 2726 人，乡镇（街道）残联、村（社区）残协专职委员共计 22622 人，10 个地市级残联配备了 8 名残疾人领导干部，62%的县级残联配备了残疾人干部。

全省现有省级助残社会组织 5 个，各级残疾人专门协会 577 个，市级各类专门协会全部建立，县级已建比例为 97.6%。

九、服务设施

残疾人服务设施建设得到全面发展。截至 2022 年底，全省已竣工的各级残疾人综合服务设施 77 个，总建设规模 16.4 万平方米，总投资 4.3 亿元；已竣工各级残疾人康复设施 40 个，总建设规模 12.3 万平方米，总投资 5.8 亿元；已竣工的各级残疾人托养服务设施 50 个，总建设规模 12.6 万平方米，总投资 1.9 亿元。

2022 年甘肃省残疾人事业发展统计公报

2022 年，全省残疾人工作以习近平新时代中国特色社会主义思想为指导，全面贯彻党的二十大精神、省第十四次党代会精神，认真贯彻落实习近平总书记对甘肃重要讲话重要指示批示精神、关于残疾人工作的重要论述，坚持系统思维，坚持稳中求进工作总基调，完整、准确、全面贯彻新发展理念，深入实施《甘肃省“十四五”残疾人保障和发展规划》，更好统筹发展和安全，全面推进残疾人事业高质量发展。

一、康复

2022 年，残疾人康复服务水平不断提升。残疾人精准康复服务行动目标任务圆满完成，13.3 万持证残疾人及残疾儿童得到基本康复服务，其中 0-6 岁残疾儿童 0.6 万人。得到康复服务的人中有视力残疾人 1.3 万、听力残疾人 1.3 万、言语残疾人 0.06 万、肢体残疾人 6.6 万、智力残疾人 0.9 万、精神残疾人 1.5 万、多重残疾人 1.2 万。4.6 万残疾人得到各类基本辅助器具适配服务。（见图 1）

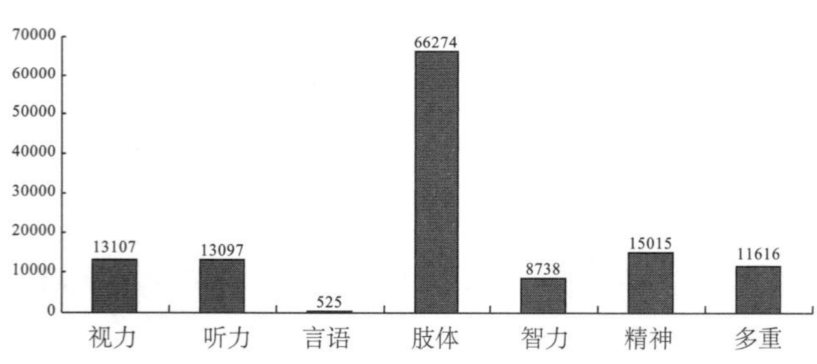

图 1　全省各类别残疾人得到基本康复服务情况（单位：人）

加强残疾人康复机构与人才队伍建设，深化社区康复工作，实施全国残联系统康复专业技术人员规范化培训。截至 2022 年底，全省共有残疾人康复机构 209 个，其中残联办 72 个、卫生办 70 个、民政办 8 个、教育办 3 个、民办 43 个、其他 8 个。全省康复机构在岗人员 4423 人，其中，管理人员 521 人、业务人员 3439 人、其他人员 463 人。

二、教育

2022 年全省共有特殊教育普通高中班（部）1 个。在校生 165 人，毕业生 27 人。残疾人中等职业学校（班）2 个，在校生 336 人，毕业生 71 人，有 424 名被普通高等院校录取。

三、就业

截至 2022 年底，全省城乡持证残疾人就业人数为 26.4 万人，其中按比例就业 0.7 万人，集中就业 0.2 万人，个体就业 1.5 万人，公益性岗位就业 0.3 万人，辅助性就业 0.3 万人，灵活就业（含社区、居家就业）7.3 万人，从事农业种养加 16.2 万人。（见图 2）

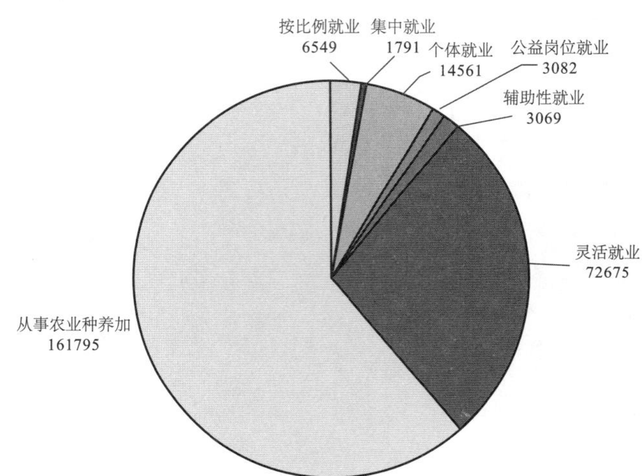

图 2　全省城乡持证残疾人就业情况（单位：人）

盲人按摩事业稳步发展，全年培训盲人保健按摩 402 名，盲人医疗按摩 190 名；保健按摩机构达 400 个，医疗按摩机构达 40 个。

四、社会保障

截至 2022 年底，全省残疾居民参加城乡社会养老保险人数 96.5 万；22.1 万人享受参保个人缴费资助政策，占比 95.5%。41 万残疾人领取养老金。

残疾人托养服务工作稳步推进，残疾人托养服务机构 162 个，为 5823 名残疾人提供托养服务。1 万残疾人接受居家服务。

五、宣传文化

2022 年，以“促进残疾人就业，保障残疾人权益”为主题，组织第三十二次“全国助残日”活动。策划拍摄的微电影《生活的冠军》在全省第六届践行社会主义核心价值观“强国复兴有我”主题微电影创作展播活动中荣获一等奖。甘肃省盲人歌手王春淼、“全国自强模范”任宝仓、残奥健儿李甜甜在北京冬残奥会开幕式、火炬接力、赛场上展现甘肃残疾人风采。选树宣传自强典型和助残先进 50 余人次，推荐 4 名优秀残疾人当选年度“陇人骄子”及候选人、“中国残疾人事业新闻人物、助残新闻人物”提名奖，甘肃省 3 件作品在第十六届残疾人事业好新闻评选活动中获奖，甘肃省选送的 6 个节目在第十届全国残疾人文艺汇演中全部获奖。

截至 2022 年底组织播出省、市（州）残疾人专题广播节目 24 个、电视手语栏目 11 个，省、市（州）、县（市、区）三级公共图书馆共设立盲文及盲文有声读物阅览室 58 个，全省共开展残疾人文化季活动 284 场次，省市残联共举办残疾人文化艺术类的比赛及展览 17 次。

六、体育

残疾人体育活动丰富活跃。成功举办省第十一届残运会暨第五届特奥会，省特奥会共有 12 个代表队 195 名运动员参赛。产生金牌 278 枚、银牌 179 枚、铜牌 116 枚；省残运会共有 11 个代表队 516 名运动员参赛，产生金牌 281 枚、银牌 246 枚、铜牌 179 枚，打破 32 项全省残运会纪录。全省组织开展残疾人群体活动 246 次，参加人数 1.8 万人次。

七、维权

制定或修改关于残疾人的专门法规、规章 1 个，制定或修改保障残疾人权益的规范性文件 20 个。全省县级以上人大常委会开展《中华人民共和国残疾人保障法》执法检查和专题调研 16 次；政协开展视察和专题调研 11 次。全省开展普法宣传教育活动 4 次，4100 余人次参加；举办省级法律培训班 3 个，18000 人次参加。全省残联协助人大代表、政协委员提出议案、建议、提案 5 件，办理议案、建议、提案 13 件。

省市县三级无障碍环境建设与管理法规、政府令和规范性文件共出台 47 个；68 个市（州）、县（市、区）开展无障碍环境建设；开展无障碍环境建设检查 56 次，组织无障碍环境建设工作培训 1343 人次。

八、组织建设

2022 年，全省市（州）、县（市、区）全部建立残联。乡镇（街道）已建立残联 1362 个，已建立社区（村）残协 1.7 万个。省市县乡残联工作人员达 4432 人，乡镇（街道）、村（社区）选聘残疾人专职委员 1.6 万人。14 个市州残联全部配备了残疾人领导干部，77 个县级残联配备了残疾人干部。

共建立各类残疾人专门协会 512 个，其中省级专门协会 5 个，市级专门协会 77 个，县级专门协会 430 个。助残社会组织 46 个。

九、服务设施

2022 年底，已竣工的综合服务设施 93 个，总建筑面积 12.3 万平方米，总投资 3 亿元；已竣工的各级残疾人康复设施 40 个，总建设规模 22.2 万平方米，总投资 6 亿元；已竣工的各级残疾人托养服务设施 41 个，总建设规模 10.6 万平方米，总投资 3 亿元。

2022 年青海省残疾人事业发展统计公报

2022 年，青海省残联坚持以习近平新时代中国特色社会主义思想为指导，认真落实习近平总书记关于残疾人事业的重要论述，全面贯彻党的二十大精神，推进残疾人事业高质量发展。

一、康复

44853 名残疾人得到基本康复服务，22550 名残疾人得到基本辅助器具适配服务。得到康复服务的持证残疾人中，有视力残疾人 5815 名、听力残疾人 6536 名、言语残疾人 725 名、肢体残疾人 24235 名、智力残疾人 3189 名、精神残疾人 1589 名、多重残疾人 2702 名，未评残 62 名。

截至 2022 年底，有残疾人康复机构 68 个。康复机构在岗人员达 1414 人，其中，管理人员 228 人，业务人员 1040 人，其他人员 146 人。

二、教育

共有特殊教育普通高中（部、班）1 个，在校生 140 人，其中聋生 140 人。残疾人中等职业学校（班）2 个，在校生 253 人，毕业生 29 人。

三、就业

城乡持证残疾人就业人数为 49509 人，其中按比例就业 4460 人，集中就业 1466 人，个体就业 2633 人，公益性岗位就业 1588 人，辅助性就业 671 人，灵活就业（含社区、居家就业）19249 人，从事农业种养加 21202 人。

开展农村困难残疾人实用技术培训，为 2085 人次残疾人赋能。48 个残疾人就业帮扶基地共安置 712 名残疾人就业，带动 465 户残疾人家庭增收。

共培训盲人保健按摩人员 34 人次、盲人医疗按摩人员 216 人次。现有保健按摩机构 129 个，医疗按摩机构 13 个。

四、社会保障

截至 2022 年底，参加城乡居民基本养老保险的残疾人数达 126240 名。47890 名残疾人领取养老金。60 岁以下参保的残疾人中，35623 名重度残疾人和 31260 名非重度残疾人得到参保缴费资助。

开展残疾人托养服务的各级各类机构达 72 个，其中寄宿制服务机构 19 个，日间照料机构 14 个，综合性服务机构 29 个。1617 名残疾人通过寄宿制和日间照料服务机构接受了托养服务，2837 名残疾人接受居家服务。

五、宣传文化

截至 2022 年底，共有省级残疾人专题广播节目 1 个、电视手语栏目 1 个，地级残疾人电视手语栏目 9 个。

各级公共图书馆设立盲文及盲文有声读物阅览室 16 个，开展残疾人文化周活动 82 场次，省地两级残联艺术团 2 个。

六、体育

进一步推进残疾人体育融入全省体育工作大局，组织举办青海省第十八届运动会田径等 4 个残疾人比赛项目、第四届全民健身大会三人制聋人篮球等 5 个残疾人项目的比赛，共决出金牌 71 枚，银牌 58 枚，铜牌 46 枚。落实青海省参加东京残奥会、全国残特奥会运动员及教练员奖金 519 万元，2 名优秀运动员荣获“青海青年五四奖章”和“青海三八红旗手”荣誉称号。第八届残疾人环湖赛纳入全国第 12 届残疾人健身周活动，并首次举办线上展示活动。完成残疾人康复体育关爱家庭项目 1800 户，残疾人康复健身示范点 30 个。

七、维权

制定或修改关于残疾人的专门法规和规章：省

级 2 个、地级 1 个；制定或修改保障残疾人权益的规范性文件：省级 2 个、地级 1 个、县级 1 个。县级以上人大开展《中华人民共和国残疾人保障法》执法检查和专题调研 2 次；政协开展视察和专题调研 2 次。开展省级普法宣传教育活动 123 次，35839 人次参加；各地残联办理建议、提案 5 件。

共出台了 5 个省、地、县级无障碍环境建设与管理法规、政府令和规范性文件；开展无障碍环境建设检查 34 次，无障碍培训 10 人次。

八、组织建设

2022 年，市县乡共有残联 462 个，各地市已建残联 8 个，县（市、区）已建残联 45 个，乡镇（街道）已建残联 409 个，社区（村）已建残协 4607 个。

省市县乡残联工作人员 1169 人，乡镇（街道）残联、村（社区）残协专职委员总计 1887 人。地级配备了残疾人领导干部的残联 5 个，县级配备了残疾人干部的残联 14 个。

残疾人专门协会 270 个，助残社会组织 7 个。

九、服务设施

截至 2022 年底，已竣工的各级残疾人综合服务设施 21 个，总建设规模 73859.6 平方米，总投资 21960.0 万元；已竣工的各级残疾人康复设施 8 个，总建设规模 60373.0 平方米，总投资 24250.0 万元；已竣工的各级残疾人托养服务设施 30 个，总建设规模 59670.0 平方米，总投资 18104.2 万元。

2022年宁夏回族自治区残疾人事业发展统计公报

2022年，在自治区党委、政府的坚强领导下，在中国残联的精心指导下，在自治区政府残工委成员单位和社会各界的大力支持下，宁夏残联系统坚持以习近平新时代中国特色社会主义思想为指导，认真学习贯彻党的二十大精神，全面落实自治区第十三次党代会决策部署，紧扣“完善残疾人社会保障制度和关爱服务体系，促进残疾人事业全面发展”目标，着力补短板、强弱项，固底板、扬优势，不断推动残疾人事业全面发展。

一、康复

提请自治区政府出台《宁夏残疾预防行动计划（2021-2025年）》，贯彻落实《“十四五”残疾人康复服务实施方案》，推动“十四五”残疾预防和残疾人康复工作高质量发展。落实好自治区政府民生实事，将0-6岁残疾儿童救助时段由按满月计算调整按整年计算，圆满完成残疾儿童早期干预项目试点，开展送康复上门服务，3215名0-6岁残疾儿童、2541名7-17岁残疾儿童得到康复救助。持续开展残疾人精准康复服务行动，62686名残疾人得到基本康复服务，19333名残疾人得到基本辅助器具适配服务。得到康复服务的60475名持证残疾人中，有视力残疾人6250名、听力残疾人5874名、言语残疾人486名、肢体残疾人29967名、智力残疾人4123名、精神残疾人9608名、多重残疾人4167名；还有2211名未持证残疾儿童得到康复服务。

实施“爱心接力、循环使用”辅助器具免费借用公益项目，新建免费借用点266个，累计建成517个，惠及残疾人1.8万人次。全年免费为100名重度肢体残疾人适配电动站立式轮椅、80名肢体残疾人实施“重塑未来”矫治手术、100名脊髓损伤残疾人提供个性化、专业化、精准化康复训练。与宁夏国龙慈善基金会合作实施“国龙爱心助残”项目，免费为161名残疾人实施骨关节置换手术。积极争取社会捐赠救助，免费为350名白内障患者实施复明手术。

加强残疾人康复机构规范化建设，持续深化社区康复工作。截至2022年底，有残疾人康复机构53个。康复机构在岗人员达1751人，其中，管理人员172人，业务人员1297人，其他人员282人。

二、教育

出台《“十四五”特殊教育发展提升行动计划》，持续巩固残疾儿童义务教育阶段入学率。截至2022年底，全区义务教育阶段适龄残疾儿童共有6898人，入学6750人，入学率达到97.85%。共有特殊教育普通高中（部）1个，在校生70人，其中聋生62人，盲生8人。残疾人中等职业学校（部）1个，在校生24人，毕业生14人。有376名残疾人被普通高等院校录取。实施扶残助学项目，资助残疾学生375名。建立自治区级国家通用手语和盲文讲师团，516人接受国家通用手语和通用盲文培训。

三、就业

城乡持证残疾人就业人数为68954人，其中按比例就业6092人，集中就业1294人，个体就业4414人，公益性岗位就业1828人，辅助性就业1240人，灵活就业（含社区、居家就业）23470人，从事农业种养加30616人。

2022年，城乡持证残疾人新增就业6743人，其中城镇新增就业2168人，农村新增就业4575人。开展农村困难残疾人实用技术培训，为2733人次残疾人赋能。64个残疾人就业帮扶基地共安置929名残疾人就业，带动1977户残疾人家庭增收。

现有盲人保健按摩机构85个，盲人医疗按摩机构10个，共培训盲人保健按摩人员60人次、盲人医疗按摩人员110人次。

四、社会保障

截至2022年底，参加城乡居民基本养老保险的残疾人数为13.1万名，6.1万名残疾人领取养老金。

60 岁以下参保的残疾人中，3.9 万名重度残疾人和 6133 名非重度残疾人得到参保缴费资助。参加城乡居民基本医疗保险的残疾人 18.4 万名，享受参保个人缴费资助 16.0 万名，其中全额代缴 9.4 万名，部分代缴 6.6 万名。10.2 万名困难残疾人享受生活补贴、9.9 万名重度残疾人享受护理补贴。

残疾人托养服务工作稳步推进，开展残疾人托养服务的各级各类机构达 94 个，其中寄宿制服务机构 23 个，日间照料机构 22 个，居家服务机构 40 个，综合性服务机构 9 个。为 8069 名有需求的残疾人提供了托养服务，其中寄宿制机构中托养残疾人 891 人，日间照料机构中托养残疾人 420 人，接受居家服务 6758 人。

五、宣传文化

印发《“十四五”提升残疾人文化服务能力实施方案》，召开全区自强模范记者见面会，开展全区残疾人优秀文艺节目基层巡演，举办“喜迎二十大、永远跟党走”全区第四届中华经典诵读大赛暨全区残疾人专场比赛。组织开展残疾人文化周、文化进社区、进残疾人家庭、“书香中国•阅读有我”全民阅读等群众性文化活动 226 场次，惠及残疾人 4.6 万人（次）。为 3645 户残疾人家庭实施了“五个一”文化关爱服务项目。开展残疾人艺术类比赛及展览 25 场次。

截至 2022 年底，共有自治区级残疾人专题广播节目 1 个、电视手语栏目 1 个，地市级残疾人专题广播节目 1 个、电视手语栏目 6 个，自治区、市、县（区）残联开通新媒体官方账号 24 个。各级公共图书馆设立盲文及盲文有声读物阅览室 29 个，区市县三级残联艺术团 3 个。

六、体育

开展冰雪运动季、残疾人健身周、全国特奥日等群众性体育活动 189 场次，参与人数 1.4 万人次。开展残疾人体育比赛 3 次，参赛残疾人运动员 393 人次。培育残疾人运动员训练基地 2 个，聘用教练员 25 人。

七、维权

截至 2022 年底，全区保障残疾人权益的省级规范性文件有 3 个、县级有 3 个。县级以上人大开展《中华人民共和国残疾人保障法》执法检查和专题调研 1 次；政协开展视察和专题调研 1 次。开展省级普法宣传教育活动 2 次，1.8 万人次参加；举办省级残疾人工作者法律培训 2 场，614 人次参加。各级残联建成法律援助站 27 个，为残疾人提供法律援助案件 150 件。开办就业年龄段残疾人意外伤害综合保险“圆梦护航保”，各级财政累计投入资金 595.7 万元，共承保就业年龄段残疾人 11.2 万人次，共为 419 名残疾人进行了意外伤害理赔，理赔总金额 241 万元。全区各级各部门共受理特殊困难残疾人上门代办事项 5.3 万件，办结 5.2 万件，惠及残疾人 5.0 万人（次）。各地残联办理建议、提案 18 件。

无障碍建设法规、标准进一步完善。全区共出台了 9 个区、市、县级无障碍环境建设与管理法规、政府令和规范性文件；全区开展无障碍环境督导检查 68 次，无障碍业务培训 418 人次，向检察机关提供案件线索 134 条，立案 40 件，发出诉前检察建议 10 件。2022 年度，为 4046 户残疾人家庭实施了无障碍改造，为 120 名残疾人发放了残疾人机动轮椅车燃油补贴。

八、组织建设

2022 年，市县乡共有残联 273 个，5 个地市残联已全部成立，22 个县（市、区）已建残联 21 个，乡镇（街道）已建残联 247 个，社区（村）已建残协 2850 个。

各级残联工作人员 790 人，乡镇（街道）残联、村（社区）残协专职委员总计 2983 人。有 4 个地市级残联配备了残疾人领导干部，县级残联普遍配备了残疾人工作人员。

全区共建立各类残疾人专门协会 135 个，其中自治区级专门协会已建 5 个，地市级专门协会已建 25 个，县级专门协会已建 105 个。助残社会组织 42 个。

九、服务设施

截至 2022 年底，已竣工的各级残疾人综合服务设施 13 个，总建设规模 26647.0 平方米，总投资 6556.3 万元；已竣工的各级残疾人康复设施 23 个，总建设规模 160184.9 平方米，总投资 56278.7 万元；已竣工的各级残疾人托养服务设施 15 个，总建设规模 36744.0 平方米，总投资 12433.0 万元。

2022 年新疆维吾尔自治区残疾人事业发展统计公报

2022 年，在自治区党委、人民政府的正确领导和中国残联的指导下，新疆残联紧紧围绕党中央、国务院关于残疾人事业的决策部署，全面贯彻党的二十大精神，落实习近平总书记关于残疾人工作的重要指示批示精神，持续推动残疾人事业发展，确保完成全年目标任务。

一、康复

贯彻落实《国家残疾人预防行动计划（2021—2025 年）》，制定《自治区残疾预防行动计划（2021—2025 年）》，进一步加强残疾预防工作。持续开展残疾人精准康复服务工作，2022 年，全疆共有 8.7 万名残疾人得到基本康复服务，得到康复服务的持证残疾人中，有视力残疾人 1 万名、听力残疾人 0.8 万名、言语残疾人 0.05 万名、肢体残疾人 4.2 万名、智力残疾人 0.6 万名、精神残疾人 1 万名、多重残疾人 1 万名。全年共有 2.9 万名残疾人得到基本辅助器具适配服务。

大力推动对口援疆残疾儿童康复救助“启明行动”现场观摩会，并启动全疆 11 个援疆地州市开展对口援疆残疾儿童康复救助工作。

截至 2022 年底，全疆共有残疾人康复机构 178 个。康复机构在岗人员达 2797 人，其中，管理人员 311 人，业务人员 2190 人，其他人员 296 人。

二、教育

推动出台《自治区“十四五”特殊教育发展提升行动计划》，继续实施“爱心天使”助学项目，对 329 名考入普通高等院校（本科、大专）家庭生活困难的残疾学生给予一次性资助。

截至 2022 年底，全疆共有特殊教育普通高中 2 个，共有在校生 266 人，其中聋生 237 人，其他残疾学生 29 人。残疾人中等职业学校 2 个，在校生 395 人，毕业生 123 人，毕业生中 17 人获得职业资格证书。

三、就业

制定印发《自治区促进残疾人就业三年行动方案（2022—2024 年）》，积极开展促进残疾人就业十大行动，持续推进残疾人按比例就业工作，组织开展就业援助月活动。

截至 2022 年底，城乡持证残疾人就业人数为 18.3 万人，其中按比例就业 2.3 万人，集中就业 0.4 万人，个体就业 1.8 万人，公益性岗位就业 0.7 万人，辅助性就业 0.2 万人，灵活就业（含社区、居家就业）4.9 万人，从事农业种养加 8.1 万人（图 1）。开展农村困难残疾人实用技术培训，为 0.2 万人次残疾人赋能。88 个残疾人就业帮扶基地共安置 467 名残疾人就业，带动 678 户残疾人家庭增收。

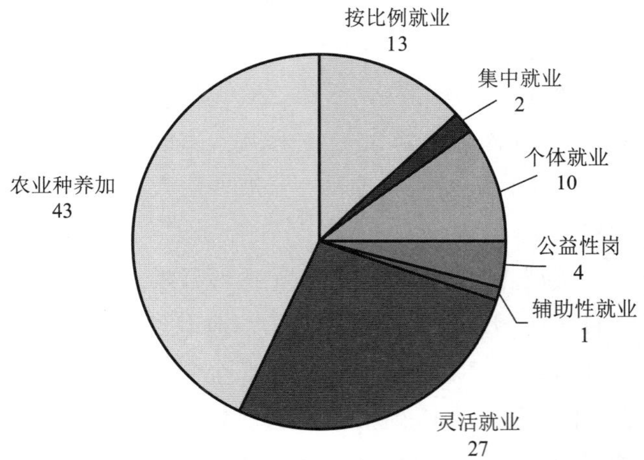

图 1　2022 年自治区城乡持证残疾人就业人数分布状况（单位：%）

四、社会保障

截至 2022 年底，全疆参加城乡居民基本养老保险的残疾人数达 33.7 万名。60 岁以下参保重度残疾人中，8.2 万名享受到个人缴费资助政策，有 10.1 万名残疾人领取养老金。

残疾人托养服务机构 180 个，其中寄宿制托养服务机构 73 个，日间照料机构 77 个，综合性托养服务机构 29 个。3104 名残疾人通过寄宿制和日间照料服务机构接受了托养服务。22 名残疾人接受居家服务。

五、宣传文化

截至2022年底，自治区设立电视手语栏目1个；地级残疾人专题广播节目1个、电视手语栏目2个。全疆各级公共图书馆共设立盲文及盲文有声读物阅览室15个，共开展残疾人文化周活动102场次。为视力障碍人士开通家庭“光明影院”，丰富他们的业余文华生活。

六、维权

2022年，全疆有2个县级修改保障残疾人权益的规范性文件。县级以上人大开展《中华人民共和国残疾人保障法》执法检查和专题调研2次；政协开展视察和专题调研1次，自治区残联开展普法宣传教育活动1次，100余人次参加。

残疾人参政议政工作稳步开展，各地残联协助人大代表、政协委员提出议案、建议、提案14件，办理议案、建议、提案8件。

全疆各级共出台了4个无障碍环境建设与管理法规和规范性文件，开展无障碍环境建设检查40次，无障碍培训134人次。制定《关于“十四五”推进困难重度残疾人家庭无障碍改造工作的指导意见》，全年完成困难重度残疾人家庭无障碍改造7802户。会同有关部门出台《自治区无障碍环境建设“十四五”实施方案》。积极发挥自治区人大基层立法联系点作用，推动法治建设工作。

七、组织建设

2022年，全疆已建地级残联14个，县级残联97个，乡镇（街道）级残联861个，社区（村）已建残协9863个。

全疆共有地、县、乡残联工作人员2459人，乡、镇（街道）残联、村（社区）残协专职委员总计2772名。地市级配备了残疾人领导干部的残联7个，县级配备了残疾人干部的残联42个。成立地方各级残疾人专门协会492个，其中自治区级专门协会已建5个，地级专门协会已建68个，县级专门协会已建417个，助残社会组织12个。

八、服务设施

截至2022年底，已竣工的各级残疾人综合服务设施80个，总建设规模28万平方米，总投资6.7亿元；已竣工的各级残疾人康复设施41个，总建设规模20.3万平方米，总投资4.7亿元；已竣工的各级残疾人托养服务设施57个，总建设规模11万平方米，总投资1.9亿元。

2022 年新疆兵团残疾人事业发展统计公报

2022 年，在兵团党委的坚强领导下，在中国残联的关心指导下，在各级残工委委员单位支持配合、社会各界积极参与下，兵团残联认真贯彻落实习近平总书记关于残疾人事业的重要论述精神和党中央、国务院关于新时代残疾人事业新部署新要求，以喜迎党的二十大、学习宣传贯彻党的二十大精神为主题主线，扎实做好各项重点工作任务，兵团残疾人事业迈上新台阶，残疾人获得感、幸福感、安全感进一步增强。根据 2022 年度残疾人事业统计数据，公报如下：

一、康复

2022 年，将残疾儿童康复救助补贴项目列入兵团党委“为群众办实事”项目，将救助补贴标准从 1.2 万元/人•年提高到 2 万元/人•年，并对符合条件的残疾儿童家庭发放生活补贴 5000 元，全年共有 162 名残疾儿童接受康复救助，做到了“应康尽康”“应救尽救”。持续开展康复专业技术人员继续医学教育，派员参加国家级培训 16 人次，兵团本级举办康复专业人员师资培训班 2 期、培训 61 人次。推动兵团、师市级医联体参与中国康复研究中心的康复医联体建设，组织兵团、师市、团场残疾人康复中心的康复技术人员参加中国康复研究中心在线康复培训 200 余人次。

2022年，兵团共6940名残疾人得到基本康复服务，2092名残疾人得到基本辅助器具适配服务。得到康复服务的持证残疾人中，有视力残疾人409名、听力残疾人303名、言语残疾人7名、肢体残疾人2430名、智力残疾人428名、精神残疾人2858名、多重残疾人428名。

截至2022年底，有残疾人康复机构35个。康复机构在岗人员达1114人，其中，管理人员129人，业务人员586人，其他人员399人。

二、教育

2022 年，兵团残联配合兵团教育部门加大《“十四五”特殊教育发展提升行动》实施，进一步完善随班就读支持保障服务体系建设，重点做好控辍保学、规范送教上门服务等，残疾儿童少年义务教育入学率达 97%。组织实施“彩票公益金助学”项目，安排资金 40 余万元，资助 191 名家庭经济困难残疾儿童少年接受教育。积极推广国家通用手语和国家通用盲文，举办 1 期 30 人的通用手语师资培训班，在兵团卫视、六师五家渠市和八师石河子市电视台等开办手语栏目。

三、就业

2022 年，兵团城乡持证残疾人就业人数为 20421 人，其中，按比例就业 7937 人，集中就业 734 人，个体就业 2217 人，公益性岗位就业 580 人，辅助性就业 176 人，灵活就业（含社区、居家就）6166 人，从事农业种养加 2611 人。开展农村困难残疾人实用技术培训，为 2501 人次残疾人赋能。29 个残疾人就业帮扶基地共安置 162 名残疾人就业，带动 101 户残疾人家庭增收。

截至 2022 年底，兵团共培训盲人保健按摩人员 190 人次、盲人医疗按摩人员 182 人次。现有保健按摩机构 232 个，医疗按摩机构 14 个。

四、社会保障

2022 年，兵团参加城乡居民基本养老保险的残疾人数达 22909 名。5170 名残疾人领取养老金。60 岁以下参保的残疾人中，8333 名重度残疾人和 2439 名非重度残疾人得到参保缴费资助。

开展残疾人托养服务的各级各类机构达 29 个，其中寄宿制服务机构 21 个，综合性服务机构 7 个。228 名残疾人通过寄宿制和日间照料服务机构接受了托养服务，37 名残疾人接受居家服务。

五、宣传文化

2022 年，会同兵团文明办、教育局等部门联合制定《关于进一步推进兵团扶残助残文明实践活动的实施意见》。积极发挥 50 个“残健融合”文化站（点）宣传文化主阵地作用，并利用残疾人就业宣传年、第三十二次“全国助残日”等，广泛开展“书香兵团残疾人书画大赛”系列活动和文化进社区、进残疾人家庭“五个一”等各类活动 380 余场，覆盖 1.34 万人次。

截至 2022 年底，兵团共有省级残疾人电视手语栏目 1 个，地级残疾人专题广播节目 1 个、电视手语栏目 2 个。各级公共图书馆设立盲文及盲文有声读物阅览室 2 个，开展残疾人文化周活动 180 场次，省地两级残联艺术团 1 个。

六、体育

2022 年，兵团建设 7 个残疾人体育健身示范点。积极开展优秀残疾人运动员选拔储备，并开展一期历时 3 个月的竞技体育培训班，积极备战粤港澳大湾区全国残疾人运动会。

七、维权

2022 年，制定印发《兵团残联系统开展法治宣传教育第八个五年规划（2021—2025 年）》，扎实推进残联系统法治建设，举办 1 期 62 人的兵团残联系统干部依法行政培训班。兵团共有残疾人法律救助工作站 149 个。各级公共法律服务平台为 300 余人次残疾人提供法律咨询服务，受理残疾人维权信访诉求 225 人次，均予以妥善解决，结案率 100%。各师市残联对 2562 户有需求的残疾人家庭实施无障碍改造。

八、组织建设

2022 年，兵团各级共有残联 35 个，其中县（市、区）已建残联 14 个，乡镇（街道）已建残联 20 个，社区（村）已建残协 795 个。省市县乡残联工作人员 141 人，乡镇（街道）残联、村（社区）残协专职委员总计 175 人。县级配备了残疾人干部的残联 3 个。残疾人专门协会 60 个，助残社会组织 15 个。

九、服务设施

截至 2022 年底，兵团已竣工的各级残疾人综合服务设施 2 个，总建设规模 1200 平方米，总投资 211 万元；已竣工的各级残疾人康复设施 11 个，总建设规模 84462 平方米，总投资 28768.2 万元；已竣工的各级残疾人托养服务设施 36 个，总建设规模 81128.2 平方米，总投资 14341.7 万元。

附录

Appendix

关于使用 2010 年末全国残疾人总数及各类、不同残疾等级人数的通知

残联〔2012〕25 号

各省、自治区、直辖市及计划单列市残联，新疆生产建设兵团残联，黑龙江农垦总局残联：

根据第六次全国人口普查我国总人口数，及第二次全国残疾人抽样调查我国残疾人占全国总人口的比例和各类残疾人占残疾人总人数的比例，推算了 2010 年末我国残疾人总人数及各类、不同等级的残疾人数，现通知如下：

全国残疾人总数为 8502 万人。

各类残疾人的人数分别为：视力残疾 1263 万人；听力残疾 2054 万人；言语残疾 130 万人；肢体残疾 2472 万人；智力残疾 568 万人；精神残疾 629 万人；多重残疾 1386 万人。

各残疾等级人数分别为：重度残疾 2518 万人；中度和轻度残疾人 5984 万人。

以上数据可在工作中使用并对外公开。

中国残疾人联合会

二〇一二年三月五日

中国残联统计调查项目目录

审批项目一览表

统计调查项目名称	批准文号	有效期截止时间
中国残疾人事业统计调查制度	国统制〔2021〕102 号	2024 年 9 月
全国残疾人基本服务状况和需求信息数据动态更新	国统制〔2021〕70 号	2024 年 6 月
全国残疾人家庭收入状况调查制度	国统制〔2022〕 30 号	2025 年 2 月

中国残疾人联合会文件

残联发〔2006〕1号

关于印发《全国残联系统统计工作管理办法》的通知

各省、自治区、直辖市及计划单列市残联，新疆生产建设兵团残联、黑龙江农垦总局残联：

为了加强统计工作的管理，规范统计调查行为，提高统计调查的整体效益，充分发挥统计工作的服务和监督作用，中国残联依据《中华人民共和国统计法》《中华人民共和国统计法实施细则》《部门统计调查管理暂行办法》，结合工作实际，对原有的《中国残联系统统计工作暂行规定》《中国残联系统专项业务统计调查项目管理暂行办法》《中国残联机关统计资料管理暂行办法》等进行了修订和整合，制定了《全国残联系统统计工作管理办法》，现予以印发，请遵照执行。

中国残疾人联合会
二〇〇六年一月三日

全国残联系统统计工作管理办法

一、总　则

第一条　为了科学、有效地组织全国残联系统统计工作，规范统计调查行为，提高统计调查的整体效益，充分发挥统计工作的服务和监督作用，依据《中华人民共和国统计法》（以下简称《统计法》）、《中华人民共和国统计法实施细则》（以下简称《实施细则》）、《部门统计调查管理暂行办法》，结合工作实际，制定本办法。

第二条　全国残联系统统计工作的基本任务是：对全国残疾人事业的发展状况和残联系统的业务工作进行统计调查、统计分析、统计预测和统计监督，为国家和各级人民政府制定与残疾人事业相关的政策、法规提供依据，为领导运筹决策和残联系统工作的发展提供有效的服务。

第三条　全国残联系统统计工作由：中国残疾人事业统计年报制度、中国残疾人事业统计快报制度、中国残疾人事业基础统计台账制度、专项业务统计调查工作组成。

第四条　各级残联应加强统计现代化建设，积极利用信息技术手段，使残疾人事业统计数据更加科学、准确、及时，逐步实现残疾人事业统计数据的电子化和统计数据的社会共享与服务。

二、统计机构、职责和统计人员

第五条　全国残联系统统计工作实行统一领导、分级负责。中国残联负责全国残疾人事业统计工作的组织、协调与管理，并对地方残联统计工作进行指导，具体由中国残联设置的统计机构负责组织实施。地方各级残联的统计工作由地方各级残联设置的统计机构或统计主管部门负责管理和组织实施，并接受上级残联统计机构和同级人民政府统计部门的指导、监督与管理。

第六条　中国残联的统计机构设在中国残联信息中心，负责组织、协调和管理全国残联系统的统计工作。其主要职责是：制定残疾人事业统计调查计划和项目，制定统计标准；组织协调各级残联搜集、整理、提供统计资料，管理统计资料的发布，开展统计分析、统计预测和统计监督工作；指导、检查全国残联系统统计工作，组织统计业务经验交流，开展全国残联系统统计科学研究；做好统计人员培训工作；制订全国残联系统统计工作现代化规划。

各省级残联应设置统计机构或明确统计主管部门并设专职统计人员，负责指导本行政区域内各级残联统计工作，组织管理本级残联的统计工作。其主要职责是：在完成好中国残联和上级残联下达的各项统计调查工作的同时，为本级残疾人事业提供各项统计数据，并开展统计调查活动。

各地级市残联应明确统计主管部门并设专（兼）职统计人员，其主要职责是：在完成好中国残联和上级残联下达的各项统计调查工作的同时，为本级残疾人事业提供各项统计数据，并开展统计调查活动。

各县级残联应明确统计工作主管部门或主管负责人，确定兼职统计人员。其主要职责是：做好基础数据工作，建立统计台账，完成好中国残联和上级残联下达的统计调查任务，为本级残疾人事业提供各项统计数据，并开展统计调查活动。

第七条　各级残联统计人员应保持相对稳定。统计人员的调动，应当征得本级统计主管部门或统计工作负责人的同意；省级专职统计人员的调动，应当征得中国残联统计机构的同意。统计人员调动工作或离职，应当由经过统计业务培训、能够胜任统计业务工作的人员接替，并办理交接手续。各级残联的统计人员应取得同级人民政府统计机构颁发的统计上岗证，具有残联系统业务知识和计算机操作能力。

三、统计报表制度的编制、修改与审批

第八条　中国残疾人事业统计年报、快报制度和统计台账制度中的指标、指标涵义、调查范围、

分类目录、计算方法和统计报表表式、统计编码以及报送时间，由中国残联统一规定，按照国家统计局的要求报送国家统计局进行审批备案。按规定程序经国家统计局批准或备案的统计报表，在报表的右上角标明制表机关名称、表号、批准或备案机关名称及其批准文号。被调查的部门、人员应当准确、及时地按报表规定填报。

不符合前款规定的统计报表（包括以搜集数字为主的调查提纲）是非法报表，被调查的部门可以拒绝填报。

第九条 中国残疾人事业统计年报、快报和统计台账应根据中国残疾人事业发展的需要及时进行调整和补充。中国残联各业务部门因工作需要，调整和补充有关指标时，应进行充分论证并与中国残联统计管理部门联系与协商，经中国残联理事会批准后，报国家统计局批准或备案。

四、统计台账管理

第十条 为了规范中国残联系统统计工作，做到依法统计，发挥统计服务和监督作用，根据《中华人民共和国统计法》和国家相关统计工作的规定，中国残联将制定中国残疾人事业统计台账制度，加强统计台账的管理与数据的报送。

第十一条 中国残疾人事业统计台账（卡）充分利用电子网络化的方式、将科学合理、准确实用的动态管理，与中国残疾人事业统计报表制度相衔接。台账填写内容要符合法律法规政策的要求，填写对象真实、准确；先填卡，后建账，做到由台账中提取统计数字。

第十二条 各级残联必须依据中国残疾人事业统计台账（卡）中的数据，报送中国残疾人事业统计快报、年报和各项专项业务统计调查的统计报表，做到填报统计报表的数据全面、准确、及时、数出一门。

第十三条 中国残疾人事业统计台账在统一格式、统一软件下实施，由各级地方残联统计人员协调业务部门和人员用计算机或纸质台账、台卡方式进行专门管理。统计人员发生变动时，要严格履行交接手续。

第十四条 省级、地（市）级残联都应建立电子化台账。有条件的县级残联也要实行电子化台账，各级残联应积极推动电子化台账建设，加强统计台账的管理工作。在没有实行全面电子化台账之前，将实行电子化台账和纸质台账、台卡的同时保存。

第十五条 中国残疾人事业统计台账、台卡按中国残疾人事业统计报表逐级汇总上报。

五、专项业务统计调查管理

第十六条 中国残联和地方各级残联开展的专项业务统计调查，以及残联各业务部门与其他部门或单位联合组织实施的统计调查，其调查的统计指标与中国残联年报、快报指标交叉重复或需要对外公布统计数据的统计调查，均属于专项业务统计调查管理范畴。

第十七条 中国残联系统各级统计机构统一管理和协调本级业务部门专项业务统计调查。

第十八条 专项业务统计调查项目必须符合国家统计局《部门统计调查项目管理暂行办法》的基本原则与要求。专项业务统计调查项目的立项必须有充分的理由。调查要有明确的目的和资料使用范围。调查项目应当与中国残联职能范围和各项业务工作相对应。

第十九条 中国残联系统各级统计机构通过建立审批备案制度、调查项目公布制度、跟踪检查制度、举报制度，对会内专项业务统计调查进行管理。

第二十条 专项业务统计调查项目中的统计标准和分类必须与政府综合统计机构规定使用的标准和分类相一致。涉及政府综合统计机构规定以外的专业标准和分类，要与国家有关标准或行业标准相一致。尚无国家标准和行业标准的，必须严格按照标准化及分类科学的原则进行归纳和设计，并在使用前征求政府综合统计机构的意见。

第二十一条 中国残联新增设的统计调查项目在制定好统计调查方案后，须提交中国残联统计机构审核，报国家统计局批准后统一组织实施。

地方残联新增设的统计调查项目，由本级残联统计机构统一管理，报上级残联统计机构和同级人民政府统计局批准后组织实施。地方残联制发的统计调查表内容、指标涵义、计算方法、完成期限等，均不得与中国残联制发的有关统计调查表相抵触。

六、统计资料的管理与发布

第二十二条 残联系统统计资料实行归口管理。全国性残联系统 统计资料，由中国残联统计机构统一管理；地方性残联系统统计资料，由地方残联统计机构或统计人员统一管理。统计机构和统计人员必须建立统计工作责任制和统计资料整理、审查、管理制度，不断提高工作质量和工作效率，保证残联系统统计资料的准确、及时。

各级残联的文件、报告、简报、情况反映、信息等引用综合性的统计数字，必须经本级统计机构或统计人员复核。对外提供和公布的统计资料，必须经本级统计机构或统计人员统一复核和办理并由主管理事长批准。任何部门和个人不得擅自公开和使用未经正式公布的残联系统统计资料。

第二十三条 各级残联统计机构、统计人员必须建立健全统计资料档案，对原始记录、统计台账和综合分析等统计资料，按有关规定保管，不得损坏。对于属于国家秘密的残联系统统计资料，要按照《中华人民共和国保守国家秘密法》、国家统计局《统计资料保密管理办法》等有关规定，妥善保管。

七、奖励和惩罚

第二十四条 各级残联对有下列表现之一的残联统计机构或者人员，给予表扬或奖励：

一、在改革和完善残联系统统计制度、统计方法等方面，有重要贡献的；

二、在完成规定的残联系统统计调查任务，保障残联系统统计资料的准确性、及时性方面，做出显著成绩的；

三、在进行残联系统统计分析、统计预测和统计监督方面取得重要成绩的；

四、在运用和推广现代化信息技术方面，有显著效果的；

五、在残联系统统计科学研究方面有所创新的；

六、坚持实事求是，依法办事，同违反统计法规和本办法的行为作斗争，表现突出的。

第二十五条 各级残联对有下列行为之一的机构或者人员，给予批评或处分：

一、虚报、瞒报、拒报残联系统统计资料的；

二、伪造、篡改残联系统统计资料的；

三、无故迟报残联系统统计资料的；

四、侵犯统计机构、统计人员行使统计法规及本办法所规定的职权或打击报复统计人员的；

五、违反统计法规及本办法，未经批准，自行编制发布残联系统统计报表的；

六、违反统计法规及本办法，未经核定批准，擅自对外提供或公布残联系统统计资料的。

八、附 则

第二十六条 本办法由中国残联负责解释。

第二十七条 本办法自发布之日起试行。

中华人民共和国统计法

（1983 年 12 月 8 日第六届全国人民代表大会常务委员会第三次会议通过。根据 1996 年 5 月 15 日第八届全国人民代表大会常务委员会第十九次会议《关于修改〈中华人民共和国统计法〉的决定》修正。2009 年 6 月 27 日第十一届全国人民代表大会常务委员会第九次会议修订。）

第一章 总 则

第一条 为了科学、有效地组织统计工作，保障统计资料的真实性、准确性、完整性和及时性，发挥统计在了解国情国力、服务经济社会发展中的重要作用，促进社会主义现代化建设事业发展，制定本法。

第二条 本法适用于各级人民政府、县级以上人民政府统计机构和有关部门组织实施的统计活动。

统计的基本任务是对经济社会发展情况进行统计调查、统计分析，提供统计资料和统计咨询意见，实行统计监督。

第三条 国家建立集中统一的统计系统，实行统一领导、分级负责的统计管理体制。

第四条 国务院和地方各级人民政府、各有关部门应当加强对统计工作的组织领导，为统计工作提供必要的保障。

第五条 国家加强统计科学研究，健全科学的统计指标体系，不断改进统计调查方法，提高统计的科学性。

国家有计划地加强统计信息化建设，推进统计信息搜集、处理、传输、共享、存储技术和统计数据库体系的现代化。

第六条 统计机构和统计人员依照本法规定独立行使统计调查、统计报告、统计监督的职权，不受侵犯。

地方各级人民政府、政府统计机构和有关部门以及各单位的负责人，不得自行修改统计机构和统计人员依法搜集、整理的统计资料，不得以任何方式要求统计机构、统计人员及其他机构、人员伪造、篡改统计资料，不得对依法履行职责或者拒绝、抵制统计违法行为的统计人员打击报复。

第七条 国家机关、企业事业单位和其他组织以及个体工商户和个人等统计调查对象，必须依照本法和国家有关规定，真实、准确、完整、及时地提供统计调查所需的资料，不得提供不真实或者不完整的统计资料，不得迟报、拒报统计资料。

第八条 统计工作应当接受社会公众的监督。任何单位和个人有权检举统计中弄虚作假等违法行为。对检举有功的单位和个人应当给予表彰和奖励。

第九条 统计机构和统计人员对在统计工作中知悉的国家秘密、商业秘密和个人信息，应当予以保密。

第十条 任何单位和个人不得利用虚假统计资料骗取荣誉称号、物质利益或者职务晋升。

第二章 统计调查管理

第十一条 统计调查项目包括国家统计调查项目、部门统计调查项目和地方统计调查项目。

国家统计调查项目是指全国性基本情况的统计调查项目。部门统计调查项目是指国务院有关部门的专业性统计调查项目。地方统计调查项目是指县级以上地方人民政府及其部门的地方性统计调查项目。

国家统计调查项目、部门统计调查项目、地方统计调查项目应当明确分工，互相衔接，不得重复。

第十二条 国家统计调查项目由国家统计局制定，或者由国家统计局和国务院有关部门共同制定，报国务院备案；重大的国家统计调查项目报国务院审批。

部门统计调查项目由国务院有关部门制定。统计调查对象属于本部门管辖系统的，报国家统计局备案；统计调查对象超出本部门管辖系统的，报国家统计局审批。

地方统计调查项目由县级以上地方人民政府统计机构和有关部门分别制定或者共同制定。其中，由省级人民政府统计机构单独制定或者和有关部门共同制定的，报国家统计局审批；由省级以下人民政府统计机构单独制定或者和有关部门共同制定的，报省级人民政府统计机构审批；由县级以上地方人民政府有关部门制定的，报本级人民政府统计机构审批。

第十三条 统计调查项目的审批机关应当对调查项目的必要性、可行性、科学性进行审查，对符合法定条件的，作出予以批准的书面决定，并公布；对不符合法定条件的，作出不予批准的书面决定，并说明理由。

第十四条 制定统计调查项目，应当同时制定该项目的统计调查制度，并依照本法第十二条的规定一并报经审批或者备案。

统计调查制度应当对调查目的、调查内容、调查方法、调查对象、调查组织方式、调查表式、统计资料的报送和公布等作出规定。

统计调查应当按照统计调查制度组织实施。变更统计调查制度的内容，应当报经原审批机关批准或者原备案机关备案。

第十五条 统计调查表应当标明表号、制定机关、批准或者备案文号、有效期限等标志。

对未标明前款规定的标志或者超过有效期限的统计调查表，统计调查对象有权拒绝填报；县级以上人民政府统计机构应当依法责令停止有关统计调查活动。

第十六条 搜集、整理统计资料，应当以周期性普查为基础，以经常性抽样调查为主体，综合运用全面调查、重点调查等方法，并充分利用行政记录等资料。

重大国情国力普查由国务院统一领导，国务院和地方人民政府组织统计机构和有关部门共同实施。

第十七条 国家制定统一的统计标准，保障统计调查采用的指标涵义、计算方法、分类目录、调查表式和统计编码等的标准化。

国家统计标准由国家统计局制定，或者由国家统计局和国务院标准化主管部门共同制定。

国务院有关部门可以制定补充性的部门统计标准，报国家统计局审批。部门统计标准不得与国家统计标准相抵触。

第十八条 县级以上人民政府统计机构根据统计任务的需要，可以在统计调查对象中推广使用计算机网络报送统计资料。

第十九条 县级以上人民政府应当将统计工作所需经费列入财政预算。

重大国情国力普查所需经费，由国务院和地方人民政府共同负担，列入相应年度的财政预算，按时拨付，确保到位。

第三章 统计资料的管理和公布

第二十条 县级以上人民政府统计机构和有关部门以及乡、镇人民政府，应当按照国家有关规定建立统计资料的保存、管理制度，建立健全统计信息共享机制。

第二十一条 国家机关、企业事业单位和其他组织等统计调查对象，应当按照国家有关规定设置原始记录、统计台账，建立健全统计资料的审核、签署、交接、归档等管理制度。

统计资料的审核、签署人员应当对其审核、签署的统计资料的真实性、准确性和完整性负责。

第二十二条 县级以上人民政府有关部门应当及时向本级人民政府统计机构提供统计所需的行政记录资料和国民经济核算所需的财务资料、财政资料及其他资料，并按照统计调查制度的规定及时向本级人民政府统计机构报送其组织实施统计调查取得的有关资料。

县级以上人民政府统计机构应当及时向本级人民政府有关部门提供有关统计资料。

第二十三条 县级以上人民政府统计机构按照国家有关规定，定期公布统计资料。

国家统计数据以国家统计局公布的数据为准。

第二十四条 县级以上人民政府有关部门统计调查取得的统计资料，由本部门按照国家有关规定公布。

第二十五条 统计调查中获得的能够识别或者推断单个统计调查对象身份的资料，任何单位和个人不得对外提供、泄露，不得用于统计以外的目的。

第二十六条 县级以上人民政府统计机构和有关部门统计调查取得的统计资料，除依法应当保密的外，应当及时公开，供社会公众查询。

第四章　统计机构和统计人员

第二十七条　国务院设立国家统计局，依法组织领导和协调全国的统计工作。

国家统计局根据工作需要设立的派出调查机构，承担国家统计局布置的统计调查等任务。

县级以上地方人民政府设立独立的统计机构，乡、镇人民政府设置统计工作岗位，配备专职或者兼职统计人员，依法管理、开展统计工作，实施统计调查。

第二十八条　县级以上人民政府有关部门根据统计任务的需要设立统计机构，或者在有关机构中设置统计人员，并指定统计负责人，依法组织、管理本部门职责范围内的统计工作，实施统计调查，在统计业务上受本级人民政府统计机构的指导。

第二十九条　统计机构、统计人员应当依法履行职责，如实搜集、报送统计资料，不得伪造、篡改统计资料，不得以任何方式要求任何单位和个人提供不真实的统计资料，不得有其他违反本法规定的行为。

统计人员应当坚持实事求是，恪守职业道德，对其负责搜集、审核、录入的统计资料与统计调查对象报送的统计资料的一致性负责。

第三十条　统计人员进行统计调查时，有权就与统计有关的问题询问有关人员，要求其如实提供有关情况、资料并改正不真实、不准确的资料。

统计人员进行统计调查时，应当出示县级以上人民政府统计机构或者有关部门颁发的工作证件；未出示的，统计调查对象有权拒绝调查。

第三十一条　国家实行统计专业技术职务资格考试、评聘制度，提高统计人员的专业素质，保障统计队伍的稳定性。

统计人员应当具备与其从事的统计工作相适应的专业知识和业务能力。

县级以上人民政府统计机构和有关部门应当加强对统计人员的专业培训和职业道德教育。

第五章　监督检查

第三十二条　县级以上人民政府及其监察机关对下级人民政府、本级人民政府统计机构和有关部门执行本法的情况，实施监督。

第三十三条　国家统计局组织管理全国统计工作的监督检查，查处重大统计违法行为。

县级以上地方人民政府统计机构依法查处本行政区域内发生的统计违法行为。但是，国家统计局派出的调查机构组织实施的统计调查活动中发生的统计违法行为，由组织实施该项统计调查的调查机构负责查处。

法律、行政法规对有关部门查处统计违法行为另有规定的，从其规定。

第三十四条　县级以上人民政府有关部门应当积极协助本级人民政府统计机构查处统计违法行为，及时向本级人民政府统计机构移送有关统计违法案件材料。

第三十五条　县级以上人民政府统计机构在调查统计违法行为或者核查统计数据时，有权采取下列措施：

（一）发出统计检查查询书，向检查对象查询有关事项；

（二）要求检查对象提供有关原始记录和凭证、统计台账、统计调查表、会计资料及其他相关证明和资料；

（三）就与检查有关的事项询问有关人员；

（四）进入检查对象的业务场所和统计数据处理信息系统进行检查、核对；

（五）经本机构负责人批准，登记保存检查对象的有关原始记录和凭证、统计台账、统计调查表、会计资料及其他相关证明和资料；

（六）对与检查事项有关的情况和资料进行记录、录音、录像、照相和复制。

县级以上人民政府统计机构进行监督检查时，监督检查人员不得少于二人，并应当出示执法证件；未出示的，有关单位和个人有权拒绝检查。

第三十六条　县级以上人民政府统计机构履行监督检查职责时，有关单位和个人应当如实反映情况，提供相关证明和资料，不得拒绝、阻碍检查，不得转移、隐匿、篡改、毁弃原始记录和凭证、统计台账、统计调查表、会计资料及其他相关证明和资料。

第六章　法律责任

第三十七条　地方人民政府、政府统计机构或者有关部门、单位的负责人有下列行为之一的，由任免机关或者监察机关依法给予处分，并由县级以上人民政府统计机构予以通报：

（一）自行修改统计资料、编造虚假统计数据的；

（二）要求统计机构、统计人员或者其他机构、人员伪造、篡改统计资料的；

（三）对依法履行职责或者拒绝、抵制统计违法行为的统计人员打击报复的；

（四）对本地方、本部门、本单位发生的严重统计违法行为失察的。

第三十八条 县级以上人民政府统计机构或者有关部门在组织实施统计调查活动中有下列行为之一的，由本级人民政府、上级人民政府统计机构或者本级人民政府统计机构责令改正，予以通报；对直接负责的主管人员和其他直接责任人员，由任免机关或者监察机关依法给予处分：

（一）未经批准擅自组织实施统计调查的；

（二）未经批准擅自变更统计调查制度的内容的；

（三）伪造、篡改统计资料的；

（四）要求统计调查对象或者其他机构、人员提供不真实的统计资料的；

（五）未按照统计调查制度的规定报送有关资料的。

统计人员有前款第三项至第五项所列行为之一的，责令改正，依法给予处分。

第三十九条 县级以上人民政府统计机构或者有关部门有下列行为之一的，对直接负责的主管人员和其他直接责任人员由任免机关或者监察机关依法给予处分：

（一）违法公布统计资料的；

（二）泄露统计调查对象的商业秘密、个人信息或者提供、泄露在统计调查中获得的能够识别或者推断单个统计调查对象身份的资料的；

（三）违反国家有关规定，造成统计资料毁损、灭失的。

统计人员有前款所列行为之一的，依法给予处分。

第四十条 统计机构、统计人员泄露国家秘密的，依法追究法律责任。

第四十一条 作为统计调查对象的国家机关、企业事业单位或者其他组织有下列行为之一的，由县级以上人民政府统计机构责令改正，给予警告，可以予以通报；其直接负责的主管人员和其他直接责任人员属于国家工作人员的，由任免机关或者监察机关依法给予处分：

（一）拒绝提供统计资料或者经催报后仍未按时提供统计资料的；

（二）提供不真实或者不完整的统计资料的；

（三）拒绝答复或者不如实答复统计检查查询书的；

（四）拒绝、阻碍统计调查、统计检查的；

（五）转移、隐匿、篡改、毁弃或者拒绝提供原始记录和凭证、统计台账、统计调查表及其他相关证明和资料的。

企业事业单位或者其他组织有前款所列行为之一的，可以并处五万元以下的罚款；情节严重的，并处五万元以上二十万元以下的罚款。

个体工商户有本条第一款所列行为之一的，由县级以上人民政府统计机构责令改正，给予警告，可以并处一万元以下的罚款。

第四十二条 作为统计调查对象的国家机关、企业事业单位或者其他组织迟报统计资料，或者未按照国家有关规定设置原始记录、统计台账的，由县级以上人民政府统计机构责令改正，给予警告。

企业事业单位或者其他组织有前款所列行为之一的，可以并处一万元以下的罚款。

个体工商户迟报统计资料的，由县级以上人民政府统计机构责令改正，给予警告，可以并处一千元以下的罚款。

第四十三条 县级以上人民政府统计机构查处统计违法行为时，认为对有关国家工作人员依法应当给予处分的，应当提出给予处分的建议；该国家工作人员的任免机关或者监察机关应当依法及时作出决定，并将结果书面通知县级以上人民政府统计机构。

第四十四条 作为统计调查对象的个人在重大国情国力普查活动中拒绝、阻碍统计调查，或者提供不真实或者不完整的普查资料的，由县级以上人民政府统计机构责令改正，予以批评教育。

第四十五条 违反本法规定，利用虚假统计资料骗取荣誉称号、物质利益或者职务晋升的，除对其编造虚假统计资料或者要求他人编造虚假统计资料的行为依法追究法律责任外，由作出有关决定的单位或者其上级单位、监察机关取消其荣誉称号，追缴获得的物质利益，撤销晋升的职务。

第四十六条　当事人对县级以上人民政府统计机构作出的行政处罚决定不服的，可以依法申请行政复议或者提起行政诉讼。其中，对国家统计局在省、自治区、直辖市派出的调查机构作出的行政处罚决定不服的，向国家统计局申请行政复议；对国家统计局派出的其他调查机构作出的行政处罚决定不服的，向国家统计局在该派出机构所在的省、自治区、直辖市派出的调查机构申请行政复议。

第四十七条　违反本法规定，构成犯罪的，依法追究刑事责任。

第七章　附　则

第四十八条　本法所称县级以上人民政府统计机构，是指国家统计局及其派出的调查机构、县级以上地方人民政府统计机构。

第四十九条　民间统计调查活动的管理办法，由国务院制定。

中华人民共和国境外的组织、个人需要在中华人民共和国境内进行统计调查活动的，应当按照国务院的规定报请审批。

利用统计调查危害国家安全、损害社会公共利益或者进行欺诈活动的，依法追究法律责任。

第五十条　本法自 2010 年 1 月 1 日起施行。

部门统计调查项目管理办法

（中华人民共和国国家统计局令第22号）

第一章　总则

第一条　为加强部门统计调查项目的规范性、统一性管理，提高统计调查的科学性和有效性，减轻统计调查对象负担，推进部门统计信息共享，根据《中华人民共和国统计法》及其实施条例和国务院有关规定，制定本办法。

第二条　本办法适用于国务院各部门制定的统计调查项目。

第三条　本办法所称的统计调查项目，是指国务院有关部门通过调查表格、问卷、行政记录、大数据以及其他方式搜集整理统计资料，用于政府管理和公共服务的各类统计调查项目。

第四条　国家统计局统一组织领导和协调全国统计工作，指导国务院有关部门开展统计调查，统一管理部门统计调查。

第五条　国务院有关部门应当明确统一组织协调统计工作的综合机构，负责归口管理、统一申报本部门统计调查项目。

第二章　部门统计调查项目的制定

第六条　国务院有关部门执行相关法律、行政法规、国务院的决定和履行本部门职责，需要开展统计活动的，应当制定相应的部门统计调查项目。

第七条　制定部门统计调查项目，应当减少调查频率，缩小调查规模，降低调查成本，减轻基层统计人员和统计调查对象的负担。可以通过行政记录和大数据加工整理获得统计资料的，不得开展统计调查；可以通过已经批准实施的各种统计调查整理获得统计资料的，不得重复开展统计调查；抽样调查、重点调查可以满足需要的，不得开展全面统计调查。

第八条　制定部门统计调查项目，应当有组织、人员和经费保障。

第九条　制定部门统计调查项目，应当同时制定该项目的统计调查制度。

统计调查制度内容包括总说明、报表目录、调查表式、分类目录、指标解释、指标间逻辑关系，采用抽样调查方法的还应当包括抽样方案。

统计调查制度总说明应当对调查目的、调查对象、统计范围、调查内容、调查频率、调查时间、调查方法、组织实施方式、质量控制、报送要求、信息共享、资料公布等作出规定。

面向单位的部门统计调查，其统计调查对象应当取自国家基本单位名录库或者部门基本单位名录库。

第十条　部门统计调查应当规范设置统计指标、调查表，指标解释和计算方法应当科学合理。

第十一条　部门统计调查应当使用国家统计标准。无国家统计标准的，可以使用经国家统计局批准的部门统计标准。

第十二条　新制定的部门统计调查项目或者对现行统计调查项目进行较大修订的，应当开展试填试报等工作。其中，重要统计调查项目应当进行试点。

第十三条　部门统计调查项目涉及其他部门职责的，应当事先征求相关部门意见。

第三章　部门统计调查项目审批和备案

第十四条　国务院有关部门制定的统计调查项目，统计调查对象属于本部门管辖系统或者利用行政记录加工获取统计资料的，报国家统计局备案；统计调查对象超出本部门管辖系统的，报国家统计局审批。

部门管辖系统包括本部门直属机构、派出机构和垂直管理的机构，省及省以下与部门对口设立的管理机构。

第十五条　部门统计调查项目审批或者备案包括申报、受理、审查、反馈、决定等程序。

第十六条 部门统计调查项目送审或者备案时，应当通过部门统计调查项目管理平台提交下列材料：

（一）申请审批项目的部门公文或者申请备案项目的部门办公厅（室）公文；

（二）部门统计调查项目审批或者备案申请表；

（三）统计调查制度；

（四）统计调查项目的论证报告、背景材料、经费保障等，修订的统计调查项目还应当提供修订说明；

（五）征求有关地方、部门、统计调查对象和专家意见及其采纳情况；

（六）制定机关按照会议制度集体讨论决定的会议纪要；

（七）重要统计调查项目的试点报告；

（八）由审批机关或者备案机关公布的统计调查制度的主要内容；

（九）防范和惩治统计造假、弄虚作假责任规定。

前款第（一）项的公文应当同时提交纸质文件。

第十七条 申请材料齐全并符合法定形式的，国家统计局予以受理。

申请材料不齐全或者不符合法定形式的，国家统计局应当一次告知需要补正的全部内容，制定机关应当按照国家统计局的要求予以补正。

第十八条 统计调查制度应当列明下列事项：

（一）向国家统计局报送的制定机关组织实施统计调查取得的具体统计资料清单；

（二）主要统计指标公布的时间、渠道；

（三）统计信息共享的内容、方式、时限、渠道、责任单位和责任人；

（四）向统计信息共享数据库提供的统计资料清单；

（五）统计调查对象使用国家基本单位名录库或者部门基本单位名录库的情况。

第十九条 国家统计局对申请审批的部门统计调查项目进行审查，符合下列条件的部门统计调查项目，作出予以批准的书面决定：

（一）具有法定依据或者确为部门公共管理和服务所必需；

（二）与现有的国家统计调查项目和部门统计调查项目的主要内容不重复、不矛盾；

（三）主要统计指标无法通过本部门的行政记录或者已有统计调查资料加工整理取得；

（四）部门统计调查制度科学、合理、可行，并且符合本办法第八条、第九条和第十八条规定；

（五）采用的统计标准符合国家有关规定；

（六）符合统计法律法规和国家有关规定。

不符合前款规定的，国家统计局向制定机关提出修改意见；修改后仍不符合前款规定条件的，国家统计局作出不予批准的书面决定，并说明理由。

第二十条 国家统计局对申请备案的部门统计调查项目进行审查，符合下列条件的部门统计调查项目，作出同意备案的书面决定：

（一）统计调查项目的调查对象属于制定机关管辖系统，或者利用行政记录加工获取统计资料；

（二）与现有的国家统计调查项目和部门统计调查项目的主要内容不重复、不矛盾；

（三）部门统计调查制度科学、合理、可行，并且符合本办法第八条、第九条和第十八条规定。

第二十一条 国家统计局在收到制定机关申请公文及完整的相关资料后，在20个工作日内完成审批，20个工作日内不能作出决定的，经审批机关负责人批准可以延长10日，并应当将延长审批期限的理由告知制定机关；在10个工作日内完成备案。完成时间以复函日期为准。

制定机关修改统计调查项目的时间，不计算在审批期限内。

第二十二条 部门统计调查项目有下列情形之一的，国家统计局简化审批或者备案程序，缩短期限：

（一）发生突发事件，需要迅速实施统计调查；

（二）统计调查内容未做变动，统计调查项目有效期届满需要延长期限。

第二十三条 部门统计调查项目实行有效期管理。审批的统计调查项目有效期为3年，备案的统计调查项目有效期为5年。统计调查制度对有效期规定少于3年的，从其规定。有效期以批准执行或者同意备案的日期为起始时间。

统计调查项目在有效期内需要变更内容的，制定机关应当重新申请审批或者备案。

第二十四条 部门统计调查项目经国家统计局批准或者备案后，应当在统计调查表的右上角标明表号、制定机关、批准机关或者备案机关、批准文号或者备案文号、有效期限等标志。

第二十五条 制定机关收到批准或者备案的书面决定后，在10个工作日内将标注批准文号或者备案文号和有效期限的统计调查制度发送到部门统计调查项目管理平台。

第二十六条 国家统计局及时通过国家统计局网站公布批准或者备案的部门统计调查项目名称、制定机关、批准文号或者备案文号、有效期限和统计调查制度的主要内容。

第四章 部门统计调查的组织实施

第二十七条 国务院有关部门应当健全统计工作流程规范，完善统计数据质量控制办法，夯实统计基础工作，严格按照国家统计局批准或者备案的统计调查制度组织实施统计调查。

第二十八条 国务院有关部门在组织实施统计调查时，应当就统计调查制度的主要内容对组织实施人员进行培训；应当就法定填报义务、主要指标涵义和口径、计算方法、采用的统计标准和其他填报要求，向调查对象作出说明。

第二十九条 国务院有关部门应当按《中华人民共和国统计法实施条例》的要求及时公布主要统计指标涵义、调查范围、调查方法、计算方法、抽样调查样本量等信息，对统计数据进行解释说明。

第三十条 国务院有关部门组织实施统计调查应当遵守国家有关统计资料管理和公布的规定。

第三十一条 部门统计调查取得的统计资料，一般应当在政府部门间共享。

第三十二条 国务院有关部门建立统计调查项目执行情况评估制度，对实施情况、实施效果和存在问题进行评估，认为应当修改的，按规定报请国家统计局审批或者备案。

第五章 国家统计局提供的服务

第三十三条 国家统计局依法开展部门统计调查项目审批和备案工作，为国务院有关部门提供有关统计业务咨询、统计调查制度设计指导、统计业务培训等服务。

第三十四条 国家统计局组织国务院有关部门共同维护、更新国家基本单位名录库，为部门统计调查提供调查单位名录和抽样框。

第三十五条 国家统计局建立统计标准库，为部门统计调查提供国家统计标准和部门统计标准。

第三十六条 国家统计局向国务院有关部门提供部门统计调查项目查询服务。

第三十七条 国家统计局推动建立统计信息共享数据库，为国务院有关部门提供部门统计数据查询服务。

第六章 监督检查

第三十八条 国家统计局依法对部门统计调查制度执行情况进行监督检查，依法查处部门统计调查中的重大违法行为；县级以上地方人民政府统计机构依法查处本级和下级人民政府有关部门和统计调查对象执行部门统计调查制度中发生的统计违法行为。

第三十九条 任何单位和个人有权向国家统计局举报部门统计调查违法行为。

国家统计局公布举报统计违法行为的方式和途径，依法受理、核实、处理举报，并为举报人保密。

第四十条 县级以上人民政府有关部门积极协助本级人民政府统计机构查处统计违法行为，及时向县级以上人民政府统计机构移送有关统计违法案件材料。

第四十一条 县级以上人民政府统计机构在调查部门统计违法行为或者核查部门统计数据时，有权采取《中华人民共和国统计法》第三十五条规定的下列措施：

（一）发出检查查询书，向检查单位和调查对象查询部门统计调查项目有关事项；

（二）要求检查单位和调查对象提供与部门统计调查有关的统计调查制度、调查资料、调查报告及其他相关证明和资料；

（三）就与检查有关的事项询问有关人员；

（四）进入检查单位和调查对象的业务场所和统计数据处理信息系统进行检查、核对；

（五）经本机构负责人批准，登记保存检查单位与统计调查有关的统计调查制度、调查资料、调查报告及其他相关证明和资料；

（六）对与检查事项有关的情况和资料进行记录、录音、录像、照相和复制。

县级以上人民政府统计机构进行监督检查时，监督检查人员不得少于2人，并应当出示执法证件；未出示的，有关部门有权拒绝检查。

第四十二条　县级以上人民政府统计机构履行监督检查职责时，有关部门应当如实反映情况，提供相关证明和资料，不得拒绝、阻碍检查，不得转移、隐匿、篡改、毁弃与部门统计调查有关的统计调查制度、调查资料、调查报告及其他相关证明和资料。

第七章　法律责任

第四十三条　县级以上人民政府有关部门在组织实施部门统计调查活动中有下列行为之一的，由上级人民政府统计机构、本级人民政府统计机构责令改正，予以通报：

（一）违法制定、实施部门统计调查项目；

（二）未执行国家统计标准或者经依法批准的部门统计标准；

（三）未执行批准和备案的部门统计调查制度；

（四）在部门统计调查中统计造假、弄虚作假。

第四十四条　县级以上人民政府有关部门及其工作人员有下列行为之一的，由上级人民政府统计机构、本级人民政府统计机构责令改正，予以通报：

（一）拒绝、阻碍对部门统计调查的监督检查和对部门统计违法行为的查处；

（二）包庇、纵容部门统计违法行为；

（三）向存在部门统计违法行为的单位或者个人通风报信，帮助其逃避查处。

第四十五条　县级以上人民政府统计机构在查处部门统计违法行为中，认为对有关国家工作人员依法应当给予处分的，应当提出给予处分的建议，将处分建议和案件材料移送该国家工作人员的任免机关或者监察机关。

第八章　附　则

第四十六条　中央编办管理机构编制的群众团体机关、经授权代主管部门行使统计职能的国家级集团公司和工商领域联合会或者协会等开展的统计调查项目，参照部门统计调查项目管理。

县级以上地方人民政府统计机构对本级人民政府有关部门制定的统计调查项目管理，参照本办法执行。

第四十七条　本办法自2017年10月1日起施行。国家统计局1999年公布的《部门统计调查项目管理暂行办法》同时废止。